GIRT
BY SEA

GIRT BY SEA

RE-IMAGINING AUSTRALIA'S SECURITY

LA TROBE
UNIVERSITY PRESS
IN CONJUNCTION WITH BLACK INC.

REBECCA STRATING & JOANNE WALLIS

Published by La Trobe University Press,
in conjunction with Black Inc.
Wurundjeri Country
22–24 Northumberland Street
Collingwood VIC 3066, Australia
enquiries@blackincbooks.com
www.blackincbooks.com
www.latrobeuniversitypress.com.au

La Trobe University plays an integral role in Australia's public intellectual life, and is recognised globally for its research excellence and commitment to ideas and debate. La Trobe University Press publishes books of high intellectual quality, aimed at general readers. Titles range across the humanities and sciences, and are written by distinguished and innovative scholars. La Trobe University Press books are produced in conjunction with Black Inc., an independent Australian publishing house. The members of the LTUP Editorial Board are Vice-Chancellor's Fellows Emeritus Professor Robert Manne and Dr Elizabeth Finkel, and Morry Schwartz and Chris Feik of Black Inc.

9781760644512 (paperback)
9781743823538 (ebook)

 A catalogue record for this
book is available from the
National Library of Australia

Book design and typesetting by Beau Lowenstern
Cover image © VizArt
Index by Belinda Nemec

Joanne: For Tom, Sam and Ben

Bec: For Lincoln

CONTENTS

INTRODUCTION

Australia is an island continent. An inescapable feature of its geography is that it is 'girt by sea'.[1] Australia has the world's third-largest maritime jurisdiction, covering over 8 million square kilometres, and its zone of maritime search-and-rescue responsibility is a staggering 53 million square kilometres – around one tenth of the Earth's surface – making it the world's largest. The vast surrounding oceans and seas have long connected Australia with the rest of the world via trade, travel and submarine cables. Even today, 99 per cent of goods imported in volume come by sea.

Australia is also a nation of over 8200 islands, some of which house communities with distinctive languages and cultures. These islands lie across multiple oceans and seas, linking Australia to its neighbours in Southeast Asia, the Pacific Islands, New Zealand and South Asia. A growing number of migrants to Australia come from these regions. More than 17 per cent of the Australian population can be classified as 'Asian Australian', and 1.3 per cent were born in Pacific Island countries.[2] An increasing amount of Australia's trade and investment is with these regions too: more than 65 per cent of Australia's two-way trade is with Asia, and nearly one-third is with China.[3]

Yet, while Australia has deepened defence cooperation with many neighbouring states, when push comes to shove it continues to look well beyond the oceans and regions that surround it to the distant horizons of the United States for its ultimate security guarantee. Australia's investors also continue to look beyond Australia's immediate region to the United States, the United Kingdom and the European Union, which are the three largest destinations for outbound Australian investment, by far.[4] And the favour is reciprocated: the same economies are Australia's three largest sources of inbound investment.[5]

We were reminded of this tendency in September 2021, when Australia's then prime minister, Scott Morrison, announced the AUKUS security partnership with the United States and the United Kingdom, under which Australia plans to acquire a new fleet of nuclear-powered submarines built in collaboration with the three partners. This initiative replaced Australia's existing program to develop conventional submarines in cooperation with the French, whose bid had originally been chosen over what many viewed a superior one from the Japanese.

Having effectively been wedged on the AUKUS issue by the departing Coalition government, Anthony Albanese's Labor government doubled down on it. Its 2023 *Defence Strategic Review* declared that Australia's defence policy would be based on 'an enhanced and expanded Alliance with the United States' and its new nuclear-powered submarines would give the Royal Australian Navy the necessary 'enhanced lethality' to adapt to 'the significant changes in Australia's strategic circumstances.'[6] These 'significant changes' principally concern the rising power and influence of China, in and beyond Asia, and the challenge this presents to US primacy and the key international rules and principles that underpin regional order.

The AUKUS agreement reflects how the maritime domain has become a frontline theatre over the last decade for 'competition that operates on multiple levels – economic, military, strategic and diplomatic' – between China and the United States and its partners.[7]

The agreement also reveals Australia's underlying assumption that the military should play the leading role in national security. The nuclear-powered submarines that are the first pillar of AUKUS are projected to cost Australia up to $368 billion – an eye-watering sum.[8] The *Defence Strategic Review* is similarly revealing, confirming that 'defence funding will increase over the next decade above its current trajectory'.[9] What the government hasn't made clear is how strengthening Australia's military power – or its naval power specifically – will ensure peace and prosperity.[10]

Despite this, the Albanese government has prioritised a defence-led approach to security since its election in 2022, focusing its efforts on a defence review during its first year in office. The *Defence Strategic Review* emphasised that Australia should use 'all elements of national power'[11] and in his statement in the review Defence Minister Richard Marles agreed that Australia's strategic interest requires the deployment of 'all elements of our national power in statecraft'.[12] But with so much attention – and spending – already committed to expanding Australia's defence capabilities, there is a real risk that other mechanisms for securing Australia will continue to be overlooked and that attention and resources will be diverted away from the non-military security challenges facing Australia, which will be generated by a diverse range of interlinked and complex causes.

In the maritime domain, rising sea levels pose significant threats to the homes, economies and livelihoods of coastal communities in and beyond Australia. And the COVID-19 pandemic exposed the vulnerabilities of global maritime supply chains. If security threats are as likely to come from intersecting economic, environmental, political and health crises as from a great power war, we should comprehensively and holistically rethink how to pursue Australia's security, looking beyond the expansion of the country's military capabilities.

Unfortunately, security debates rarely take stock of the full range of security challenges faced by Australia. With the exceptions of Australia's first national security strategy, released by the Gillard government in 2013, and the Turnbull government's *2017 Foreign Policy White Paper*, which came three prime ministers ago, government reviews and white papers (used by governments to outline their proposals for future policy) have focused mostly on defence. Over the past ten years, we've seen defence white papers released in 2013 and 2016, the *Defence Strategic*

Update in 2020 and the *Defence Strategic Review* in 2023. Marles has committed the government to releasing a national defence strategy in 2024, which will be updated biennially.[13]

The maritime domain is in many ways a case study in the difficulties of achieving a 'joined-up' approach to national security, one in which the different government departments and agencies work together to implement a coherent strategy. Indeed, when the Department of Home Affairs quietly released a civil maritime security strategy in 2022, it chose to focus on the non-military risk to Australia and Australia's maritime domain[14], deliberately excluding military operations from its scope. But it doesn't make sense for Australia to take a siloed approach to maritime security when the challenges emerging in and from the seas are strategic, economic, environmental and human in nature.

This book is our attempt to apply a fresh lens to Australia's national security – one that takes a balanced view of the diverse challenges we face and resists assumptions about the stability of the existing regional order. This has required us to interrogate the constructed idea of 'Australia' that foreign and defence policymakers are seeking to defend, and to think critically about the meaning of 'security'. Given the Australian public voted against adopting an Aboriginal and Torres Strait Islander Voice to Parliament in the 2023 referendum, we think it's time to critically re-evaluate what and whose security we mean when we say 'Australia's security'.

We focus specifically on the security issues that play out in the maritime regions crucial to Australia's interests: the north seas (the Torres Strait and the Timor, Arafura and Coral seas), the Western Pacific, the South China Sea, the South Pacific, the Indian Ocean and the Southern Ocean. By doing so, we hope to reorientate Australia's strategic imagination, drawing its gaze back from distant horizons to interrogate and foreground the security opportunities and threats it faces closer to home.

We look at each maritime region's historical importance to Australia, examine the contemporary security issues at play and analyse their relevance to Australia's national security. We then critically assess

Australia's current policy approach and consider what it could do differently. By imagining what *could* be, we have sought to identify new and potentially challenging ideas to enrich existing debates on Australia's security.

HOW DOES AUSTRALIA IMAGINE ITSELF?

In a speech delivered in London in January 2023, Australian foreign minister Penny Wong caused controversy by suggesting that states such as Australia should reflect on their colonial heritage and broaden the scope of what counts as their national history. While 'such stories can sometimes feel uncomfortable', she said, 'understanding the past enables us to better share the present and the future [and] helps open the world to us'.[15]

Although Wong's comments were criticised in some circles, they are part of a wider conversation about history, identity and demography that is crucial to the work of understanding how Australia imagines and projects its identity – that is, what 'Australia' means domestically and on the international stage. The historical legacies of imperialism continue to shape Australia's attitudes to its neighbours, and their attitudes to Australia. As Wong puts it, 'One of the most important ways our countries can modernise our relationships is in the story we tell the world about who we are, which is, of course, the starting point of our foreign policies'.[16]

Telling a more complete story about Australia means acknowledging Australia's history prior to the arrival of the First Fleet at Sydney Cove on 26 January 1788. What is now a unitary nation-state known as Australia is a relatively recent invention. For millennia, First Nations peoples lived across Australia in an intricate patchwork of nation, language and social groups. The concept of *maradhal* in the Wiradjuri language encapsulates the truth that the years prior to European settlement 'were not pre-history but history'.[17]

This has implications for how we conceive of 'national' security. Archaeologists have found international Indigenous trade networks, spanning thousands of kilometres of maritime area, that are thousands of years old.[18] Yet discussions on Australian security rarely account for First Nations' approaches to foreign relations through historical and contemporary political and cultural practices.[19] Far greater consideration needs to be given to how Indigenous Australians understand Australia's security and their own.

The national security community must also recognise that the concept of 'Australia' is contested. When the British arrived in 1788, they began Australia's first large-scale conflict: the Frontier Wars between the European colonists and First Nations people, who resisted colonisation. The Frontier Wars were Australia's longest conflict, lasting into the 1930s, and led to the deaths of at least ten thousand Indigenous people in 410 massacres.[20]

Although there is now greater discussion of the Frontier Wars in mainstream Australian discourse,[21] the national security community seldom talks about how the contemporary Australian nation-state was borne from conflict or that First Nations peoples never ceded sovereignty. This history must be acknowledged if we are to understand the impact it has on how Australia imagines itself today, how it is seen by others and how it understands and pursues its security.

The contested nature of Australia's identity also needs to be taken into account when interrogating Australia as a referent object – that is, as an entity and/or idea needing protection. This kind of interrogation is rare. Most analysts take for granted that they are concerned with the physical security of Australia's territory, infrastructure and population.

The *2016 Defence White Paper*, the most authoritative contemporary statement of Australia's strategic interests, defines a 'secure, resilient Australia' as one that is 'protected against attack or the threat of attack and coercion and where Australia exercises full sovereignty over its territories and borders'.[22] Its territories and borders include Australia's northern approaches, maritime jurisdiction and offshore territories. Potential threats encompass non-geographic threats, such as cyber-attack, anti-satellite weapons and ballistic missiles, as well as 'unexpected shocks, whether natural or man-made'.[23]

In February 2023, Defence Minister Richard Marles stated that the government's first responsibility is 'to provide for the safety and security of its people' and, most significantly, their sovereignty. He defined sovereignty as 'the capacity of a people, through their government, to determine their own circumstances and to act of their own accord, free from any coercive influence'.[24]

However, this definition is complicated by the contested nature of Australia. What Australian people determine are 'their own circumstances' and how they want 'to act' will differ according to many factors. And not all Australians are included in and given equal opportunities to influence debates. This, in turn, has consequences for what 'circumstances' the government understands that it needs to protect and how it should protect them.

While the Labor government has made positive steps towards being more inclusive, notably through its support for the Voice to Parliament referendum and a First Nations foreign policy, the Australian national security community – government, policymakers, academics and commentators – hasn't always sought to develop a sufficiently comprehensive understanding of the 'Australia' that needs to be secured and how that can be achieved. The unsuccessful Voice to Parliament campaign demonstrates that Australia still has work to do when it to comes to imagining a more inclusive society, including in terms of security.

When Australia's ambassador for gender equality, Stephanie Copus Campbell, released a video in early 2023, conservative commentators criticised her rather innocuous statement that gender equality assists regional security. One shock jock commented that gender equality wouldn't help Australia deal with China.[25] However, the *2016 Defence White Paper* acknowledges that a secure and prosperous Indo-Pacific region is vital to Australia's national interests – and research has demonstrated that societies in which women enjoy the same rights as men are more likely to be stable, secure and prosperous.[26] What this example highlights is a temptation in some quarters to shut down more inclusive ways of conceptualising and pursuing national security if they perceive them to be products of identity politics.[27]

We argue that we need to secure multiple dimensions of Australia: its physical territory, infrastructure and population, but also its institutions of governance, economy, environment and society.[28] We understand that the security of society requires an intersectional approach, involving the protection of people of different genders, ethnic and racial identities, sexual orientations, faiths, customs, languages and cultures.

Our belief that there are multiple dimensions of Australia that need to be secured means we also have broader notions of how that security should be achieved than many mainstream analysts. While we recognise that the military plays an important role in securing Australia's physical territory, securing other aspects of Australia requires many other tools of statecraft.

REIMAGINING AUSTRALIA'S SECURITY

In the spirit of keeping our minds and imaginations open, we attempt in this book to rethink how the Australian government should pursue Australia's security. To do this, we have asked ourselves several questions.

First, what would it look like if Australia were to move beyond a siloed approach to strategic and foreign policy, in which different arms of statecraft operate relatively separately, towards a holistic approach, in which all arms of statecraft work in coordination to grapple with the complexity of interrelated security threats?

Second, how could a more comprehensive, nuanced and contingent understanding of the range of security opportunities and threats facing Australia reshape strategic and foreign policymaking?

Third, as a regional partner, how could Australia be confident in its strengths, ambitious on foreign and strategic policy, but humble about its limitations? What would it mean if Australia were to accept that it doesn't always have the answers and might have things to learn from its neighbours, and if it were to apologise for, and learn from, its mistakes?

Fourth, could Australia be a determined regional player that pursues its national interest, while also being empathetic when its interests don't neatly align with the interests of others? Could Australia accept that its neighbours and regional partners won't always share its perceptions about regional threats or its view on the best ways to address them?

Fifth, how could Australia lead when it needs to but work with others and follow their lead when appropriate? Australia's Asian and Pacific partners regularly emphasise that they value inclusivity. Are there more opportunities for Australia to seek multilateral responses to certain challenges that draw together the largest possible number of partners into cooperative initiatives?

Finally, how would Australia's understanding of security change if it were to see Asian and Pacific states and actors from a more relational and situational perspective rather than a hierarchical one, based on the relative power of states? And what possibilities would emerge if Australia were to focus on building long-term relationships (in which Australia's interests would sometimes win and sometimes lose out) instead of short-term and transactional ones?

Guided by these questions, we reimagine Australia as a regional actor – one which can develop a coherent security strategy by working with old and new allies and partners to shape the regional order in ways that ensure its security. In the remainder of this book, we set out how this could occur, with a focus on the maritime domain.

We are interested in Australia's strategic imagination, because using our imaginations can open us up to other futures and perspectives. Australia can't imagine away real challenges – climate change, for instance, is inexorable, and its consequences must be faced – but it can devise new ways of meeting those challenges. It can identify a range of roads it could take rather than continuing down one assumed path. And we can use our imaginations to try to understand and empathise with the perspectives of other nations with which Australia's future is intertwined.

1
———

AUSTRALIA'S STRATEGIC IMAGINATION

Australia's strategic imaginary was shaped by geography, its sense of place in the world and a developing understanding of itself as a middle power.[1] Following Federation in 1901, during its incremental emergence as an independent sovereign state responsible for its own international relations, Australia developed four key dynamics in its thinking about foreign and strategic policy:

1. Australia believes that it needs security guarantors but is separated by the 'tyranny of distance' from those states that could reasonably be expected to play such a role.[2]
2. Australia fears being 'abandoned' by the 'great and powerful friend[s]' it has chosen as its security guarantors.[3]
3. Australia is uncertain about whether it should seek security from its region or from within its region – depending, typically, on the potential adversaries it might be anxious about at the time.[4]
4. Australia values an international order that is based on rules, preferably rules that purport to be liberal.[5]

These dynamics have meant that throughout most of its history of statehood, Australia has understood its security interests as intimately linked with those of a patron.

After Federation, Australia's strategic policy was guided by the principle of Commonwealth Defence, whereby Australia – as a dominion of the British Empire, with sovereignty over domestic affairs but not international relations – would contribute to, and coordinate with, UK policy.

The government began to develop a more independent foreign and strategic policy after World War I. Its first significantly independent step was to sign the 1919 Treaty of Versailles – the first political treaty to be negotiated and signed by Australian officials – which formalised peace with Germany and established the League of Nations. The treaty exemplified the government's belief that international order should be created through collectively made rules, in this case crystallised in the Covenant of the League of Nations.

Australia's independence was then enhanced by the 1926 Balfour Declaration, which recognised Australia, and other British dominions, as autonomous and equal in status to Britain. Still, elements of the Australian government remained reluctant to claim too much independence. Australia didn't formally adopt the Statute of Westminster until 1942, eleven years after the British parliament passed it in 1931. The statute recognised that Australia was under the authority of the Crown and not the British government.

Australia's belief in its dependence on a security guarantor has always been tinged with uncertainty about its guarantor's reliability, stretching back to the late nineteenth century, when colonial governments were disappointed by Britain's reluctance to respond to the encroachment of other European powers in the South Pacific. Post-Federation, the Australian government was unhappy when Britain did not address Australia's anxieties about German colonies in its neighbourhood during World War I, but instead required Australia to send its imperial forces to distant battles in Europe and the Middle East.[6]

It was Britain's inability to play a decisive role in defending Australia during World War II that made it clear to Australia that its national interests would not always match those of its guarantor. When Australia became concerned that the United Kingdom could not defend it from Japan's advance, Australia pursued a policy of collective security, under the auspices of the international rules-based order created by the newly formed United Nations, and through an alliance with its perceived wartime saviour, the United States. This culminated in the Australia, New Zealand and the United States (ANZUS) Security Treaty in 1951.

The ANZUS alliance encouraged the government to expand its strategic imagination by transitioning to an ambitious policy of forward defence.[7] Australia would act at the far edges of its air and sea approaches in Asia and Southeast Asia and, as a 'dependent ally', would support allies in the expectation that they would come to Australia's aid if needed.[8] Accordingly, Australian troops were deployed to conflicts in Malaya and Korea in the late 1940s and 1950s, and in South Vietnam between 1962 and 1972.

Despite making these 'insurance payments', the government's confidence in forward defence was shaken by the British withdrawal from 'east of Suez' in 1967 and US president Richard Nixon's announcement in 1969 of the 'Guam Doctrine', whereby the United States expected Asian states to be self-reliant. The Australian government's 1968 strategic basis paper glumly concluded that Australia must be prepared to deal with situations 'which directly threaten our territorial interests and [in] which we could not reasonably rely on receiving help from our allies'.[9] The 1970s therefore saw Australia's strategic policy shift towards 'self-reliance within an alliance framework', an approach articulated in Australia's first defence white paper in 1976.[10]

Many of its neighbours in Asia, and some in the Pacific, had emerged from colonisation during this period, so the government also began to grapple more seriously with how it should approach its region. These efforts crystallised in the 'defence of Australia' doctrine, laid out in the 1987 defence white paper. The doctrine had two fundamental elements: maintaining and developing Australia's independent defence and strategic capabilities, within the framework of its alliance, and promoting strategic stability and security in Australia's near region.[11]

Coincidentally, it was in 1986 that the government finally moved to make Australian law independent of the British parliament and courts, with the passage of the *Australia Act*.

The end of the Cold War created space for the government to imagine a role for Australia on the international stage and to once again emphasise the importance of collective security, particularly under the United Nations.[12] This saw Australia involved in the first Gulf War in 1990, the UN Transitional Authority in Cambodia in 1991, the UN Operation in Somalia in 1993 and the UN Assistance Mission for Rwanda in 1994. But the government continued to be occupied by its own region,[13] adopting the policy of regional defence in 2000, which held that Australia should play a larger role in securing its region,[14] as it did when it led the International Force East Timor (INTERFET) to respond to the violence that broke out after the Timorese people voted overwhelmingly for independence from Indonesia in 1999.

Australia encountered a frustrating dynamic as the leader of INTER-FET: the reluctance of its security guarantor to provide substantive support. In the lead-up to the intervention, the Howard government's efforts to secure a commitment of ground troops from the United States were unsuccessful. While the United States did provide vital communications and intelligence assets, helicopter mobility and strategic lift,[15] its reluctance to commit ground troops to the cause prompted then defence minister John Moore to wryly comment, 'Well, so much for the ANZUS Treaty.'[16] The government was particularly disappointed because it had hoped a US Army presence would constitute a 'tripwire', ensuring American support in the event of conflict between Indonesia and Australia.[17]

Notably, after the 9/11 terrorist attacks in 2001, the Australian government quickly invoked the ANZUS Treaty – the first time it had been activated – and threw its support behind the United States during the subsequent war on terror, playing active roles in the Afghanistan and Iraq wars, and investigating the potential for terrorism in its near region. That potential became reality in October 2002, with the bombing of a nightclub in Bali, Indonesia, which killed eighty-eight Australians. Those attacks were followed by the bombing of the Marriott Hotel in Jakarta in August 2003 and the bombing of the Australian embassy in Jakarta in September 2004. Subsequently, the government's security imaginary began to recognise a range of non-traditional threats, such as terrorism and transnational crime, though the government's interest in these threats was sidelined in the following decade by the rise of China.

Australia has long been cast as a 'liminal state', located in Asia but culturally bound to distant Anglosphere states.[18] Such identity dilemmas have driven the third dynamic of Australian security policy – namely, whether it should seek security *within* Asia or *from* Asia. Historically, Australian security policy has been framed in relation to an 'other' that has typically been Asian.[19] Fear of an Asian invasion is an established trope in Australian culture, literature and politics, shaping its foreign, defence and immigration policies.[20]

In the twenty-first century, the 'other' is undoubtedly China. According to Lowy Institute opinion polling, most Australians now see China as presenting a 'military threat' to Australia.[21] In a 2021 Australia Institute poll, the proportion of Australians (42 per cent) fearing an attack from China was not much lower than the proportion of Taiwanese who gave the same response (51 per cent). Nationalism, populism and a rise in anti-China sentiment, particularly during the COVID-19 pandemic, has been fuelled by hairy-chested rhetoric about China by certain politicians and commentators.[22] This has not been helped by China's coercive diplomacy, which culminated in sweeping economic sanctions against Australia in 2020.

There are legitimate reasons for the government to be concerned about China. China became Asia's largest economy in 2010, and after a decade of President Xi Jinping's rule its global role has been transformed – economically, militarily and politically. While its economic growth slowed during the pandemic, China's GDP has expanded by more than 100 per cent during Xi's administration.[23] China now has the world's largest army (although not the most powerful) and the second-highest military expenditure, behind the United States.[24] Xi's doctrine is framed around the 'national rejuvenation' of China and the restoration of its international status to an 'unspecified rightful position' following the long century of humiliation (1839–1949).[25] Deng Xiaoping's famous exhortation that China should 'disguise its ambitions and hide its claws' is no longer a guiding principle of its foreign policy. Australia and its allies and partners are, and should be, concerned about what this means for their ability to shape international rules and the rules-based order they promote. Yet the continuation of China's rise is far from assured: its economy slowed during the pandemic; it faces looming challenges with unemployment, social unrest and declining birth rates; and its military spending is still less than one-third of the United States'.

Two seemingly contradictory visions of China have emerged. The first is of a country that comes to threaten Australian (and global) peace and security by dominating Asia and the Pacific, mobilising its economic and military might to match its intentions and potentially pulling Australia into war. Defence experts have told Australians to 'prepare for a high-intensity conflict in our own strategic environment' as they hear the 'drums of war'.[26] The second vision is of a country whose authoritarianism and 'internal contradictions' in politics and economics will ultimately lead to its collapse. According to this narrative, China 'has a long way to go to match the capabilities, flexibility, innovation and training of first-rank military forces such as those of the US and Australia'.[27]

It can be difficult to reconcile the 'China threat' and 'China failure' narratives. Taken to their fullest extent, either could be dangerous. An economically and politically weaker China may take more international risks. But an all-consuming, one-dimensional fear of China on Australia's part could be used to justify more military spending and adventurism, with conflict becoming a self-fulfilling prophecy. This is known as a security spiral, in which states seeking security through military build-up can instead provoke competition. In 2021, world military expenditure surpassed US\$2 trillion for the first time, with China doing its bit to encourage this militarisation.[28] On the other hand, underplaying the extent to which Asia's security order continues to evolve and clinging to an old order that no longer exists also involves risks. Defending Australia's interests in a multipolar region is now the reality and priority.

Australian governments' bipartisan determination to pursue self-reliance within the context of a close US alliance has shaped the strategic imagination since 2001,[29] particularly as concerns about Australia's vulnerabilities to threats arising from or through Asia and the Pacific have grown.[30] Australia's anxiety about its geography and desire to keep the United States engaged in the region encouraged the government to redefine its region of strategic interest as the 'Indo-Pacific' in 2013, although the term was first used in official Australian defence discourse in 1976.[31] The *Defence White Paper 2013* defined the Indo-Pacific as the region 'connecting the Indian and Pacific oceans through Southeast Asia'.[32]

The Indo-Pacific concept was explicitly linked to the government's goal to strengthen the rules-based order in the region, including the 'United Nations, international laws and conventions and regional security architectures'.[33] The government sees the rules-based order as important because, as a middle power, Australia 'does not have the capacity to unilaterally protect and further our global security interests'.[34] It does not want bigger powers to be able to unilaterally impose their will upon smaller and middle powers. (These political narratives tend to focus on China's coercive capacities and intent, rather than those of the United States.) However, the government has expressed mounting concern that the rules-based order is 'under increasing pressure' as 'newly powerful countries want greater influence and to challenge some of the rules'. It has committed itself to working with the United States and 'like-minded partners' to maintain it.[35]

Today, the influence of geography on Australia's security imaginary means that the four longstanding dynamics of its strategic and foreign policy continue to be influential. Australia's strategic policy is still one of qualified self-reliance.[36] This policy was explicitly endorsed in the 2023 *Defence Strategic Review*, which stated that 'in the context of the [US] Alliance and the deteriorating strategic environment, Australia must be more self-reliant so we are able to contribute more to regional stability'.[37] The translation of this policy into practice was exemplified by the 2021 announcement of the AUKUS security partnership, which signalled that the government sees its future efforts to defend itself as inextricably reliant in some measure on the United States and the United Kingdom. Even once its fleet of nuclear-powered submarines is established, Australia will be unable to sustain it without ongoing assistance from either the United States, the United Kingdom or both, since Australia does not have a sophisticated domestic nuclear capability.

While much of the response to AUKUS has focused on whether Australia's 'sovereignty' will be infringed by this reliance on the United States and/or the United Kingdom, this ignores the fact Australia already relies on the United States and, to a lesser extent, on other partners to sustain and support other aspects of its military capabilities. This means that Australia can't defend itself without relying on continued US support.

Most of Australia's procurements are either US-built or compatible with US systems. As the *2016 Defence White Paper* states, 'Australia sources our most important combat capability from the United States', and interoperability with the United States is a key strategic goal.[38] To be 'interoperable', states need to purchase the right kind of technology from common suppliers. This means that about 60 per cent of Australia's defence spending is on US equipment.[39] Indeed, in the period 2014–18, Australia became the world's fourth-largest arms importer, with its procurements increasing by 37 per cent since the previous four-year period.[40] US-built purchases included the twelve EA-18G 'Growler' aircraft built by US multinational Boeing, the seventy-two F-35 Joint Strike Fighters outlined in the *2016 Defence White Paper* (the single biggest Air Force procurement, at $17 billion), fifteen P-8 Poseidon maritime surveillance and patrol aircraft, and the GM-158C Long Range Anti-Ship Missiles that cost $800 million.

While Australia's dependence on the United States for its defence capability can be read negatively, on the positive side it has meant Australia can afford sophisticated equipment and technology that would have been prohibitively expensive for it to develop and manufacture itself.

The strategic policy framework that the *2020 Defence Strategic Update* outlines signalled Australia's willingness to project military power and deter actions against itself. The focus of the previous white paper was the preservation of the rules-based order. What is striking about the 2020 document is that it highlights how concerned Defence had become about the extent to which Australia's regional security environment had deteriorated.

That concern is echoed in the 2023 *Defence Strategic Review*, which recognises that the United States is no longer 'the unipolar leader of the Indo-Pacific'[41] and identifies 'intense China–United States competition' as 'the defining feature of our region'.[42] The review singles out China's 'assertion of sovereignty over the South China Sea', among other activities, as threatening the region's rules-based order.[43] The review also observes that China is 'engaged in strategic competition in Australia's near neighbourhood'.[44]

The review warns that regional military modernisation means Australia 'cannot rely on geography or warning time' for its protection. And while it acknowledges that 'there is at present only a remote possibility of any power contemplating an invasion of our continent', it also notes that 'the threat of the use of military force or coercion against Australia does not require invasion'.[45] It therefore concludes that Australia requires 'a new, holistic approach to Australian defence planning and strategy', and a national defence strategy that supports, among other things, 'whole-of-nation strategies', 'an enhanced and expanded alliance with the United States' and 'a focus on deterrence through denial, including the ability to hold any adversary at risk'.[46]

WHAT DILEMMAS DOES AUSTRALIA FACE IN PURSUING ITS SECURITY?

The government faces several dilemmas in pursuing Australia's security, both in and beyond its maritime domains.

First, global power has shifted, and the centre of strategic gravity is now in Asia, with China being a great power and peer competitor of the United States. The 2023 *Defence Strategic Review* recognises this, and even the United States itself appears to have moved away from policies of 'primacy' in the region.

But while the Australian security community is well aware of this reality, it isn't necessarily internalised in its debates. These still often proceed as though the United States remains an unchallenged great power, in part because the United States remains so central to how it imagines its security that it is difficult to see a future in which it is no longer dominant. Australia's approach has thus been guided by a desire to keep the United States as engaged and present in the region as possible. But just because something is difficult doesn't mean it shouldn't be done. Australia needs to imagine a future in which China is a great power that can shape the international order and which Australia must live alongside, potentially according to a new set of rules. This future is possible and warrants deeper thought, even if it isn't desirable or inevitable.

Second, Australia's perception that it needs a security guarantor has left it vulnerable to the limits of its guarantors' commitment and capabilities. Having been let down by the British during World War II, Australia has depended on the United States since the 1950s. However, as Australia was reminded by Nixon's Guam Doctrine, American support is not guaranteed. And nor is it unconditional or free, as Donald Trump made clear to US allies during his presidency. This knowledge has seen Australian leaders make expensive decisions to support US interventions, not least in Vietnam and Iraq. The cost of the alliance and uncertainty about US commitment to Australian security leaves Australia with a dilemma: should it continue to rely on the United

States? This question, which goes back to when the ANZUS Treaty was signed in 1951, has become more acute as US frailties have grown. The 6 January 2021 riots following the election of Joe Biden, and the swing of the Republican Party to the populist, isolationist right, raise serious questions about the future of American democracy. If the United States experiences democratic backsliding or succumbs to isolationism, can Australia depend on it for defence in its times of need?

We are not advocating that Australia step away from ANZUS, although we note that the text of the ANZUS Treaty commits the United States to very little other than consulting Australia should its territorial integrity, political independence or security in the Pacific be threatened. Australia's reliance on US defence matériel (and its subsequent sustainment) and its deep interoperability with the US military means that its defence capability is inextricably linked to the United States. But there needs to be more open debate about a plan B: if Australia can't depend on the United States, how will it otherwise seek its security? In what ways can Australia better pursue its independence within the alliance structure and keep a range of strategic options open in future, particularly as it asserts an increasingly important role in Asia and the Pacific?

Third, how does Australia resolve the paradox that it seeks security both from and within Asia and the Pacific? To get around this dilemma, the Australian government has led the global adoption of the 'Indo-Pacific' label to describe its region of strategic interest. Its emphasis on the Pacific rather than Asia draws the United States into its strategic neighbourhood, countering China's efforts to exclude Washington from the emerging Asian order. It also highlights the position of the maritime domain on the frontline of emerging challenges to Australia's national interests, regional stability and the liberal 'rules-based order' that successive governments have sought to defend. However, the Indo-Pacific lacks a logic as a 'region': there is no unifying geographic, cultural, historical or political rationale behind it. It is the strategic equivalent of a Rorschach test: for some, it reflects the interconnectedness of the

Indian and Pacific oceans through economic interactions and key trading routes; for others, it's merely a political construct designed to support the containment of China. It's also a problematic term because Australia's security interests are not uniform across the Indo-Pacific. The maritime threats to Australia are too complex and interdependent to be negotiated by a 'one-size-fits-all' strategic system. Australia has very different interests, histories and policy approaches across its key maritime domains.

Fourth, for several decades after World War II, Australia saw collective security, under the auspices of the United Nations, as key to international peace and security. Australia continues to play an active role in the United Nations, most recently as a member of the Security Council in 2013 and 2014, and prioritises the preservation of a rules-based order created by the UN charter and UN treaties. But with tensions between the United States and China rising leading to greater obstruction to UN decision-making, Australia has sought alternative 'strategic' minilateral arrangements, exemplified by the Quadrilateral Security Dialogue (now known just as 'Quad') with the United States, India and Japan, and its AUKUS trilateral agreement. How these minilateral arrangements relate to multilateral institutions or bilateral alliances is still being played out, but they signal a shift away from the US-led 'hub-and-spokes' Asian alliance system, in which the United States is the 'hub' and its allies – Australia, Japan, South Korea, the Philippines and Thailand – are the 'spokes'.

Fifth, as a middle power, Australia has long relied on the rules-based order to protect its interests on the international stage and has been emphasising its importance over the last decade. Foreign Minister Penny Wong declared in 2022 that 'we know we will always be better off in a world where the rules – whether they govern trade or the maritime domain, or the environment or military engagement – are clear, mutually negotiated and consistently followed'.[47] In the *2016 Defence White Paper*, which infamously features the term fifty-six times, a 'stable Indo-Pacific region and rules-based global order which supports our interests', is ranked as the third most important strategic defence interest, weighted equally with defending the Australian mainland from attack.

However, the extent to which the rules-based order constrains and binds powerful states is questionable – it failed, for instance, to prevent Russia's invasion of Ukraine in 2022. And even nations that purport to uphold the rules-based order, such as the United States and Australia, do so selectively and, as we discuss in Chapter 7, can have different perspectives of certain 'rules', even if they broadly agree on the legitimacy of regimes such as the United Nations Convention on the Law of the Sea (UNCLOS). The rules-based order was largely created by the United States and its allies and partners after World War II and therefore reflects their interests and values at that time. The maritime rules-based order – underpinned by UNCLOS, the so-called constitution for the oceans – is also complex. UNCLOS was negotiated in the 1970s, and while newly decolonised and developing states were integral to the creation of new norms and maritime zones, dilemmas persist in terms of what rules are privileged, whose interests they serve and their suitability for managing contemporary challenges, including new and emerging global security matters.

Australia therefore must ask itself two questions: Is the rules-based order legitimate? And is Australia (and its close partners) sufficiently compliant with the rules-based order to justify its continued existence? These may lead to further questions: If the rules-based order is no longer legitimate, what will replace it? And will Australia face an international system in which order is instead determined by power?

Sixth, how should Australia balance its interests and its values? Australia prides itself on being a liberal-democratic country and a 'good international citizen'[48] but doesn't always act accordingly, either at home or overseas, as we discuss in Chapter 2. Its treatment of Indigenous Australians and refugees, and its participation in the invasion of Iraq, for instance, fall well short of good international citizenship. Australia is likely to face even more acute dilemmas if strategic competition between the United States and China worsens, as it may be tempted to turn a blind eye to human-rights abuses and breaches of international law in the states that it is partnering with in pursuit of its perceived strategic interests. This was highlighted by the September 2023 controversy over Canada's allegations that the Indian government sponsored the assassination of a Canadian Sikh leader on Canadian soil.

WHAT IS MARITIME SECURITY AND WHY IS IT IMPORTANT TO AUSTRALIA'S SECURITY?

For all of Australia's 'fear of abandonment' and anxiety about the 'tyranny of distance', its geography is a strategic asset – its littoral oceans and seas act as a buffer between the Australian mainland and any potential invader. Even as technological advances give potential adversaries the capability to project power across greater distances, Australia's maritime geography shields Australia from invasion and attacks on big population centres such as Melbourne and Sydney.

On the other hand, Australia has vast coastlines and maritime area to defend but is constrained by the size of its population and budget, which are congruent with its status as a prosperous but middle-sized state.

Past white papers have considered maritime dimensions of conventional defence challenges such as deterring attacks and coercing adversaries; achieving and maintaining air and sea control; protecting key sea lines of communication; denying adversaries access to forward operating bases; and deploying joint task forces to support the operations of regional partners. The *Defence Strategic Review* is no exception in this respect, arguing that 'an enhanced lethality surface combatant fleet, [which] complements a conventionally-armed, nuclear-powered submarine fleet, is now essential'.[49]

Defence planners have viewed the so-called 'air–sea gap' of Australia's northern approaches – the maritime and air space separating

Australia from the nations of Southeast Asia, particularly the archipelagos to Australia's north – as crucial to protecting Australia from territorial invasion and key to its forward-defence capabilities (projecting power through the deployment of forces into the region).

The 1942 Battle of the Coral Sea was a pivotal victory for US and Australian forces in World War II, a conflict in which Australia was exposed to ninety-seven air attacks from Japanese fighters and bombers. Japan targeted Darwin's port and harbour, as well as towns across Northern Australia, to interrupt the Allies' use of Darwin's port facilities for forward defence. As we argue in Chapter 2, it is little wonder that this experience was formative for Australia's defence policy: it remains the only foreign attack on the Australian continent by another state since the British invasion of 1788.

Australia's desire for a security guarantor is also linked to its maritime geography. It has, after all, allied itself with the United States and, before that, the United Kingdom – both dominant global maritime powers. AUKUS is symbolic of the historical role the maritime has played in Australia's great power relationships.

It was not all smooth sailing: the United States opposed Australia's efforts to establish itself and New Zealand as the dominant powers in the Pacific through the 1944 Canberra Pact, which Washington regarded as imposing on its own sphere of interest. But in 1951, less than a decade later, the Australian and US navies signed the Radford–Collins agreement, in which they agreed to share responsibility for protecting sea lines of communication in the South Pacific and Eastern Indian Ocean.

The Radford–Collins agreement was born of Australia's experiences in World War II, the emergence of Cold War conflicts and the formation of the People's Republic of China, the combined impact of which generated concerns about protecting maritime trade. Defence planners in Canberra were uncertain about whether the United States would or could assist Australia if its maritime trade were threatened,[50] particularly as, in 1950 the United States 'did not view Australia as within its area of responsibility, nor did it believe it should in any way automatically safeguard Australia's sovereignty or its interests'.[51] The declaration of the Australia, New Zealand and Malaya (ANZAM) region forced the United States' hand, as it overlapped with its Pacific theatre.[52] An operational agreement rather than a treaty, the Radford–Collins agreement offered a way for Australia (on behalf of ANZAM) and the United States to divide areas of maritime responsibility between their navies in the event of conflict and to coordinate in ensuring the free flow of maritime trade.

Keeping sea lines of communication open is vital for Australia, the fifth-largest maritime trading country in the world. In 2020–21, Australia's maritime exports were worth $354.8 billion. Even as the pandemic caused enormous difficulties with shipping, this represented an increase of 1.3 per cent in real terms from the previous year.[53] To the north, the sea lanes through neighbouring archipelagic nations remain important for the transit of fuel resources necessary for energy security and defence operations. Over the past two decades, Australia's dependency on imported transport fuels has only increased, growing from around 60 per cent in 2000 to over 90 per cent in 2013.[54]

This reliance on maritime trade means that the Australian government supports the principle of *mare liberum* (or 'the free seas'), with 'freedom of navigation' as its central norm. But this norm is interpreted differently across Asia and the Pacific, and the maritime domain has increasingly become a site of geostrategic competition between the United States and China. China's maritime activities in domains such as the South and East China seas have sparked concerns about its broader intentions to reshape international order for Australia and other US allies and partners. Some of China's activities have prevented smaller Southeast Asian states from accessing their sovereign rights to maritime resources such as fish, oil and gas within the maritime zones generated under international law.

China has also been growing its navy: the People's Liberation Army Navy comprises an estimated 355 ships and will likely grow to a force of 420 capable and modern vessels by 2025 and to 460 by 2030.[55]

China has also been building artificial islands through dredging and landfill in the South China Sea to house military installations, which have environmental as well as strategic implications.

So-called grey zone or hybrid warfare tactics are also increasing in East Asia's maritime domains. Non-military assets, such as coastguard, fishing and survey vessels, are being used for strategic purposes, and more navy vessels and aircraft are conducting transit operations in contested areas, intensifying the risk of unplanned conflict. While not new, when grey zone tactics are used in contests for naval and air superiority, flouting the rules that govern the world's oceans, this is likely to have consequences for Australia's peace and prosperity.

Despite the importance of the maritime to Australia's security, Australia is often perceived as 'seablind'. 'A sense of the sea and surroundings is not generally apparent', observed one commentator, while another argued that 'the country lacks a maritime consciousness to guide defence policy'.[56] The 2023 *Defence Strategic Review* addresses some of these concerns, arguing that Australia's 'strategic circumstances now require that our naval capability contributes effectively to the [Australian Defence Force's] ability to shape our strategic environment, deter potential adversaries and deny their ability to achieve objectives contrary to our national interests'.[57] It therefore recommends that Australia needs a surface combatant fleet that includes a 'mix of Tier 1 and Tier 2 surface combatants, consistent with a strategy of a larger number of smaller surface vessels'. The Review argues that this will 'significantly increase [the Royal Australian] Navy's capability through a greater number of lethal vessels with enhanced long-range strike (maritime and land) and air defence capabilities'.[58] The government has accepted this recommendation.

The *Defence Strategic Review* outlines an explicit focus on the development of anti-access / area-denial capabilities (A2/AD). The use of the term 'A2/AD' is interesting, not just because it hasn't previously been used in Australia's official defence strategy but also because it was previously shorthand for China's air-and-maritime-missile-based defensive approach to shutting out the US military from what it considers to be its 'near seas': the Taiwan Strait and the South and East China seas. The Review outlines that Australia's A2/AD strategy will encompass long-range capabilities to prevent an adversary from entering an operational area (sea or air) and shorter-range capabilities to limit 'freedom of action' within an operational area.

While the review's A2/AD strategy of denial is sound, Australia needs to look beyond these traditional defence concepts to get a full understanding of its security. In the maritime domain, this involves 'civil' maritime security.

In April 2022, the Department of Home Affairs released the Australian Government Civil Maritime Security Strategy, which received little of the fanfare that met the 2023 *Defence Strategic Review* upon its release in May 2023.[59] The review explicitly excludes 'military operations' and 'maritime safety', focusing only on 'non-military risk to Australia and Australia's maritime domain', including such risks as people smuggling, terrorism, transnational serious and organised crime, and illegal, unreported and unregulated fishing.[60] The 2020 *Guide to Australian Maritime Security Arrangements* (GAMSA) similarly identified maritime security threats as unauthorised maritime arrivals, maritime terrorism, prohibited imports and exports, illegal exploitation of natural resources, illegal activity in protected areas, compromises to biosecurity, marine pollution and piracy, robbery or violence at sea.[61]

These civil maritime security threats reflect that the oceans are home to lucrative resources, such as fish, minerals, oil and gas. While these can provide food security, jobs, economic development, energy and coastal communities' livelihoods, they are assets that states (and other actors) fight over as well. They also reflect that oceans are a medium for transportation and exchange of people, goods and ideas. Undersea cables, for example, transport 99 per cent of international data to and from Australia and are integral to the modern digital economy.

Many of these civil threats emerge not from states or their militaries but from non-state actors, ranging from small-scale fishers to powerful criminal syndicates. This means that an array of government agencies is involved in Australia's maritime security, including the Royal Australian Navy, the Australian Federal Police and state police forces, Home Affairs, Australian Border Force and the Australian Fisheries Management Authority. Unlike many other regional states, Australia has no official coastguard.

Civil maritime security threats are also transnational and cross-jurisdictional, because they can transcend national borders and exist in a network involving not just states but also individuals, corporations, private security companies and so on. These challenges often interact with land as well as the water, particularly in 'littoral' spaces. They can emerge from people, but from natural disasters, climate change and pandemics as well. They can also overlap with 'conventional' military security challenges – for instance, illegal fishing in Australia's vast exclusive economic zone intersects with such pressing concerns as drug and human trafficking, piracy, irregular maritime arrivals and 'maritime militias' that use fishing vessels to advance their strategic goals.[62]

Civil maritime security threats are regulated by both Australian domestic law and a range of international laws that constitute the maritime rules-based order – stable patterns of state behaviour, clear and coherent rules governing ocean space and resources, and effective mechanisms for resolving maritime disputes. The most significant international component of maritime order is the 1982 UNCLOS, which established the overarching framework for instituting rules to govern ocean spaces. It provides many coastal states – such as Australia – with vast benefits and entitlements. Under UNCLOS, Australia claims an exclusive economic zone – a maritime area in which it has sovereign rights to and jurisdiction over natural resources – that is bigger than its land territory. Many states view the legitimacy of UNCLOS as crucial to the creation and maintenance of order across maritime domains.

Even with this framework in place, the politics of the oceans are messy and complex. Difficulties in policing and domain awareness across maritime geographies create governance issues that even advanced surveillance technologies cannot fully address. There are different and contested maritime jurisdictions. The rights of coastal and navigating states differ according to the zone: a territorial sea is (mostly) under the control of a coastal state; within an exclusive economic zone, a coastal state has 'sovereign rights' but not absolute control; the high seas are a 'global commons' and not controlled by any one state.

Australia's size and geography mean that it has benefited from the maritime rules-based order established around UNCLOS. Any move to a hierarchical maritime order – in which the sheer power of states, rather than agreed upon laws, determines access to maritime resources and vital sea lanes – would challenge its security. Former Australian prime minister Malcolm Turnbull's 2017 speech at the annual IISS Shangri-La Dialogue encapsulated this fear of a new world order in which the big fish eat the small and 'might' wins out over 'right'.[63]

As the *Defence Strategic Review* recognises, maritime security is not just a 'home game'.[64] The 'away game' intercepts problems before they arrive at Australian shores. Effective responses to these security challenges are often only achieved in collaboration with others. Transnational maritime security issues present common challenges to coastal states across the Asian and Pacific regions, but they remain at odds over how to govern their maritime jurisdictions and the high seas.

Indeed, Asia's more demanding geopolitical environment has compelled some states to rethink their approaches to maritime security. New Zealand and the United Kingdom, for instance, recently released new maritime security strategies.

Australia has no document outlining a comprehensive and integrated maritime security strategy, let alone one that takes a holistic view on oceans security and order. The *Australia's Oceans Policy* document, released in 1998, outlined a novel and ambitious plan for an integrated, ecosystem-based approach to ocean governance, but its 'silent demise' reflected jurisdictional problems, an absence of clear lines of responsibility and a lack of political will for implementing 'joined-up' approaches.[65]

In 2004, a Joint Standing Committee on Foreign Affairs, Defence and Trade inquiry recommended that the Australian Defence Force (ADF) implement a 'modern maritime strategy', which it narrowly defined as a strategy that involves 'air, sea and land forces operating jointly to influence events in the littoral together with traditional blue water maritime concepts of sea denial and sea control'. It identified sea denial (denying the enemy's ability to use the sea), sea control (commanding the use of the sea for oneself) and power projection as three key features of such a strategy.[66]

A decade later, there had been little movement on defining a comprehensive maritime strategy. For example, the term does not appear in the *2016 Defence White Paper*, despite its ambitious plan to renew the Royal Australian Navy through the modernisation of its maritime capabilities and the procurement of submarines and other surface combatants.

The *2020 Defence Strategic Update* made it clear that the government believed that Australia's maritime security outlook had deteriorated considerably in the years since the *2016 Defence White Paper*. Its *2020 Force Structure Plan* promised a $75-billion investment in Australia's maritime capability, with massive shipbuilding plans for the acquisition or upgrade of up to twenty-three different classes of navy and army maritime vessels.[67] Before long, those spending projections were blown out of the water by the AUKUS announcement. Since 2021, Australia's plans to develop a fleet of nuclear-powered submarines – the first pillar of AUKUS – has dominated national security conversations.

There have been mixed messages from the Coalition and Labor governments about why Australia needs to invest in nuclear-powered submarines. As new technologies make conventional submarines more visible (especially because they must rise to the surface to 'snort', or take in air, more regularly than nuclear-powered submarines), leaders have argued that the superior capabilities of nuclear-powered submarines are necessary for regional security. They have also pointed out that nuclear-powered submarines could contribute to regional deterrence efforts, and in seas closer to China; be deployed to protect Australia's own territory and maritime domain; and be used to protect sea lines of communication and vital trade routes.

The Australian government's pursuit of nuclear-powered submarines becomes more explicable when viewed in light of the US strategy of 'integrated deterrence'. A key element of the Biden administration's Indo-Pacific strategy,[68] integrated deterrence prioritises closer defence and technology cooperation, supply-chain integration and interdependence with regional allies across warfighting domains to empower allies and counter coercion and aggression, including against those who seek to 'undermine the rights of sovereign nations at sea'.[69] Australia's plan to develop nuclear-powered submarines reflects the increasing enmeshment of Australia's regional security interests with the United States', which was bedded down in the 2023 *Defence Strategic Review*.

While Australia's recent moves to go all in on the US alliance are not surprising, we are concerned they may lead to the government narrowing its understanding of Australia's maritime security challenges down to just their military aspects. In the following chapters, we adopt a broader view:[70] we understand maritime security to encompass strategic, economic, human and environmental dimensions. We argue that Australia should seek a maritime regional order in the Indo-Pacific that promotes inclusive prosperity, a sustainable environment and a human-rights-based approach to issues such as labour exploitation on commercial vessels, indigenous rights at sea and irregular maritime migration.

2

AUSTRALIA'S 'NORTH SEAS'

In 2022, eight Elders from the Torres Strait Islands of Boigu, Poruma, Warraber and Masig made history with an international legal complaint that accused the Australian government of violating their fundamental human rights by failing to address climate change.[1] The group, known as the Torres Strait 8, submitted its complaint to the United Nations Human Rights Committee, a body of independent legal experts that monitors the implementation of the 1976 International Covenant on Civil and Political Rights, of which Australia is a signatory.

The media reported that the Morrison government had asked the committee to dismiss the claim on the grounds that Australia could not 'be held individually responsible' because climate change is a global problem. The government argued that Australia was 'already doing enough', and that the future impacts were too uncertain to warrant doing more.[2]

In 2014, the federal and Queensland governments had pledged $26.2 million for coastal defence in six Torres Strait communities, while simultaneously cutting $534 million from Indigenous programs (including $3.5 million from the Torres Strait Regional Authority).[3] Sea walls were built in 2017, but it took only six months for the tides to start breaking through.

In September 2022, the committee found that the Australian government had failed to adequately protect Torres Strait Islanders from the adverse impacts of climate change, violating 'their right to enjoy their culture and be free from arbitrary interferences with their private life, family and home'.[4]

This case offers an interesting lens through which to consider the dilemmas facing Australia's strategic imagination. One such dilemma relates to the planning horizons used to predict security threats and determine responses to them. There is an assumption that we will have time to deal with the climate crisis – that it exists as a future problem – which is not supported by the evidence.[5] The Torres Strait is one of Australia's most climate-vulnerable areas: the rise of its sea levels is predicted to double the global average.[6] Torres Strait Islander advocates have expressed a desire to remain on the islands and maintain their cultural and economic connection to the seas. However, the low-lying islands in Australia's north seas are exposed to extreme periodic flooding, erosion and coastal inundation. Powerful king tides have become even more destructive due to climate change.[7] Changing tides and weather patterns may ultimately force the eight hundred inhabitants of Saibai and Boigu to relocate.[8] For them, the consequences of climate change are not a far-off prospect.

Another dilemma, and an enduring one, is that, as a middle power, Australia has long relied on international law, institutions (such as the United Nations) and rules but is not always willing to match its rhetoric with action. Governments have found it difficult to balance their perceived interests and values when it comes to strategic and foreign policy.

An additional dilemma highlighted by this case is that the meaning of 'security' is open to interpretation. What is security, and whose security is the government trying to protect? Who decides? Climate change means that the oceans, long a source of livelihood and connection for Australia's coastal communities, increasingly constitute a threat. How is the Australian state responsible for ensuring economic and human security for these communities?

While climate change is a significant challenge in Australia's north seas (which we define as the Torres Strait and the Timor, Arafura and Coral seas), geopolitics means conventional defence challenges are also present in the region. The island-hopping of Japan in Southeast Asia and the Pacific during World War II is a salient reminder of why the archipelagos to Australia's north matter for the territorial defence of the Australian mainland.

As we mention in Chapter 1, the air–sea gap between Australia and the Indonesian archipelago has been seen as integral to Australia's security, providing strategic buffers or 'moats' that can be mobilised to keep threats away from Australia's mainland.[9] Historically, Australia has considered Indonesia another buffer to powerful Northeast Asian states, and, at times, a strategic dilemma in and of itself.

The 1987 defence white paper, in particular, prioritised the defence of the air–sea gap to protect Australian territory, based on an understanding that threats were likely to emerge from its northern air and maritime approaches. The 2023 *Defence Strategic Review* also prioritised the Australian Defence Forces's ability to deter attacks on Australian territory and 'hold forces at risk' in its northern maritime approaches.[10] It recommended enhancing and upgrading the network of bases across northern Australia that provide 'support, denial and deterrence', and rectifying fuel and supply issues that hinder their operation.

Northern Australia also plays an important role in Australia's alliance with the United States, particularly as a site for defence activities and joint facilities. Its location makes it both a stage from which the Australian Defence Force and its US counterpart can conduct 'forward defence' and a southern gateway for the United States to the Indo-Pacific region.

In some areas, Australia is only separated from its northern neighbours, the littoral states of Indonesia, Timor-Leste and Papua New Guinea, by very narrow stretches of water. Australia's most northerly islands, Boigu and Saibai, two of more than 270 islands making up the Torres Strait Islands, lie less than seven kilometres from the PNG mainland. The low-lying and swampy Boigu is actually a geological extension of the PNG mainland, which can be seen from the island.[11]

It is sometimes easy to forget that Australia was a colonial power in Papua New Guinea. Indeed, veteran Australian journalist Sean Dorney has described Australia's attitude to its history in Papua New Guinea as that of an 'embarrassed colonialist', given how little public discussion there is about the role it played there.[12]

This geographic closeness of Papua New Guinea, Timor-Leste and Indonesia to Australia has also played an important role in contests over maritime boundaries and attendant rights to valuable maritime resources – in particular, oil and gas.

Since the 1960s, Australia has primarily expressed its maritime priorities in the Timor Sea by pursuing its commercial and hydrocarbon claims there, which in part drove Australia's support for Indonesia's illegal occupation of Timor-Leste. A close look at Australia's historical and contemporary engagement with the north seas reveals a great deal about some of the unflattering features of Australia's strategic imagination: its settler-colonial mindset, its refusal to deal substantially with climate change, and its 'extractivism' – a conflation of security and commercial interests.

But if Australia is to address maritime security threats in the north seas it will need to improve relations with its neighbouring states, which will require it to reset its security imagination and habits of engagement. Non-traditional security threats such as illegal fishing are likely to become increasingly prevalent, as are the catastrophic effects of climate change. Cooperation with, and between, local communities and regional neighbours on shared and common interests is fundamental to both regional development *and* the protection of Australia's interests.

WHY HAVE THE NORTH SEAS HISTORICALLY MATTERED TO AUSTRALIA?

Australia's north seas have been historically important for their marine resources and trade. While Australia has been described as 'seablind', such claims can overlook the rich history of pre-colonial relations and trading routes of First Nations in the Arafura and Timor seas, the Torres Strait and the Coral Sea.[13]

Torres Strait Islanders have long associations with Sea Country, and the oceanic origins of some clans are described in their oral histories. Laurie Bamblett, a Wiradjuri man, quotes Yanyuwa elder Dinah Norman Marrngawi as saying: 'Let me tell you something, the sea, the saltwater, the waves are my mothers, the sea is my mother, it is my mother's ancestor.'[14]

Aboriginal histories and archaeology show that Indigenous Australians established trade links with other coastal clans in Asia, such as the Makassar people, centuries ago. In around 1700, trade links were initiated between the Aboriginal people of northern Australia and the Makassar people on the island of Sulawesi (part of contemporary Indonesia), which saw hundreds of fishers sail across the seas each year.[15] Victor Briggs' book *Seafaring* highlights how these sailors and navigators used sophisticated methods to create trade networks and cultural connections that were grounded in environmental consciousness and connection to land and sea.[16] The fishers traded in trepangs – also known as sea cucumbers – which remain popular in Asian cuisine and a valuable marine commodity. This tradition of pre-colonial maritime trade has been recognised in recent rulings on Australian native title.

The north seas region and its sea routes continue to be vital for trade and marine resources, but, as we've discussed, it now plays a special role in defence. This has not always been the case. Despite the known strategic importance of the north seas, they were not well defended prior to World War II. The attacks launched in and from the seas during the war revealed the significance of the air–sea gap for continental security.

On 20 January 1942, Australian warship HMAS *Deloraine* sunk a Japanese I-124 submarine, one of four that was sent to lay mines off the coast of Darwin.[17] The captain and seventy-nine sailors were killed. As a symbol of how far Australia and Japan's security relations have come since, this event was commemorated by the two countries during the multinational naval Exercise Kakadu in 2014.

A month after the Japanese submarine was sunk, on 19 February 1942, Darwin was attacked by Japanese aircraft flying from aircraft carriers, the main one being the 1st Carrier Air Fleet of *Akagi*, *Hiryū*, *Kaga* and *Sōryū*, and a fleet of accompanying warships. In the first raid, the aircraft carriers launched 188 aircraft. Darwin was also attacked by aircraft flying from land bases in the Dutch East Indies (contemporary Indonesia). Japan's intent was to restrict Australian and US capacities to fight in areas north of the Australian mainland, and to prevent a response to its invasion of Timor Island, which occurred that night.[18] The targets were primarily Australian and US ships and port facilities in Darwin Harbour. There were 297 Australians and Americans killed in the attack, which remains the only foreign attack on Australia's continent since Federation. The raid occurred just four days after the fall of Singapore, which led to the capture of more than fifteen thousand Australian soldiers. This put to bed any lingering belief among Australian policymakers that Britain would be prepared and able to protect its East Asian dominions.

As a result, Australia turned to the United States. After the bombing of Pearl Harbor in December 1941, leaders in Washington realised Australia's geostrategic importance. While the United States already had a presence in Australia, this intensified in March 1942, when US general Douglas MacArthur – Supreme Allied Commander, South-West Pacific Area – moved his command of US Pacific forces from the Philippines to Australia. By 1943, 150,000 Americans were stationed across Australia. Australians largely welcomed the US forces, and MacArthur's political influence and advisory role in Canberra was notable, including his close relationship with Prime Minister John Curtin.[19] With few options, the Curtin government elected to surrender a large degree of sovereignty by placing Australian forces under MacArthur's command. Since then, debates over Australia's strategic dependence on the United States and the nature of US influence on Australian policy have been perennial.

After the arrival of the Americans, Allied forces were attacked by Japan during the Battle of the Coral Sea, which from 4 May to 8 May involved a major naval and air engagement. Japan's aim was to cut off the sea lines of communication between Australia and the United States that were vital to the provision of troops and supplies. Japan set up a base in Tulagi in Solomon Islands and aimed to take Port Moresby in Papua New Guinea next. From there, the Japanese Air Force intended to attack Queensland ports and airfields and protect Japanese-held islands in the South Pacific. Three Japanese aircraft carriers, *Shōhō*, *Zuikaku* and *Shōkaku*, protected by a formation of frigates, headed to Port Moresby but were intercepted in the Coral Sea by the Allied fleet led by the US Navy, which knew of Japan's plan through signals intelligence. Confusion reigned as combatants struggled to recognise enemy targets: at one point, a Japanese aircraft almost landed on a US aircraft carrier. On 7 May, the US Navy attacked *Shōhō*, which became the first Japanese aircraft carrier to be sunk during the war. The main battle on 8 May saw ships destroyed and hundreds of troops on both sides killed, largely by air battle. The war revealed a valuable lesson about defending sea lines of communication in Australia's near seas, particularly those vital to supply lines in the South Pacific.

The Battle of the Coral Sea was Japan's first operational failure of the war. It played an important role in the United States' most decisive naval engagement a month later, the Battle of Midway. That battle began after the Japanese military launched an attack on the United States, falsely believing it had sunk the heavily damaged US carrier *Yorktown* in the Coral Sea. US codebreakers were able to forewarn the US fleet, including the repaired *Yorktown*, of the planned Japanese attacks.

Both these battles demonstrated the importance of intelligence and domain awareness, particularly in vast maritime contexts. The confusion over which ships belonged to which state affirms the importance of modern-day efforts to enhance 'interoperability' between allies and partners through training exercises that prepare forces to work together during the chaos of wartime. For Australia, it was merchant sea fleets that kept supply lines open – a timely reminder of their value, given Australia's plans to invest in a merchant shipping fleet, which we discuss in our conclusion to this book.

While unsuccessful, Japan's advance during World War II heightened Australia's anxieties about its vulnerability to threats at sea and in the airspace above the north seas. This means that the north seas are now a maritime area of special import in Australian defence planning and the defensive concept of 'sea denial' – which aims to prevent 'the use of the sea' by an adversary – remains a central pillar of Australian strategic planning.[20]

The 1986 Dibb review and the 1987 defence white paper shifted Australia's focus from forward defence to self-reliance and the defence of Australia. The Dibb review made it clear that Australia's maritime environment was a central element of national security, as the air–sea gap to Australia's north 'would present a formidable obstacle to any aggressor'.[21] According to the review, two contingencies of possible threat to continental Australia should be considered in force structure planning: if a hostile power were to gain access to military bases in Cocos and Christmas Islands or, worse, Papua New Guinea, it would be inimical to Australia's security interests.[22] It was therefore seen as vital that Australia demonstrate its independent military capability in these maritime areas. At the time, Soviet interests in the South Pacific precipitated concerns that Moscow would be able to 'penetrate' the air–sea gap.[23]

The 1987 defence white paper states that Australia's first aim of 'defence self-reliance' would be to defend itself and its 'uniquely Australian interests' with its own resources and a defence plan grounded in the realities of its maritime geography. Such an approach would prevent an aggressor attacking Australia in its sea and air approaches, 'gaining a foothold on any part of our territory, or extracting political concessions from [Australia] through the use or threat of military force'.[24] It prioritised air and sea defences through a 'multilayered detection system' in Australia's area of direct military interest, primarily in the north.[25] Australia's close defence relationship with Papua New Guinea, based on 'historical ties', was also emphasised 'because of the potential strategic implications . . . should a hostile power gain lodgement or control in Papua New Guinea'.[26] 'Defence in depth' – meaning the use of multiple layers of defence – 'would give forces the ability to track and target adversary forces, mount maritime and air operations in the air–sea gap and offensive strike and interdiction missions, and have the defensive capabilities to defeat hostile incursions'.[27] A similar approach based on denying sea and air approaches to enemy forces was adopted in the 1994 defence white paper.

From the late 1990s, Australia also became concerned that the 'arc of instability' to its north would leave Indonesia, Papua New Guinea and other Pacific Island countries vulnerable to failure.[28] Australia had been drawn into conflict among its northern neighbours before. It can be easy to forget that, under British command, Australia fought against Indonesia in a British and Commonwealth force in the mid-1960s. The undeclared war, known as 'Konfrontasi' or the Indonesian Confrontation, occurred mostly in the borderlands of Borneo from 1963 to 1966 and was driven by Indonesia's concerns about the newly established Federation of Malaysia and Britain's ongoing influence in the region.

In 1999, the Indonesian foreign minister announced that Indonesia would hold a referendum in the territory that is now the independent state of Timor-Leste, allowing Timorese people to choose between autonomy within Indonesia or independence. The overwhelming majority of Timorese voted for independence. After the referendum result was announced, the Indonesian military and their supporting Timorese militias engaged in widespread violence.

On 15 September 1999, the UN Security Council authorised Australia to lead International Force East Timor – which became known as INTERFET – in a humanitarian intervention to restore peace and security. Australia's deployment in Timor-Leste was its biggest overseas military operation since the Vietnam War and the first time it had led a major peace-enforcement operation. It caused a serious rift in Australia's relationship with Indonesia. Military links were severed and the Indonesian Parliament demanded the termination of the 1995 Agreement on Maintaining Security, under which the two states were to promote cooperative security activities and consult with each other on matters affecting their common security or in the case of adverse challenges to either party or their common security interests. Many Indonesians believed Australia's next step would be to detach West Papua from Indonesia, and the Australian embassy in Jakarta was attacked. Unlike Timor-Leste, West Papua has never had the opportunity to exercise its right to self-determination. The 1969 Act of Free Choice plebiscite on the issue, initiated by Indonesia, was a sham consultation that did not meet the threshold for a free, fair and universal ballot. Consequently, many West Papuans continue to agitate for independence.

While Australia's interests in its north seas have often been defence-related, they have also been commercial. An Australian business first sought an oil concession in the Timor Sea in 1905.[29] In the 1960s, major oil discoveries there rendered hydrocarbon access and exploitation a key 'maritime security' interest shaping Australia's relations with Indonesia, Portugal and the polity now known as Timor-Leste. In 1974, the Australian oil corporation Woodside discovered gas in the Greater Sunrise field in the Timor Sea. This discovery became instrumental in driving the Whitlam government's support for Indonesia's illegal occupation of Portuguese Timor in 1975.

In the early 1970s, Australia and Indonesia negotiated continental shelf (or seabed) maritime boundaries that left a gap in the middle – the so-called 'Timor Gap' – which was an area of significant hydrocarbon potential. The area was excluded because Portugal administered the eastern half of Timor and had refused to participate in the negotiations. From 1973 to 1982, UNCLOS was being negotiated, which would establish principles for drawing a continental shelf boundary, determining who could exploit the oil and gas beneath the seabed. By the time of Indonesia's formal annexation of Timor-Leste in 1976, it was clear that the 'natural prolongation' principle the states had used to establish a continental shelf boundary much closer to Indonesia than Australia would be challenged by the 'equidistant' or 'median line' approach being discussed during the UNCLOS negotiations. Under natural prolongation, a continental shelf boundary is drawn at the natural extension of the continental shelf. Australia viewed the 'Timor Trough' – a 3500-metre trench, 40 nautical miles from Timor-Leste's coastline – as the dividing line between two continental shelves. Given this geography, natural prolongation provided Australia with more seabed than it might have otherwise received using a median-line principle. This became a source of dispute when Indonesia refused to accept a line based on natural prolongation that would have closed the Timor Gap.

Over the next fifteen years, a convenient quid pro quo emerged: Australia supported Indonesia's continuing occupation of Timor-Leste, and Indonesia agreed to a joint development scheme with Australia in the Timor Gap. The two states shelved their maritime dispute and split the profits from the Timor Gap evenly. In 1989, Australian foreign minister Gareth Evans and Indonesian foreign minister Ali Alatas infamously toasted to the formalisation of this arrangement in the Timor Gap Treaty while flying over the Timor Sea.

The Timor Sea provides one example of Australia's extractivist tendencies in its relationships with its Asian and Pacific neighbours – that is, its denial of their legitimate rights to self-determination to serve its own material and commercial interests, and in this case its strategic interest in maintaining good relations with Indonesia.

Australia's relationship with Papua New Guinea offers further examples. While Australia was still the colonial administrator in Papua New Guinea, the colonial government approved the massive Panguna gold and copper mine in the Bougainville region, operated by Bougainville Copper Ltd, in which Australian company Rio Tinto was a major shareholder. Grievances arising from the impact of the mine and the division of its revenue played a major role in the Bougainville conflict that started in the late 1980s and lasted for a decade. It's estimated up to twenty thousand people were killed during this time, and many more were displaced.

An Australian mining company, Broken Hill Pty Ltd (BHP), also opened the Ok Tedi goldmine in the Western Province of Papua New

Guinea in 1984. The mine did not have the means to adequately process waste, resulting in extensive pollution. After PNG landowners successfully sued BHP, they received compensation and a commitment from BHP to construct a new facility to contain the mine's waste. However, BHP later admitted this plan would do nothing to alleviate the existing pollution. Eventually, in 2002, BHP (then known as BHP Billiton, following a 2001 merger) withdrew from the mine and transferred its equity stake to an independent development program. In 2013 the PNG government took complete ownership of the mine.

However, Australia has also been involved in resource-sharing agreements that recognise the rights of indigenous communities to marine resources. Australia and Papua New Guinea ratified the Torres Strait Treaty in 1985 to manage shared fisheries resources, which included establishing a protected zone for the traditional fishing rights of Torres Strait inhabitants. Under the 1984 *Torres Strait Fisheries Act*, which gave effect to the fisheries elements of the Torres Strait Treaty, traditional inhabitants of the Torres Strait Protected Zone who are PNG nationals are permitted to freely access Australian waters in the protected zone to practise traditional activities – particularly fishing.[30] The treaty defines traditional fishing as 'the taking, by traditional inhabitants for their own or their dependants' consumption or for use in the course of other traditional activities, of the living natural resources of the sea, seabed, estuaries and coastal tidal areas, including dugong and turtle'.[31]

Similarly, Indonesian fishers who use traditional fishing methods are permitted under a 1974 memorandum of understanding between the Australian and Indonesian governments to operate in an area of the Timor Sea within Australia's Fishing Zone. Known as the MOU Box, the area is approximately 55,000 square kilometres and is located off the north-west coast of Western Australia.[32]

But the legal definitions of traditional fishing and fishing communities are not always adequate. For example, the 1974 memorandum of understanding doesn't allow Indonesian fishers to use motorised vessels within the MOU Box and doesn't identify specific indigenous groups, such as the Bajo, as traditional fishing communities. Indonesian fishers' rights have since been restricted by policy changes such as the banning of fishing at Ashmore Reef in 1988 and an amendment to the 1974 memorandum of understanding in 1989.[33]

While some of the agreements Australia has entered into acknowledged the importance of fishing to coastal communities in the north seas, indigenous fishers in the region continue to be criminalised and excluded from areas of cultural and economic significance. The establishment of maritime borders ultimately led to a 'situation of conflict' between Indonesian fishers engaging in traditional fishing and 'the sovereign integrity of Australia's border regime'.[34] To some, the expansion of Australia's maritime boundaries was its 'last colonial act'.[35]

THE RELEVANCE OF CONTEMPORARY SECURITY ISSUES TO AUSTRALIA'S SECURITY

For all the talk about the Indo-Pacific in Australia's security discourses, geography continues to render Southeast Asia and the South Pacific as Australia's primary areas of strategic interest. The Indo-Pacific region is so vast that it would be unrealistic for a middle power such as Australia to seek to secure it entirely. Instead, it must prioritise its immediate geographic area, which has long been perceived as a vulnerability.

But has technology made geography – particularly the air–sea gap – less relevant? Only to a limited extent. The proliferation of long-range precision missiles and space-based and hypersonic capabilities increases the potential ability of an adversary to attack the Australian mainland from afar.[36] While this has changed the calculus on the defensive value of Australia's 'strategic moat', assault over water remains 'a most difficult military operation', as T.B. Millar put it in 1985.[37]

Any potential invasion of the Australian mainland would require a hostile force to transit across oceans and seas, and the most logical way would be via the archipelagos to Australia's north. Indonesia's archipelago of 13,500 islands stretches 5000 kilometres across the northern approaches to Australia; its strategic importance to Australia has long been recognised as both a means of and a buffer against attack. As the 1986 Dibb review observed: 'The Indonesian archipelago forms a protective barrier to Australia's northern approaches . . . At the same time, we must also recognise that, because of its proximity, the archipelago to our north is the area from or through which a military threat to Australia could most easily be posed.' This threat is mitigated by the fact that 'any serious military operations against Australia would require air and naval assets capable of protecting forces that would have to cross hundreds of miles of water . . . Even the narrow Torres Strait is a hazardous stretch of water for an invader to cross'.[38]

Even now, it would be difficult for an adversary to launch and sustain an attack on Australia from the northern archipelagos. Nevertheless, sea denial in the north seas and preventing adversaries' access to bases in proximate archipelagos are security imperatives. This is influenced by factors such as Australia's diplomatic relationships with Indonesia, Papua New Guinea and Timor-Leste, the presence of a regional common interest in maintaining stability and peace, and each neighbour's own defence priorities and capabilities.

But focusing solely on defending the air–sea gap around Australia's approaches could potentially undermine a strategy designed to keep threats and conflict away from Australia's immediate region of concern. Instead, Australia takes a 'layered defence' approach, based on the idea that engaging in cooperation and collective security efforts further from Australia's shores may prevent conflict emerging closer to home. This broadly fits with conceptions of maritime security as a home-and-away game: oceans are interconnected and interdependent, so the whole must be protected in order to protect a part. Regional and global security is therefore viewed as important to Australia's territorial defence.

Australia's *2020 Defence Strategic Update* recognised that short- and medium-term threats to national security are likely to exist in the 'grey zone'. In the maritime domain, this term is increasingly used to describe the employment by states of coastguards, fishing vessels and other non-military assets to advance strategic goals such as preventing foreign ships from safely transiting through maritime areas and deterring other states and foreign actors from accessing oil, gas, fish and other resources.

While the 2023 *Defence Strategic Review* eschews the term 'grey zone', the 2020 *Defence Strategic Update* states that it involves 'activities designed to coerce countries in ways that seek to avoid military conflict . . . paramilitary forces, militarisation of disputed features, exploiting influence, interference operations and the coercive use of trade and economic levers'.[39] Grey zone tactics can be used alongside conventional military force but fall below the threshold of war and, by blurring the line between civil and military operations, make it more difficult for states to defend themselves. In the maritime, grey zone tactics can include a range of activities such as sabotage, espionage, harassment, propaganda and coercion, conducted by state-sponsored, paramilitary and non-state actors such as fishing and commercial vessels.

Illegal, unregulated and unreported (IUU) fishing is sometimes linked with the grey zone, but fisheries crimes may also be committed by sophisticated transnational criminal syndicates, supported by business executives, lawyers and tax havens, or by local fishers, sometimes unintentionally if maritime boundaries are not clearly known. It presents a broad range of security challenges. IUU fishing can undermine the ability of states to create rules around the sustainability of fishing stocks and conservation of marine environments. In Australia's north seas, for example, illegal fishers use equipment that threatens coral reefs. IUU fishing can rob coastal communities of jobs and food sources. Globally, it is also linked with other maritime security challenges such as 'seafood slavery', a term developed to capture the severe human- and labour-rights abuses that some people face while working and living on fishing vessels.

IUU fishing also has economic consequences. In 2018, the OECD (Organisation for Economic Co-operation and Development) reported that Australian fisheries are worth US$2248.4 million and provide nearly fifteen thousand jobs.[40] Globally, IUU fishing is said to cost up to US$23 billion annually, around 20 per cent of the overall seafood catch, but it is difficult to get precise and up-to-date figures on the costs of IUU fishing to the Australian economy.

We do know that there was an increase in IUU fishing in the north seas during the COVID-19 pandemic. According to the Australian Fisheries Management Authority, the number of illegal fishing boats intercepted in these seas increased from four or fewer in 2019/20 to eight in 2020/21 and then jumped to 231 in 2021/22 – a nearly thirtyfold increase in one year.[41] The intercepted boats were largely traditional or small-scale vessels from Southeast Asia.

What generated this spike? One reason was COVID-19, which pushed fish prices down and increased poverty in coastal areas in Indonesia such as the Nusa Tenggara Islands, whose economies largely relied on tourism. The legal fishing industry also contracted.[42] A second reason was that territorial disputes and sustainability issues in the South China Sea have pushed vessels south. In March 2017, a Darwin court cited the territorial disputes in the South China Sea as one of the reasons a group of Vietnamese men had been fishing illegally in Australian waters. The men claimed 'they had been pushed from their traditional fishing territory in the Spratly Islands over the past few years by China, which now controls parts of the region.'[43]

In the 'grey zone', states are increasingly using fishing fleets to achieve their strategic ends, such as preventing other actors from legitimately accessing maritime areas or resources within them. The most prominent example is China's 'maritime militia' in the South China Sea, which we will discuss at greater length in Chapter 4. There are concerns that Chinese fishing fleets are now fanning out from the South and East China seas to more distant waters. The scale of the fishing can result in environmental damage, as occurred in the Galapagos, where a Chinese fishing 'armada' logged 73,000 hours of fishing in just one month.[44]

In 2020, when China's ministry of commerce announced a $204-million deal to establish a 'comprehensive multi-functional fishery industrial park' project on Daru Island in Papua New Guinea's

Western Province, the plan's environmental and security implications were questioned. The MOU offered little detail, but it was expected that Chinese-backed commercial vessels would be allowed to fish in the Torres Strait, raising concerns among Torres Strait fishing communities in Australia.[45] The fishing park would also give China a foothold only a few kilometres from Australia[46] and open the door to more Chinese fishers trawling an area that Australia considers its strategic neighbourhood.

Australia's concerns about Chinese fleets in the north seas is reasonable. In 2017, Timorese and Australian officials, with the help of the activist organisation Sea Shepherd, apprehended a fleet of fifteen Chinese fishing boats. Timor-Leste had granted the fleet a twelve-month permit to fish inside its exclusive economic zone for US$312,450. The fleet was permitted to fish for tuna, but Timorese and Australian officials found an estimated 40 tonnes of sharks and rays on board. The Chinese company that was granted the permit, Hong Long Fisheries, had the same owners as Pingtan Marine Enterprises, which was banned from Indonesian waters following accusations of theft. Pingtan had claimed that under the Timor licence each of its ships could reap annual revenue of approximately US$3 million. China's actions were described at the time as a form of 'state-sponsored illegal fishing'.[47] However, the crew and boats were later released without charge.

Some of the reactive panic within Australia's national security community to Chinese MOUs in Papua New Guinea is less reasonable. Since the Daru announcement in 2020, China has made no substantive progress on implementing its plans to establish a fishing park (admittedly, the COVID-19 pandemic may have contributed to this). And in 2021, the PNG government said it was not formally considering a proposal for a 'New Daru City', a project that had been floated by Hong Kong–registered company WYW Holding Limited to transform the port town into a business, commercial and industrial zone. Indeed, the project has been described as a 'mirage' that will 'never eventuate'.[48]

The substantive dangers posed by grey zone 'threats' is also often unclear. Foreign 'coercion', 'interference' and 'influence' are terms invoked in discussions of China's role in Australia and neighbouring countries, but these concepts are poorly defined and differentiated from each other. This matters, because if there is confusion about what the threats are, countering them becomes more difficult. For instance, a recent report produced by an Australian think tank provides examples of 'Chinese maritime coercion' in Southeast Asia and the Pacific.[49] The only two Pacific examples relate to Papua New Guinea: one is the Daru fishing park and the other a Chinese state-owned company expanding the Momote Airport. But no evidence is provided to demonstrate that either development would necessarily subject Papua New Guinea to 'maritime coercion' or that Papua New Guinea was forced to enter into these agreements.

AUSTRALIA'S CURRENT POLICY APPROACH

Today, northern Australia is viewed as an 'alliance hub', ideal for joint operations facilitated by the Australia–US Force Posture Initiatives (AUSFPI). The Australian Signals Directorate station at Joint Defence Facility Pine Gap, established in 1966, is one of the most important covert surveillance bases for the United States outside its own territory. Along with the North West Cape facilities, Pine Gap aids US surveillance of East Asia, including China.

In 2010, the Gillard government announced US Marine Corps troops would be deployed to Darwin to conduct training and exercises with the Australian Defence Force, aiming to enhance military cooperation and regional security through capacity building, interoperability and warfighting for combined and joint operations. They were to be deployed on a rotational basis for about six months.

The first rotation of the US Marine Rotational Force – Darwin began in 2011 with Australia hosting about two hundred US Marines. Today, more than 2500 Marines are on rotation at any one time.[50] The arrangement expanded in 2014 to include the rotation of US Air Force personnel and 'increased logistics and sustainment support for US surface and subsurface vessels in Australia' to enhance maritime cooperation between the allies.[51] In February 2020, a $1.1-billion upgrade to the Tindal air force base in northern Australia was announced to provide access for US war planes.

The 2022 Australia–US Ministerial Consultations (or AUSMIN) formalised the AUSFPI. The two allies also decided more stores, munitions and fuel 'in support of US capabilities' would be located in Australia, and agreed to continue a US rotational presence in Australia across air, land and maritime domains. This presence would include the Bomber Task Force and the US Navy.

These developments highlight the increasing geostrategic importance of Australia (particularly northern Australia) to the United States. It also highlights Australia's deepening commitment to the US alliance. As we have mentioned, the 2023 *Defence Strategic Review* endorsed the expansion of the US military presence in Australia, recommending that Australia's future strategy prioritise 'an enhanced and expanded Alliance with the United States, including key US Force Posture Initiatives in Australia'.[52]

All of this means there is a good chance the US presence in northern Australia will continue to grow, and rapidly. In March 2022, when the US Marine Corps stood up its first Marine Littoral Regiment in Hawaii, defence experts suggested that northern Australia could be an ideal location for another such regiment given the importance of areas that bridge land and sea. Australia has a 'large shore-based population', 'expansive coastal regions and offshore islands' and it is surrounded 'by a complex web of interlocking littorals' that link the region together, most notably the archipelago of the north (Indonesia, the Philippines, Papua New Guinea, Fiji, the Marshall Islands, Solomon Islands, Tuvalu and Vanuatu).[53]

But there are gaps in Australia's policies when it comes to other areas of maritime security. Australia has not updated its national action plan to prevent, deter and eliminate IUU fishing since 2014, despite the rise in IUU activities regionally.[54] It also hasn't addressed the jurisdictional issues within Australia: fishing is managed by state, territorial and federal authorities, and this can cause problems. For instance, the Rowley Shoals (south of the Timor Sea) formally come under Western Australia's jurisdiction, but WA authorities say they need more support from the federal government to combat IUU fishing there. Disputes over the allocation of responsibility for policing Australia's exclusive economic zone reflect the need for greater connection between the agencies working in maritime security domains and an overarching maritime security strategy that holistically assesses and responds to threats in and from the maritime domain.

Over the last twenty years, Australian authorities have destroyed approximately 1500 boats and prosecuted more than two thousand foreign (mainly Indonesian) nationals engaged in illegal fishing in its waters.[55] Traditional Indonesian vessels have been allowed access to the MOU Box in Australia's fishing zone north-west of Broome since 1974, but IUU fishing occurs because of opportunistic fishing in and around the MOU Box.[56] Fishers have also shifted away from 'traditional' fishing activities in Australian waters and towards the use of motorised vessels, which is against the rules.

Australia and Indonesia work together closely to combat IUU fishing, running annual coordinated patrols between Australia's Maritime Boundary Command, the Indonesian Coast Guard (BAKAMLA), the Indonesian Directorate General of Surveillance for Marine and Fisheries Resources (PSDKP) and the Australian Fisheries Management Authority at the Australia–Indonesia boundary in an operation known as Operation Gannet.[57] In February 2020, the two neighbours entered into an expanded information-sharing agreement that could see the Australian Defence Force provide greater support for maritime domain awareness.

With its Indonesian counterparts, the Australian Fisheries Management Authority runs public information campaigns in eastern Indonesia and other key states such as Vietnam and Papua New Guinea, raising awareness about the consequences of getting caught IUU fishing in Australia's exclusive economic zone. This approach has contributed to the number of foreign fishing vessels operating illegally in Australian waters falling from 367 in 2005/06 to four in 2018/19. These campaigns were suspended during the COVID-19 pandemic, which subsequently saw a corresponding increase in IUU fishing in Australia's northern waters.[58]

Australia participates in a range of bilateral fishing agreements and arrangements with neighbouring countries such as Timor-Leste and Papua New Guinea, including cooperative patrols on fisheries surveillance and enforcement in the Arafura and Timor seas.[59] But while the Australian government has prioritised deterrence and maritime border protection, it has neglected its commitment under the 1989 update to its 1974 MOU with Indonesia 'to make arrangements for co-operation in developing alternative income projects in Eastern Indonesia for traditional fishermen traditionally engaged in fishing'.[60]

Australia's contemporary relationship with Indonesia has the qualities of a diplomatic rollercoaster. After Timor-Leste achieved independence in 2002, the relationship improved, in large part because the two states needed to cooperate to respond to terrorism and border-security threats following the Bali bombings in October 2002, the Marriott Hotel attacks in August 2003, the Australian embassy bombings in September 2004 and the Bali bombings in October 2005. High-level strategic dialogue and military talks resumed, and law enforcement and intelligence agencies cooperated on both traditional and non-traditional security threats. The relationship improved further after the Indian Ocean tsunami of 2004: Australia responded quickly and generously, providing humanitarian support, emergency relief, engineering assistance and aeromedical evacuation. Australia also announced a $1-billion aid program. In 2005, Australia resumed training members of the Indonesian military.

But in mid-2006, when Australia granted asylum to forty-three asylum seekers from Indonesia's West Papua province, Indonesia recalled its ambassador to Australia. To assuage Indonesian concerns that Australia supported West Papuan self-determination, Australia and Indonesia signed the Agreement on the Framework for Security Cooperation (the Lombok Treaty) in November 2006,[61] providing for enhanced defence cooperation. Both parties agreed they would not support activities that would threaten the stability, sovereignty or territorial integrity of the other. However, relations were again tested in 2013, when it was reported that Australia had spied on President Susilo Bambang Yudhoyono and nine other high-level Indonesian officials.[62] Australia scrambled to rebuild bridges with Indonesia, and in 2014 the two countries' foreign ministers signed an agreement to promote intelligence cooperation and create a 'joint understanding on a code of conduct'.[63]

Relations were tested yet another time in 2015, when Indonesia executed two Australian drug smugglers. Prime Minister Tony Abbott maintained that he respected Indonesia's sovereignty but stressed that Australia stood against the death penalty and the bilateral relationship had suffered because of the executions.[64] But Australia quickly backtracked, sending its recalled ambassador back to Indonesia after only a few weeks.[65] Its subsequent efforts to rebuild its relationship with Indonesia were so successful that the two states were able to agree to a comprehensive strategic partnership in August 2018.[66]

Reflecting the ebbs and flows of the relationship, by November 2018 the relationship was strained once more – this time because the Australian government announced it was considering following the United States' lead and moving the Australian embassy in Israel from Tel Aviv to Jerusalem.[67] When the two states didn't sign a planned bilateral free trade agreement at that year's East Asia Summit, the official reason given was 'translation issues', but the embassy announcement was widely believed to be what scuppered the deal, given the domestic pressure it put on Indonesian president Joko Widodo.[68] Yet again, Australia scrambled to mend the relationship, and the Indonesia–Australia Comprehensive Economic Partnership Agreement was signed in March 2019 and came into force in July 2020.[69]

The bilateral relationship with Indonesia remains a delicate one for Australia: it cannot rely on shared history, culture and interests to strengthen cooperation as it does with allies and partners such as the United States and New Zealand. This challenge isn't unique to Australia's relationship with Indonesia, but it is of particular importance given Indonesia's geographic proximity.

Maritime security cooperation is currently strong between the two states, but the fact they don't always agree is reflected in their differing stances on other maritime issues. For instance, they hold different opinions on some key provisions of UNCLOS, including the right of transit passage through Indonesia's archipelagic sea lanes. Indonesian authorities regard archipelagic waters as an 'integral part of their national territory . . . [and] tend to view such waters as equivalent to their land territory, sometimes diminishing or discounting altogether the concessions (including navigation rights) given to maritime states as the trade-off for recognition of the archipelagic concept'.[70] Australia, on the other hand, supports the right of transit passage to states navigating through archipelagic sea lanes.

Disagreements on maritime boundaries have the potential to flare up. Many maritime boundaries are dual boundaries, meaning they delineate both the exclusive economic zone of a country and its continental shelf. But this is not the case with Australia and Indonesia: their maritime boundaries, set in 1971 and 1972, only established the limits of their respective continental shelves – essentially the seabed boundary determining access to hydrocarbon resources. This was not an exclusive economic zone boundary, because this concept was not formalised until the 1982 UNCLOS. The 1997 Perth Treaty, negotiated over two decades later, determined the exclusive economic zone limits between the two countries in accordance with equidistance principles – in other words, it identified the boundary line as being an equal distance from each coast. While the provisions in the Perth Treaty have so far been observed, Indonesia has never ratified the treaty. In 2021, an Indonesian border negotiator told an Australian newspaper that talks between Australia and Indonesia on maritime boundaries had restarted in December 2019 but were stalled by the COVID-19 pandemic. In response, the Department of

Foreign Affairs and Trade insisted that the meetings had only concerned 'technical amendments'. There have been hints that Indonesia wishes to address the treaty or reopen discussions over continental shelf boundaries, an unattractive prospect for Australia, given changes to international law since the 1970s and the benefits that current boundaries provide.

Revived discussions around the Australia–Indonesia maritime boundary are a consequence of Australia and Timor-Leste's agreement on a maritime boundary in 2018. The agreement, negotiated through a world-first UN compulsory conciliation initiated in 2016, showed Australia's willingness to drop its 'natural prolongation' argument in favour of a median line between the two states. Consequently, Timor-Leste's continental shelf boundary is much closer to Australia than Indonesia's.

The five decades of Australian government policy preceding this momentous boundary treaty with Timor-Leste provides one of the best examples of Australia's evasion of the rules-based order when it suits its interests. In 2002, three months before Timor-Leste's independence, Australia excluded itself from compulsory jurisdiction on maritime boundary disputes under UNCLOS. While legal, the move prevented Timor-Leste from taking Australia to court to resolve the maritime boundary between them and confirmed Australia's confidence in its 'natural prolongation' argument was shaky. The 2002 Timor Sea Treaty signed on the day of Timor-Leste's independence placed a moratorium on maritime boundary delimitation, instead establishing a joint petroleum development area much like that which Australia and Indonesia had agreed upon in the Timor Gap. What was different was that Timor-Leste received a 90–10 split of profits but Australia retained the rights to offshore processing.

Ironically, Australian leaders' and officials' incessant use of the term 'rules-based order' to put pressure on China following the 2016 South China Sea arbitral tribunal ruling proved to be Australia's undoing. Timor-Leste's leaders and supporters weaponised Australia's rhetoric against it, pointing out its double standard in condemning China's behaviour in the South China Sea but refusing to negotiate boundaries with the Timorese. Allegations that Australia had spied on Timor-Leste during the 2004 negotiations of the 2007 Treaty on Certain Maritime Arrangements in the Timor Sea (CMATS) also re-emerged, raising questions about whether the Australian government had met its obligations under the 1969 Vienna Convention on the Law of Treaties to negotiate 'in good faith'. While this agreement may have been technically within the rules, it was hardly in the spirit of them.

A compulsory conciliation under UNCLOS was initiated by Timor-Leste because other legal strategies could not directly address the issue of maritime boundaries.[71] Australia initially disputed the Conciliation Commission's jurisdiction, which led critics to again draw parallels between Australia's behaviour and that of China in its response to the arbitration proceedings brought against it by the Philippines.[72] Australia attempted to deflect criticisms by arguing that it was acting within the rules-based order by maintaining a commitment to the CMATS Treaty, but the accusations of hypocrisy proved persuasive. Both parties ultimately engaged with the conciliation process in good faith, which was central to its success.

The new Maritime Boundary Treaty, ratified in August 2019, was widely cast as a diplomatic victory for the small state. Notably, the Australia–Timor-Leste maritime boundary did not actually conform to equidistance principles set out in UNCLOS across the whole boundary. Instead, it reflected a flexible pragmatism that enabled both states to find a compromise. Australia declared the resolution of the treaty an 'example of the rules-based order in action'.[73]

This episode demonstrates that, far from lacking savvy, Australia's neighbours can take Australia's strategic anxiety about China's regional influence and access to nearby maritime infrastructure and leverage it to their advantage. This behaviour has since continued. In 2018, it was leaked to the media that Timorese officials had suggested turning to China's Belt and Road Initiative for the funds to realise Dili's pipeline ambitions for the Greater Sunrise field, presumably to pressure Australia to support or invest in its development plans.[74] And in 2022, Timorese president José Ramos-Horta launched an audacious public bid to compel Australia to support Timor-Leste's plans for Greater Sunrise. Timor-Leste's leaders envisage the Tasi Mane project as an oil and gas processing hub on its south coast that would develop the resources from Greater Sunrise, as outlined in its national 2011–2030 Strategic Development Plan. Estimated to cost US$16–18 billion, Timorese leaders say Tasi Mane would provide an 'industrial base' to the Timorese economy, which is already heavily reliant on oil and gas revenue from the Timor Sea. Ramos-Horta threatened to turn to China if Australia did not step up to support its development. While Australia has been reluctant to support the project because of concerns about its commercial viability and cost, Timor Leste's leaders have form in changing Canberra's mind.

Some Timorese politicians disagree about the viability of the Tasi Mane plan, and an independent report commissioned as part of the Timor Sea Conciliation found it relied on optimistic accounting.[75] But the Timor-Leste government has staked Timor-Leste's future development on the plan and is unlikely to change course. Developing Greater Sunrise is also an urgent priority for the Timor-Leste government, whose sovereign wealth fund, which includes profits from its other resource projects, is rapidly declining. Because the Australian government identifies Australia as a major development partner in Timor-Leste and the Pacific,[76] and Timor-Leste is facing an economic cliff as oil and gas reserves in other areas of the Timor Sea dwindle, a negotiated solution seems the best option for both states. This would require a nuanced understanding of the multidimensional factors involved in the security challenges that Australia faces, as well as an acknowledgement of how Australia's past decision-making has contributed to Timor-Leste's current development challenges.

The politics of China's increasingly visible presence in Australia's region, particularly via its Belt and Road Initiative, are also evident in Australia's relations with Papua New Guinea. A 'modern-day' Battle of the Coral Sea is playing out, involving submarine cables rather than submarine warfare.[77] In 2018, the Turnbull government, acting on security advice, banned Chinese telecommunications corporation Huawei from operating in Australia's 5G network. In the same year, the government announced that Australia would finance the Coral Sea Cable System, a deep-sea high-speed internet connection between Papua New Guinea, Solomon Islands and Australia, countering another bid by Huawei. However, while PNG prime minister James Marape accepted Australia's funding and building of the Coral Sea Cable, his government then contracted Huawei to build Papua New Guinea's domestic network, which connects to the cable.

Still concerned about Huawei's growing presence in Papua New Guinea and the South Pacific, the Australian government funded Australian telco Telstra's July 2022 acquisition of Digicel Pacific, the largest private telecommunications company in the South Pacific. While the Albanese government downplayed the deal by calling it a commercial investment, its decision reflected an uncomfortable reality: Australia's regional development agenda is shaped by strategic priorities. Regional partners that have complicated histories with Australia may not be sold on the idea that the Australian government will treat them more ethically or provide greater assurance of their long-term sovereignty than Beijing.

WHAT SHOULD AUSTRALIA DO DIFFERENTLY?

Northern Australia is set to play an even more important role in Australia's national security than it previously has, as demonstrated by recent developments in the Australia–US alliance and the 2023 *Defence Strategic Review*'s emphasis on the north seas. Some of Australia's key foreign- and defence-policy dilemmas are playing out in the region, the most significant being how to grapple with a changing security environment in which the threat of direct attack by another country remains low but is nonetheless one that defence planners must prepare for and deter.

As the 2023 *Defence Strategic Review* tells us, more states will soon use new technologies to project power across greater distances and Australia will not be able to rely on the advantages of its isolated geography to the extent it has in the past. Australia increasingly views 'national defence' as reliant on deterring threats that can move over and through the north seas.

In April 2023, the Albanese government announced it would increase its investment in Australia's northern bases to the tune of $3.8-billion over four years.[78] It justified the spending by arguing that the Australian Army and Air Force need to be better equipped for 'littoral operations in northern land and maritime spaces', which would involve the development of a long-range strike capability, central to a deterrence-by-denial strategy.[79]

The government's focus on the Army and Air Force is a reminder that it is not only the Navy that operates in maritime environments: effective maritime defence strategy requires a joined-up approach within the Australian Defence Force. This seems easier in theory than in practice, as the Navy, Air Force and Army remain relatively siloed. It should also include other stakeholders, such as civil society groups and the shipping industry.

Another dilemma in the north seas is how to maintain the US security guarantee without compromising Australia's foreign and strategic policy-making independence. While Australian support for the US alliance is generally strong, military basing has been electorally controversial. The media reported that in 2010 the Gillard government had a last-minute case of cold feet prior to its announcement of the US Marine Rotational Force – Darwin, fearing a backlash from the Labor Party's left faction.

There have been two key concerns about US military basing: the first is that Australia risks ceding its sovereignty to the United States (successive Australian leaders have been keen to emphasise that Pine Gap is a *joint* defence facility, even if it was built and paid for by the Americans); the second is that basing unnecessarily makes Australia a target for the United States' adversaries.

In some ways, these concerns are outdated and the more important question is how the practices, habits and routines of the US alliance – and the cumulative decisions of the past – ultimately shape and constrain Australia's perception of its strategic options. We will return to this question in the book's conclusion but note here that both sides are clearly determined to reinforce the importance of the alliance for dealing with new strategic challenges. It seems unlikely that Australia would roll back its investments with the United States in the north given its concerns about the shifting strategic environment.

Australia's real challenge, therefore, lies in ensuring that other states in its immediate region don't view Australia as America's 'lapdog'. It can do this by investing more in regional diplomacy (particularly public diplomacy), building sustainable partnerships beyond the defence realm, demonstrating Australia's interest in the priorities of neighbouring states and providing greater reassurance that its deterrence efforts are designed to be defensive rather than offensive.

As we said in the introduction, we wrote this book because we want to apply a fresh lens to the analysis of Australia's security. In thinking about the north seas, this means looking beyond the domain's traditional role in defence planning and alliance politics and expanding our concept of what Australian security means and who it benefits. The north seas maritime domain reveals the complexity of traditional and non-traditional security challenges and the way they often intersect with issues such as climate change, pandemics, transnational crime, and human-rights and labour issues.

We also argued that First Nations people deserve a much bigger voice in Australian security discussions. As Indigenous foreign-affairs and policy scholars James Blackwell and Julie Ballangarry point out, current defence and diplomacy efforts to engage First Nations communities still fall short of giving them 'a fair seat at the table, or full and accurate representation' in international relations.[80] This needs to be rectified. There is great potential for the government to learn from the pre-colonial international relations of First Nations peoples in the north seas and their approach to protecting the seas and oceans.

Balancing state priorities, the interests of coastal communities and Australia's regional relationships is an ongoing challenge that needs to be managed. A recent article reported that Torres Strait Islander fishing communities are increasingly concerned about illegal fishing and have accused the Australian Fisheries Management Authority and Border Force of being unwilling to crack down on incursions from PNG fishers. One Torres Strait Island leader stated, 'I fully understand that we've got to keep Papua New Guinea on-side . . . [and] not entertaining other foreign interests. But this is about First Nations people in Australia who are trying to survive.'[81] Indeed, efforts to demarcate maritime areas into discrete zones based on territorial sovereignty can overlook connections across these maritime areas, as well as connections that specific communities have with the maritime environment, which might not neatly fit within boundaries. In 2022, it was reported that a group of Indonesians in the Timor Sea had called for Australia to cede control of Ashmore and Cartier islands (technically in the Indian Ocean). Over 600 kilometres north of Broome, the islands were initially claimed by the British in the late nineteenth century for their guano deposits. It seems likely that sovereignty and maritime boundary issues will remain a part of the political landscape in Australia's north seas.

While Australia's fishing agreements with Indonesia and Papua New Guinea do take traditional practices of indigenous communities into account, more could be done to listen to First Nations voices (within and beyond Australia) in maritime governance and international relations more generally, although such efforts should not merely assist the objectives of the settler-colonial state.[82] A new agreement in 2022 between Australia and Indonesia that focused on addressing illegal fishing in Australia's fishing zone was balanced by a commitment to providing economic opportunities through 'alternative livelihoods'.[83] But it doesn't go far enough. Australia should also consider new rules and arrangements to enable fishers to use motorised vessels without it being cast as IUU fishing. This would expand economic opportunities for Indonesian fishers.

The history of the north seas does not always reflect well on Australia. Australia's extractivism led it to support Indonesia's illegal annexation of Timor-Leste, and following Timor-Leste's independence Australia behaved in such a way that critics cast it as the new coloniser of the Timor Sea. More recently, its announcement of the AUKUS security partnership raised concerns in Indonesia, with Jakarta speaking out against nuclear proliferation and nuclear-powered submarines at a UN review of the nuclear non-preliferation treaty.[84] Despite this, in 2023 Indonesia and Australia committed to developing a new defence-cooperation agreement, again highlighting how multidimensional these relationships can be. Unfortunately, the 2006 Lombok Treaty has severely limited Australia's options to publicly advocate for the civil and political rights of West Papuans, which President Widodo's administration has cracked down on in recent years. If Australia were to do so, it would unravel the treaty and nearly two decades of cooperation and trust-building between the countries, as well as cooperation on climate change and other initiatives. But by failing to do so, Australia's credentials as an upholder of the rules-based order, especially as it relates to self-determination, are thrown into question and its relationships with several Pacific Island countries are undermined.

Repairing damage arising from Australia's past behaviour requires developing and coordinating with regional partners in areas of common interest, particularly those that will contribute to regional economic development. This is already happening to some degree in maritime security between Australia and Indonesia. While not without its stumbles, such coordination and cooperation build trust that can assist with securing the economic livelihoods of coastal communities in Australia and Indonesia that rely on the maritime domain.

Many states in the Indo-Pacific are predominantly concerned with economic development and nation-building rather than strategic competition. An Indo-Pacific strategy that fails to account for the economic priorities of regional states is one that is doomed to fail. This includes maritime security strategies, because the ocean is vital to economic security as a source of jobs, food, energy resources and trade.

Australia, the United States and US partners (except for Japan) have lagged in developing an inclusive economic agenda for the Indo-Pacific, focusing instead on great power competition, which PNG and Timorese leaders have criticised. Indonesia's President Jokowi has even called for the Indo-Pacific to explicitly engage and include China, rather than implicitly trying to contain it. Indonesia, Papua New Guinea and Timor-Leste have engaged with China's Belt and Road Initiative because infrastructure is a nation-building priority. It should be noted that there are question marks over whether COVID-19 and internal economic crises will act as a handbrake on China's BRI investment – it turns out that holding debt, even if some of it can be leveraged, is not necessarily beneficial for China. On this issue, Australian politicians must keep a cool head.

Australia needs to push past the idea that it should only assist regional states with their maritime security because if it doesn't, China will. This is *an* interest but it's not the only one. As researcher and former naval officer Sam Bateman pointed out, when Australia supports the security of its neighbours it has a flow-on effect: if Papua New Guinea's 'borders and waters aren't secure, then illegal immigrants, drugs and other prohibited goods can readily move through PNG into Australia'.[85] Based purely on self-interest, there is a national security incentive to assist Papua New Guinea. If done well, such maritime assistance could also demonstrate a genuine commitment to advancing political and economic security and stability within Papua New Guinea for its own sake. To this end, the May 2023 defence cooperation agreement between Papua New Guinea and the United States has a maritime element and builds on the US partnership with Australia and Papua New Guinea on the redevelopment of the Lombrum Naval Base on Manus Island. The United States' more active defence engagement with Papua New Guinea adds a new, potentially complicated, dimension to Australia's security relationship with both states, as it seeks to balance their different priorities and ways of doing things.

Ensuring the safety of coastal communities under threat from climate change should also be a key priority. As 'ocean superpowers' with massive marine areas and similar challenges in relation to climate change and over-exploitation of their maritime domains, Australia and Indonesia have an opportunity to collaborate on some of these shared problems.[86]

When it comes to governing their often vast ocean jurisdictions, coastal Indo-Pacific states have differing capacities, including in maritime domain surveillance and intelligence. These capability gaps underscore the importance of maritime security cooperation with Indonesia and other regional states to protect fishing rights from external threats and to ensure the sustainability and conservation of fish stocks and the marine environment.

Emerging pressures suggest a risk that IUU fishing in the 'grey zone' will increase in Australian waters, and the threat may not come from Southeast Asian fishers. Does Australia have the capabilities and the governance structures to deal with it? It is doubtful. For an area of 8 million square kilometres, Australia's navy has had only eleven patrol boats supporting civilian authorities to enforce maritime law. Australia should therefore reimagine its understanding of itself as a regional actor, ditching the well-worn lens through which it has historically viewed its northern neighbours as a threat and developing something more conducive to positive and sustainable relations. One way might be to try to develop a shared regional identity as responsible users and conservators of the ocean global commons.

In the end, collaborative approaches to dealing with blue crime, including IUU fishing, are important not only for the security of littoral communities in the north seas but also for environmental and economic reasons. Canberra's influence in the northern region will be shaped by its ability to cooperate with maritime neighbours on a shared agenda. The maritime space – vital to the security of Australia, Indonesia, Papua New Guinea and Timor-Leste – is one that should continue to offer fruitful opportunities for mutually beneficial cooperation.

3

———

THE WESTERN PACIFIC

In August 2022, US House of Representatives speaker Nancy Pelosi visited Taiwan during her Asian tour. 'By travelling to Taiwan,' Pelosi said, 'we honor our commitment to democracy: reaffirming that the freedoms of Taiwan – and all democracies – must be respected.'[1] There were immediate consequences. One American commentator described her visit as 'utterly reckless, dangerous and irresponsible'.[2] China characterised it as a 'major political provocation'[3] and commenced joint military exercises around Taiwan, launching ballistic missiles over the island, instigating air and naval operations on the edge of Taiwan's claimed territorial waters and sending more than twenty fighter jets into Taiwan's air defence identification zone. It also embarked on a series of cyber attacks. In turn, the United States positioned an aircraft carrier and three other warships in waters east of Taiwan.

When asked about Pelosi's visit, Australian prime minister Anthony Albanese opted to play a straight bat. 'The level of US engagement with our Taiwanese counterparts is a matter for them,' he observed.[4] Foreign Minister Penny Wong, accomplished in the delivery of deadpan responses, pointedly added, 'All parties should consider how they best contribute to de-escalating the current tensions . . . we all want peace and stability in the Taiwan Strait.'[5]

During her visit, Pelosi praised Taiwan's 'flourishing democracy' and made it 'unequivocally clear' that the United States would 'not abandon' its commitment to Taiwan.[6] But for decades the United States' commitment to Taiwan was anything but clear. This uncertainty as to its policy in the event of a China–Taiwan conflict was deliberate, based on the principle of 'strategic ambiguity'. President Donald Trump veered close to removing that ambiguity. In his last days in office, his administration ramped up its confrontational approach to China by lifting the rules that prohibited interactions between American and Taiwanese diplomats, symbolically upgrading the US–Taiwan relationship. President Joe Biden has also been clearer on the US position, on four occasions making statements that implied the United States would support Taiwan if there were a conflict. His most recent statement, in September 2022, came when he was asked if the United States would defend Taiwan if China invaded. His response was, 'Yes, if in fact there was an unprecedented attack.'[7] After each statement, US officials were in a frenzy to walk back his comments, insisting that the principle of 'strategic ambiguity' still holds.

Given the closeness of Australia's relationship with the United States, these controversies reverberate in the Australian political arena. And that arena has not been without controversies of its own. In December 2022, a delegation of six Australian politicians travelled to Taiwan, the first visit by an Australian parliamentary delegation for several years. Albanese was again required to play a straight bat when asked about the trip, carefully specifying that it wasn't 'a government visit'. When asked about delegation's intentions, he responded dryly: 'I have no idea, I'm not going.'[8]

Both examples crystallise many of the dilemmas the Australian government faces in the Western Pacific: How should it respond to a superpower China? What must it do to maintain the US security guarantee? What are its obligations to its strategic partners? How can it preserve the US-led rules-based order? And how should it balance its interests with its values? These questions reflect the longstanding dynamics of the government's foreign- and strategic-policy thinking: fear that its security guarantor will abandon it, uncertainty about whether its own region is a source of security or threat, and a strong belief in the importance of the US-led rules-based order. They're questions that have few easy answers, making the Western Pacific the region most in need of strategic imagination.

Encompassing the Yellow Sea, the East China Sea, the Sea of Japan and the Taiwan Strait, and abutted by China, Japan, North Korea, South Korea and Taiwan (some definitions also include Russia, but that is beyond the scope of our analysis), the Western Pacific is home to flashpoints that bring Chinese interests into direct conflict with American ones. Taiwan attracts the most attention, but the Korean Peninsula is also a source of potential instability, and disputes over land features continue to inflame tensions between their claimants. That the United States and China would likely be brought into conflict if any of these flashpoints escalated means that events in the Western Pacific would reverberate far beyond the region – including in Australia.

WHY HAS THE WESTERN PACIFIC HISTORICALLY MATTERED TO AUSTRALIA?

As with the Indian Ocean, the perceived importance of the Western Pacific to Australia has fluctuated over time. In the late nineteenth century, the Australian government was concerned about Japan's expansionism, beginning with its occupation of Taiwan in 1895, after the First Sino–Japanese War, and then due to its victory in the Russo–Japanese War in the early twentieth century.

During World War I, Japan was allied with the British Empire but used the war to make territorial gains. After it ended, Japan militarised the former German islands it had acquired in the subregion now known as Micronesia. This meant the Australian government's preoccupation with Japan as a security threat continued, exacerbated by Japan's occupation of Manchuria in 1931 and its establishment of the puppet state of Manchukuo. The government's anxieties built after the Second Sino–Japanese War began in 1937. While the government supported the appeasement of Japan and hoped a compromise could be reached to prevent Japan expanding southwards, it did so behind the presumed cover of the British Empire.

After the tripartite agreement between Japan, Italy and Germany in September 1940, it became clear Japan was aligned with the fascist European powers. Demonstrating the strategic value of islands in maritime environments, Japan used its Micronesian islands as launching pads for its attack on the US base at Pearl Harbor, Hawaii, in December 1941. This saw the Second Sino–Japanese War subsumed into World War II and the British Empire and United States align with Chinese factions against Japan.

During the war, the Western Pacific served as a major staging point for Japanese campaigns into the Philippines and South Pacific, in which Australia was involved. As we discussed in the previous chapter, after the surrender of Commonwealth forces in Singapore in February 1942, the powerful Japanese Navy advanced rapidly through the South Pacific, threatening major Australian air and sea lines of communication. The tide of the war only began to turn after Allied victories in the naval battles of the Coral Sea and Midway in mid-1942.

After the war, one of the Australian government's main foreign policy objectives was to ensure Japan remained weak, with the 1946 *Appreciation of the Strategical Position of Australia* paper warning that Japan was a 'naturally aggressive nation'.[9] Although the United States led the occupation of Japan from 1945 to 1952, Australia saw its role there as being the main representative of the British Commonwealth.[10]

At first, Australian and American objectives were similar: the democratisation and demilitarisation of Japan. These objectives were also enshrined in the 1947 Japanese Constitution, which stated in article nine that Japan would renounce war and not use, or threaten to use, military force to settle international disputes. But the US approach changed with the onset of the Cold War, when it began to see Japan as a key ally. The United States adopted a more lenient occupation policy, and article nine of the Constitution was reinterpreted to allow for the creation of self-defence forces.

The Australian government was unhappy about these changes, believing that unless Japan was 'subject to effective control' it could once again 'become an aggressor'.[11] As a quid pro quo, the United States agreed to the ANZUS Treaty in 1951. This treaty sat alongside a network of bilateral treaties the United States had entered into with Japan, South Korea and Taiwan in the Western Pacific, and with the Philippines and Taiwan in Southeast Asia. These treaties were described as a hub-and-spoke system, because instead of creating a multinational treaty network along the lines of NATO (the North Atlantic Treaty Organization), the United States sought to engage with its Asian partners bilaterally, keeping itself at the centre, without actively encouraging relationships between them.

Alongside the occupation of Japan, Australia also participated in the Korean War, which had been precipitated by the division of the Korean Peninsula at the end of World War II. Although the United States had withdrawn its forces from the south and the Soviets from the north in 1948–49, after North Korea attacked South Korea in June 1950 the Americans supported South Korea and the Chinese supported North Korea. Australia threw its support behind the UN-backed assistance to the South Koreans led by the United States, reflecting Australia's concerns about communist expansion in the Western Pacific. Eventually the two sides fought to a stalemate and signed an armistice in July 1953.

World War II and the Korean War offered the Australian government some important lessons: it could no longer rely on British naval capacity for its security, and while the United States had stepped in as an alternative security guarantor, Australia's dependence on seaborne trade and the vulnerability of its sea and air lanes of communication meant it needed to expand its own maritime capability.

The government also became acutely aware that there was no multilateral mechanism in the region akin to NATO to manage potential crises (the 1954 Southeast Asia Treaty Organization, SEATO, having failed to develop). Its only mechanisms to meet potential threats were ANZUS and ANZAM (the 1949 Commonwealth defence plan between Australia, New Zealand and British-ruled Malaysia, formed to protect wartime sea communications in the area).[12] However, Australia acknowledged that the US hub-and-spoke alliance system in the region meant the United States could expect assistance from Japan, Taiwan and the Philippines.[13]

The Korean War was not the only legacy of World War II that contributed to tensions in the Western Pacific. The war also resulted in a series of consequential territorial transfers in the region, particulalry of islands. First, in the closing days of the war, the USSR captured the four southernmost islands in the Kuril Islands archipelago and Japan surrendered its claim to them under the Treaty of San Francisco. However, the USSR never signed the treaty and the issue has endured because Japan views the islands as distinct from the rest of the Kuril Islands, which it accepts are Russian. Second, the United States occupied the Ryukyu and Senkaku/Diaoyu Islands as part of its occupation of Japan. Third, in 1954 South Korea retook the Dokdo/Takeshima Islands that had been seized by Japan in 1905.

Of these territorial transfers, the US occupation of the Senkaku/Diaoyu Islands was the most divisive. In 1972, the United States handed control of the islands to Japan. This was controversial, because of their proximity to Taiwan and the Chinese mainland as well as to Japan's Okinawa.[14] In the lead-up to the transfer, both Taiwan and China claimed the islands[15] based on their discovery of them in 1403 during the Ming Dynasty and then officially administering them during the Qing Dynasty (1644–1911).[16] As advancing technologies in the 1960s made hydrocarbon resources in the seabed more readily observable and exploitable, states became increasingly aware of the economic potential of maritime areas adjacent to small land features. Japan's, Taiwan's and China's interest in Senkaku/Diaoyu (or Diaoyutai to the Taiwanese) stemmed in large part from a UN survey conducted in 1968 and 1969 that had indicated the possibility of extensive petroleum resources under the seabed around the islands.[17] Japan had occupied the islands before World War II, having officially incorporated them into its territory in 1895 as part of the Treaty of Shimonoseki (following its victory in the First Sino–Japanese War).[18] Under the treaty, which China considers one of several 'unequal treaties' forced on it by foreign powers, China ceded Taiwan to Japan 'together with all the islands appertaining or belonging to the said island of Formosa (Taiwan)'.[19] Although the treaty made no explicit reference to the Senkaku/Diaoyu Islands, the Qing Dynasty considered the area to be part of Taiwan. China later recognised the Senkaku/Diaoyu Islands as part of the US administration in Okinawa from 1945 to 1972.[20] While China and Japan signed an agreement in 1978 to shelve the issue for a future resolution,[21] Japan has since claimed it first 'discovered' the islands in 1884[22] and consequently denies there is a dispute over them.[23]

Another legacy of World War II was the revival of the Chinese Civil War between the Nationalists (the Kuomintang or KMT), under Chiang Kai-shek, and the Communists, under Mao Zedong. The Communist victory in 1949 saw Chiang Kai-shek and Nationalist forces retreat to Taiwan and its associated islands. Australia and other regional states then grew concerned about the potential for Chinese expansionism.

While the United States had initially taken a neutral stance in the Chinese Civil War, after the Korean War broke out it shifted its support to the KMT. The Menzies government in Australia was less convinced about supporting the KMT and privately debated whether Taiwan was strategically important enough to be worth defending.[24] Indeed, the 1959 Strategic Basis of Australian Defence Policy observed that 'Communist tactics in relation to the off-shore islands are unpredictable, but while the conflict is restricted to this area, Australia would not be obliged to play an active part'.[25] However, it also acknowledged that 'it might be politically desirable, in the interests of close relationships with the United States and to encourage the preservation of the forward position in Asia and Southeast Asia, to offer a token force contribution'.[26] The government was particularly wary of Chiang Kai-shek's authoritarian regime in Taipei and was concerned that the Nationalists might seek to use the United States to try to regain control of mainland China. Thus emerged the dynamic that has since characterised Australia's strategic calculations in the Western Pacific: uneasiness about its entanglement in a conflict by virtue of its obligations to the United States under the ANZUS Treaty, particularly due to provocative actions by Taiwan.

The government's strategic calculations were soon tested when China bombed small islands controlled by Taiwan in 1954, resulting in what became known as the First Taiwan Strait Crisis. Although the United States was reluctant to be drawn into a conflict that could reignite the Chinese Civil War, the strategic location of these islands encouraged it to sign a collective defence treaty with Taiwan in 1954.[27] The United States did not commit itself to defending the islands, but it did undertake to support Taiwan in the event of broader conflict with China. Concerned about an escalation of conflict, Australia coordinated with Britain, Canada and New Zealand to urge restraint and advocate for quiet diplomacy.[28] As the situation deteriorated in early 1955, the US Congress adopted the Formosa Resolution, which gave President Dwight D. Eisenhower authority to defend Taiwan and its islands. In response, the Chinese government sought negotiations with the United States in late 1955. These talks de-escalated tensions.

The Second Taiwan Strait Crisis arose when in 1958 China once more bombed islands controlled by Taiwan. This required the Australian government to again work with partners to urge restraint.[29] The United States, concerned about the strategic implications of China acquiring a foothold on the islands, resupplied Taiwanese garrisons. This ended China's bombardment and eased the crisis. However, Taiwan and China agreed to shell each other's garrisons on alternate days – a practice that continued until President Nixon initiated rapprochement between China and the United States in 1972.

The situation in the Taiwan Strait calmed during the 1960s. The Australian government continued to be ambivalent about Taiwan's claims of sovereignty over both Taiwan and mainland China. Australia advocated for the creation of two Chinas through the self-determination of Taiwan, which it saw as the only feasible way of justifying military support for Taiwan and a place for Taiwan in the United Nations, alongside China.

This caused tension in Australia's relations with Taiwan and the United States, which supported Taiwan's claim.[30] These disagreements were resolved when the government, led by Prime Minster Gough Whitlam, established diplomatic relations with China in 1972.

By the early 1970s, the Western Pacific was relatively peaceful and the government's main interest in the region was economic, focusing particularly on developing trade ties and securing new markets in Japan, South Korea and China. But the 1980s saw tensions return.

One source of tension were disputes about maritime jurisdiction under the new legal regime of exclusive economic zones created in 1982 by UNCLOS. In the East China Sea, China, Japan and South Korea dispute the location of exclusive economic zone and continental shelf boundaries. This is partly due to geography, which prevents these states from fully extending their rights under UNCLOS. While states can claim an exclusive economic zone of up to 200 nautical miles, in some parts of the East China Sea there is less than 400 nautical miles between states' coastlines. It is also due to differing interpretations and applications of maritime rules and principles.[31] The most tense of these disputes was – and still is – between China and Japan, as China claims its exclusive economic zone stretches all the way to the Okinawa Trough due to the projection of the Asian continental shelf. This is based on the principle of natural prolongation, which Japan argues is designed for continental shelf boundaries and not for exclusive economic zones. Tokyo has instead proposed that a median line be drawn to separate their exclusive economic zones, in accordance with UNCLOS and international jurisprudence that has favoured finding 'equitable solutions' in such cases of overlapping jurisdiction.

The late 1980s also saw tensions begin to escalate on the Korean Peninsula, when North Korea initiated a nuclear-weapons program. North Korea initially permitted the International Atomic Energy Agency (IAEA) to inspect its nuclear facilities, but when the IAEA identified potential discrepancies and requested permission to conduct a 'special inspection', North Korea refused. This triggered a crisis, during which North Korea repeatedly threatened to turn Seoul, the South Korean capital, into a 'sea of fire'.[32] Before the United States escalated to a military response, former US president Jimmy Carter intervened to persuade North Korean president Kim Il-sung to freeze the nuclear program, allow IAEA inspectors back into the country and negotiate with the United States on dismantling nuclear facilities. In exchange, the United States agreed to provide technological, energy, economic and diplomatic benefits. The deal was formalised in the 1994 Agreed Framework, which successfully froze North Korea's nuclear reactors for nearly a decade. Relations between North Korea and South Korea also improved during this period, due to South Korea's 'Sunshine Policy' of increased engagement with North Korea, which included business ventures, investment and family reunions between the two countries.

In the early 1990s tensions rose over Taiwan, escalating to become the Third Taiwan Strait Crisis.[33] In 1995, Taiwanese president Lee Teng-hui visited the United States to deliver a speech to Cornell University, his alma mater. Although it was billed as a private visit, the US government's decision to allow Taiwan's most senior leader to enter the country represented a reversal of American assurances to China that such a visit would not occur. In response, China conducted a series of significant military exercises and missile tests in the waters near Taiwan in the lead-up to Taiwan's 1996 presidential elections. To demonstrate its resolve in the region and deter greater Chinese actions, the United States responded in turn by deploying two carrier battle groups to the vicinity of Taiwan, including the USS *Independence* aircraft carrier, which it sailed through the Taiwan Strait.[34]

In Australia, John Howard's Coalition government was elected during the crisis. Reflecting what would become a key element of its foreign policy – full-throated support for the United States under ANZUS – the government quickly endorsed America's actions. Foreign Minister Alexander Downer observed: 'I think what we have seen in the last few days is a very clear demonstration by the United States that it is interested in maintaining its involvement in the security of the region and we obviously welcome that.'[35]

Much of the government's interest in keeping the United States engaged in Asia stemmed from its growing concern about a rising China. These concerns were shared by Japan, which was also keen to avoid instability in the region. This encouraged Australia and Japan to begin to move closer together, culminating in the 2007 Joint Declaration on Security Cooperation, which covered cooperation on non-traditional security challenges such as border security and counterterrorism,[36] and the 2008 Memorandum of Understanding on Defence Cooperation. In the 2009 defence white paper, the Australian government indicated it would 'continue to work to develop out practical defence cooperation with Japan'.[37] The bilateral relationship was then deepened by the 2014 agreement to form a special strategic partnership.[38]

Publicly, the Australian government did not yet present China's rise as a concern and continued cultivating a relationship with Beijing built on economic interests. Indeed, the *Defence White Paper* 2013 stated that 'Australia welcomes China's rise'.[39] This position was aided by a drop in tensions in the Taiwan Strait during the early 2010s, with semi-official exchanges between Beijing and Taipei reinvigorated following the election of KMT president Ma Ying-jeou, culminating in a meeting between Ma Ying-jeou and Chinese president Xi Jinping in 2015.[40] Despite this, the Australian government wasn't complacent about ongoing risks in the region. The *Defence White Paper 2013* identified 'flashpoints' on the Korean Peninsula and in the Taiwan Strait and the East and South China seas as having 'the potential to destabilise regional security'.[41] It identified that 'establishing effective mechanisms to help manage these pressure points will be increasing important', as would 'deeper understanding, clearer communication and more effective and reliable rules'.[42]

In fact, while tensions were lowering over Taiwan, they were rising on the Korean Peninsula. Many US Republicans were sceptical about whether North Korea was complying with the 1994 Agreed Framework, and in January 2002 US president George W. Bush named North

Korea, along with Iraq and Iran, as one of the members of his 'Axis of Evil'.[43] This contributed to the breakdown of the Agreed Framework in late 2002 and an increase in tensions between North and South Korea. Although the Six-Party Talks hosted by China calmed the situation for a few years, it heated up again in October 2006 when North Korea conducted its first nuclear test and then escalated when a new conservative government in South Korea abandoned the Sunshine Policy in 2008.

In 2009, North Korea withdrew from the Six-Party Talks and conducted a second nuclear test, launched a ballistic missile and announced it was abandoning the 1953 armistice. Things got worse in March 2010, when a North Korean submarine allegedly sunk a small South Korean warship, the *Cheonan*, killing forty-six South Korean Navy personnel. Then, in November 2010, in response to South Korean naval exercises, North Korea bombarded the South's Yeonpyeong Island, killing four South Korean military personnel. While new North Korean leader Kim Jong-un agreed to halt nuclear testing in 2012, this didn't last long, with North Korea conducting another nuclear test in 2013 and continuing to do so intermittently ever since. Accordingly, Australia's *Defence White Paper 2013* identified North Korea's 'nuclear program and proliferation activities' as 'a major concern'.[44]

The mid-2010s also saw indications that Australia and its allies and partners had reason to be concerned about a more activist China in the East China Sea. The first such sign followed the Tokyo Metropolitan government's purchase of the Senkaku/Diaoyu Islands from their Japanese owner in 2012.[45] This resulted in deep resentment in mainland China and Taiwan,[46] with Japanese flags burned and Japanese-made vehicles set alight in some cities.[47] In November 2013, China then implemented what it described as the East China Sea Air Defense Identification Zone, which included the Senkaku/Diaoyu Islands and overlapped with parts of the claimed air defence identification zones of Japan, South Korea and Taiwan.[48] While air defence identification zones generally require aircraft to submit their flight plans and report locations to national air-traffic control, the East China Sea Air Defense

Identification Zone applied to aircraft that were in the declared zone but not in Chinese airspace, and to commercial, not just military, aircraft. Most countries did not comply with China's requirements, and the Australian government declared it was 'opposed to any coercive or unilateral actions to change the status quo in the East China Sea'[49] – but the prospect of China enforcing its claim raised the risk of confrontation in the East China Sea.

THE RELEVANCE OF CONTEMPORARY SECURITY ISSUES TO AUSTRALIA'S SECURITY

China's declaration of its East China Sea Air Defense Identification Zone signalled its intent to develop a more muscular foreign and strategic policy. That approach has solidified since the 2016 change of government in Taiwan, which saw the pro-independence Democratic Progressive Party come to power. Although Taiwan has dropped its claim to the Chinese mainland, China maintains its claim to Taiwan and its associated islands.[50]

Most states recognised China as the only governing authority over the mainland after it took its seat on the UN Security Council in October 1971. In 1972, Australia officially ceased to recognise Taiwan as the government of mainland China and in a joint communiqué recognised China as the 'sole legitimate government of China' and acknowledged 'the position of the PRC that Taiwan is a province of the PRC'.[51] In effect, Australia adopted a 'One China Policy', whereby it recognised China but not Taiwan. However, this approach differed from China's 'One China Principle',[52] as it did not explicitly recognise Taiwan as part of China. The United States adopted a similar approach in 1979, stating that it 'acknowledges', rather than recognises, China's sovereign claim over Taiwan.[53]

In a move that has ongoing consequences, the United States' recognition of China as the only governing authority on the mainland was accompanied by its adoption of the 1979 *Taiwan Relations Act,* under which it pledged to continue giving military support to assist Taiwan in protecting itself from the use of force.[54] The Act also gave rise to the US policy of strategic ambiguity, designed to dissuade Taiwan from officially declaring independence and deter China from using military action to solve the 'Taiwan Question', as neither party can be sure whether the United States will come to Taiwan's aid or not.[55] The policy also helped to reassure treaty allies, including Australia, about the circumstances in which they might be drawn into a conflict.

But the comfort drawn from that reassurance has diminished. The Democratic Progressive Party has taken increasingly explicit moves towards declaring independence. In January 2020, President Tsai Ingwen claimed Taiwan was already an independent country called the 'Republic of China (Taiwan)' and that the mainland authorities had to 'recognise that situation'.[56] Even the KMT, long viewed as being closer to Beijing, has shifted its position in response to an electorate that increasingly identifies as 'Taiwanese' rather than 'Chinese', officially rejecting the 'One Country, Two Systems' model that Beijing had proposed for Taiwan.[57] These moves have caused consternation in China and raised the risk of conflict, particularly because, to put pressure on Taiwan, the Chinese government adopted the *Anti-Secession Law* in 2005, which stipulates that China is required to use force against Taiwan if it formally declares independence from the mainland.[58]

There is also considerable domestic pressure on the Chinese government to resolve the 'Taiwan Question', as it has identified the eventual reunification of Taiwan with the mainland as a significant step in realising the 'Chinese Dream': the 'rejuvenation of the Chinese nation'.[59] China's president, Xi Jinping, has been particularly vocal on this issue. In 2017, Xi stated that China had 'sufficient abilities to thwart any form of Taiwanese independence attempts',[60] and in 2021 he said that 'reunification must be fulfilled'.[61] Xi's public statements – underpinned by the increasing presence of Chinese aircraft in Taiwan's declared air defence identification zone,[62] sand dredging near the Matsu Islands and allegations of interference in Taiwan's political affairs – have significantly increased concerns about potential conflict.

China is gradually eroding the 'median line' down the middle of the Taiwan Strait by regularly sending warships and aircraft across it. In 2021, for instance, China sent two hundred sorties across the line in the month of October alone.[63] While China has never offically recognised this informal line – created by a US general in 1954 – it appeared to acquiesce to it for over sixty years. China has also warned other states against conducting freedom of navigation transits in the Taiwan Strait. In September 2017, when the Royal Australian Navy sailed a warship through the Taiwan Strait only two weeks after two US warships crossed the Strait, China denounced the transits as provocative.

Alongside these developments, successive administrations have indicated that the United States may move from its policy of strategic ambiguity towards a policy of 'strategic clarity'.[64] Under the Trump administration, the US Congress passed the *Taiwan Travel Act* in 2018, which allowed for high-level visits between US and Taiwanese officials.[65] And in 2019, the Congress passed the *TAIPEI Act*, which aimed to increase the scope of US–Taiwan relations and encourage other nations to officially and unofficially increase their links with Taipei.[66] In 2020, the United States lifted the 'self-imposed restrictions on the US-Taiwan relationship', allowing official contact between the United States and the governing authorities on Taiwan.[67] As we have noted, President Joe Biden has also stated on four occasions that the United States 'would defend Taiwan' if it were invaded.[68] While US diplomats walked these statements back, Biden's comments have created doubts about how long the US will continue to abide by the policy of strategic ambiguity.[69]

Parallel to these developments, the United States' ability to prevail in a future conflict with China over Taiwan has been questioned, with some arguing that the United States may lose its capacity to do so within a decade.[70] Such concerns may pressure the United States to take decisive action before it loses its military advantage. Perhaps to this end, senior Republicans have advocated in recent years for US recognition of an independent Taiwan.[71]

Tensions have also risen in the East China Sea, as China and Japan have each made more aggressive attempts to assert sovereignty over the Senkaku/Diaoyu Islands. China has begun to enter Japanese-controlled waters around the islands more frequently, with recorded entries rising from 819 in 2013[72] to 1097 in 2019.[73] In 2021, Chinese coastguard ships were spotted near the Senkaku/Diaoyu Islands for 157 consecutive days, which was the longest period since 2012. The streak was only ended by a typhoon.[74] Reflecting its recent acquisition of larger, more capable vessels, the Chinese coastguard is reportedly spending longer stretches of time in Japanese-claimed waters and has attempted to harass Japanese fishing vessels.[75] Now the biggest in the world, China's coastguard has had a military chain of command since 2018. The likelihood that these incursions would generate conflict rose in February 2021, when China adopted a law allowing the Chinese coastguard to use weapons against foreign ships if it deems they are 'illegally' entering China's waters.[76] In response, Japan claimed China is 'relentlessly continuing unilateral attempts to change the status quo by coercion near the Senkaku Islands', adding that 'Japan cannot accept China's actions to escalate the situation'.[77] Tokyo claims Beijing is incrementally annexing the Senkaku/Diaoyu Islands and gaining international recognition through these grey zone activities.

As the United States and Japan are treaty allies, it is likely the United States would become involved should these activities escalate into a conflict between China and Japan. Indeed, US president Barack Obama made a verbal commitment in 2014 to support Japan's claim to the Senkaku/Diaoyu Islands, saying that the United States would oppose any attempt to 'threaten Japanese sovereignty'.[78] The United States also has its own interest in preserving freedom of navigation and overflight for civilian and military assets in the region. Over the past decade, there have been several 'incidents', including in 2016 and 2017, involving US surveillance aircraft and Chinese fighter jets in the East China Sea, which also raise the risk of conflict.

These disputes have attracted little public attention in Australia, with a 2015 poll finding that 57 per cent of Australian respondents were unaware there was a dispute between China and Japan over the Senkaku/Diaoyu Islands,[79] and 67 per cent were unaware the US had committed to support Japan militarily in the event of conflict with China over the islands.[80] Despite this lack of public awareness, Australia has important foreign and strategic interests in the outcome of these disputes. As a treaty ally of the United States, Australia could be drawn into a US–China conflict in the East China Sea if one were to erupt. In addition, Australia is likely to come under considerable pressure to support Japan as their relationship grows closer. Beyond alliance and partnership obligations, Australia also has an interest in the sea and air lanes of communication that pass through the area.[81]

For similar reasons, Australia has an interest in stability on the Korean Peninsula. North Korea has continued to conduct sporadic nuclear tests, and the Trump administration's efforts at diplomacy, including a series of leaders' summits, generated little progress towards denuclearising the peninsula. While the government faces a dilemma about whether Australia should become involved in a conflict over the Korean Peninsula, the likelihood that such a conflict would escalate to involve nuclear weapons means it would have reason – beyond alliance obligations – to become involved. For the time being, the government continues to strongly support targeted sanctions on North Korea, playing an active role in UN sanction enforcement missions in international waters off the Korean Peninsula.[82] Australia's capacity to play any greater role in de-escalating tensions is limited by the fact that bilateral relations between the Australian government and Pyongyang are now run out of Seoul, as Pyongyang removed its embassy from Canberra in 2008.[83] Even though the United States has requested that Australia re-engage with North Korea, Australian leaders from both major parties have showed little enthusiasm.[84]

AUSTRALIA'S CURRENT POLICY APPROACH

The comments of Albanese and Wong cited at the beginning of the chapter reflect the government's longstanding policy to de-escalate tensions in the Western Pacific, balance its relationships with China and the United States, and maintain strategic ambiguity about whether it would support the United States in the event of conflict.

However, there is some suggestion that the government may harden its policy as strategic competition with China escalates. There is a strong lobby within the Australian national security community that favours providing a more explicit undertaking to support the United States should there be any conflict in the region, particularly over Taiwan. This lobby has been gathering momentum for some time. When Foreign Minister Alexander Downer said in 2004 that 'ANZUS would not necessary apply in the case of a Taiwan contingency', it generated consternation in Australian national security circles.[85] In 2008, when Taiwanese president Chen Shui-bian sought to stage a referendum on Taiwan's UN status, Prime Minister Kevin Rudd reaffirmed Australia's commitment to a 'One China Policy' and said Australia would seek diplomatic resolutions to prevent conflict.[86] This again generated widespread condemnation among the Australian national security commentariat.[87]

Australian defence policy has also begun to more explicitly acknowledge that Australia is likely to be drawn into conflicts in the Western Pacific. The 2020 *Defence Strategic Update* stated that 'Defence must be prepared to make military contributions outside of our immediate region where our interests are engaged', including 'being ready to deploy forces globally' and 'in North Asia'.[88] In November 2021, when discussing the possibility of conflict over Taiwan, Defence Minister Peter Dutton observed that it 'would be inconceivable that we [Australia] wouldn't support the US in an action if the US chose to take that action'. While Dutton later watered down his remarks, saying the government would decide 'at that time as to what was in our country's best interests', his unguarded comment suggested that a shift in position might be in the minds of at least a few Australian leaders.[89] The Labor government elected in May

2022 has restated Australia's official position as 'supporting the status quo with regard to the Taiwan Strait',[90] but the thinking – and voices – behind Dutton's comment remains influential. Indeed, the debate on Taiwan often acts as a cipher for broader questions about whether Australia should adopt a more overtly hostile approach to containing China. This more muscular position can be characterised as one of 'strategic clarity'. This position argues that the government should make a clear commitment to join with the United States and others in defending Taiwan from invasion. It holds that if the government were to do this it might deter Beijing from taking such action. In 2021, reflecting the influence of this thinking in the Australian national security community, Dutton argued that Australia should actively deter China from invading Taiwan because 'if Taiwan is taken, surely the Senkakus are next'.[91]

While the government has not yet explicitly articulated such a policy of deterrence with respect to Taiwan, it has moved towards a more actively deterrent position generally. This is evident in the increase in its defence spending, particularly its undertaking to develop nuclear-powered submarines under the AUKUS security partnership. These submarines could assist Australia to provide crucial cover for its surface ships and conduct surveillance operations in conjunction with US forces. This approach dovetails with the US government's shift to a policy of 'integrated deterrence', whereby the United States will seek to coordinate all elements of its national power and its 'unmatched network of alliances and partnerships' to deter adversaries from engaging in aggression.[92] The application of this policy is seeing the United States seek to move away from its regional hub-and-spoke alliance, instead encouraging coordination and integration between its allies, including Australia.

A more muscular approach on Taiwan is contested. An alternative position argues that the defence of Taiwan is not a vital Australian interest and therefore Australia should not become involved in any conflict over the Taiwan Strait.[93] In addition, as China's military power continues to grow, this position argues that the United States would not be able to win a war with China over Taiwan – particularly because

China has focused on developing anti-ship missiles, radars, sonars and satellites that can target missiles accurately. Hugh White, a prominent advocate of this alternative position, argues that China has developed formidable anti-access, area-denial capabilities since the 1990s which may limit the United States' ability to project military power in a Taiwan theatre.[94] There is also the potential for any US–China engagement over Taiwan to cross the nuclear threshold. To mitigate the risk this presents to Australia, White and others argue that the government should be candid with Washington and Taipei about these risks and not commit to a joint response.[95] They also argue that the government should convince the United States to abandon Taiwan, as defeat over Taiwan could spell the end of US primacy in the Western Pacific.[96] Former Australia prime minister Paul Keating is another vocal proponent of this view. He argued in November 2021 that 'Australia has no alliance with Taipei. No document that you can find.' Keating continued: 'We are committed to ANZUS for an attack on US forces, but not an attack by US forces, which means Australia should not be drawn, in my view, into a military engagement over Taiwan, US-sponsored or otherwise.'[97]

The territorial disputes in the East China Sea attract far less attention in Australia. The government's low-key strategy is one of dissuasion – working with others to convince China of the costs of unilateral actions and the importance of international law, while simultaneously using engagement to reinforce the benefits of the existing, US-led regional order.[98] In 2013, Foreign Minister Julie Bishop made clear 'Australia's opposition to any coercive or unilateral actions to change the status quo in the East China Sea', with the Department of Foreign Affairs and Trade summoning Ma Zhaoxu, China's ambassador to Australia, to explain Beijing's interests and hear Australia's concerns.[99] This sparked a minor diplomatic row. Chinese foreign minister Wang Yi later chided Bishop during her visit to China in December 2013, labelling Bishop's comments as 'irresponsible' and 'mistaken', and accusing the Australian government of 'jeopardising bilateral trust'.[100] The *2017 Foreign Policy White Paper* directly outlined the government's concerns in the

East China Sea as 'the potential for the use of force or coercion in the East China Sea and Taiwan Strait'.[101]

The Australian government maintains a policy of strategic ambiguity about whether it would intervene alongside the United States in the event of a conflict in the East China Sea. While the government supports Japan's assertion of sovereignty over the Senkaku/Diaoyu Islands, it has not given Japan clear assurances that it would come to its aid if this sovereignty were threatened. In 2014, Defence Minister David Johnston said that the 'ANZUS alliance would not commit Australia to a hypothetical conflict where the US had sent forces to support its Japanese ally'.[102] Johnston was rebuked by policymakers supportive of the US alliance, such as Opposition MP Michael Danby, who said Johnston's comments 'pulled the rug from under the feet of our mutual defence obligations to the US by signalling to China a deep reticence within the highest levels of the current Australian government over whether we would come to America's aid in some future conflict'.[103] However, public opinion seemed to agree with Johnston, with 71 per cent of poll respondents agreeing that Australia should remain neutral.[104]

But the East China Sea has an additional strategic dimension for Australia, as China's maritime claims in the region represent what the Chinese government identifies as its 'first island chain'. The concept of 'island chains' was introduced in the early 1950s by future US secretary of state John Foster Dulles, who devised an 'island-chain strategy' under which he proposed that the US could surround China and the Soviet Union with naval bases to project power and restrict sea access.[105] An island-chain approach was subsequently picked up by China as part of its contemporary maritime strategy.[106] The Chinese strategy consists of three island chains: the first runs from the Japanese island of Kyushu, down through the Ryukyu Islands and then through Taiwan towards the South China Sea; the second extends from the Japanese island of Honshu near Tokyo down through the Bonin Islands towards the Mariana Islands (including Guam), ending near Palau; and the third stretches from the Aleutian Islands and runs south across the centre of the Pacific

Ocean through the Hawaiian Islands, American Samoa and Fiji, ending at New Zealand.[107] Today, there is even talk of fourth and fifth island chains stretching into the Indian Ocean.[108] Therefore, Japan's defence of its claimed islands in the East China Sea is not just a matter of sovereign pride: it is also understood as strategically necessary for Japan, and for the United States, Australia, and their allies and partners, to restrain China from realising its island-chain strategy, and with it, potentially sea denial – if not sea control – of strategically important waterways that are critical for a trade-dependent nation such as Australia.

This prospect has led to an apparent hardening of the government's position. While there hasn't been an overt policy statement relating to the East China Sea, the 2020 *Defence Strategic Update*, the 2021 AUKUS strategic partnership (particularly Australia's planned development of nuclear-powered submarines), and the 2023 *Defence Strategic Review* suggest that the government is seeking a deterrent capability in seas closer to China than Australia.

Tensions on the Korean Peninsula also attract relatively little attention in Australian policy debates, with the government essentially adopting a policy of non-engagement towards North Korea.[109] This is despite the gravity of the threat of nuclear confrontation on the Korean Peninsula and the government's well-established history of advocating for nuclear non-proliferation. Instead, the government prefers to follow the 'maximum-pressure' policy implemented by the Trump administration in the United States, which involves using sanctions to try to force North Korea to engage in negotiations.

However, Australia has moved closer to South Korea, albeit in a low-profile way. The two states agreed to the bilateral Vision Statement for a Secure, Peaceful and Prosperous Future in 2014.[110] The Australia–South Korea relationship was then elevated to a comprehensive strategic partnership when President Moon Jae-in made a state visit to Australia in December 2021.[111] The partnership seeks to deepen bilateral cooperation on strategic and security matters, as well as economic and people-to-people exchanges.[112] Australia is now, apart from the United States, the only country to hold 2+2 foreign and defence ministerial talks with South Korea.

Another key element of the Australian government's policy approach in the Western Pacific is deepening its relationship with Japan. In 2007, Australia and Japan signed a Joint Declaration on Security Cooperation to strengthen their consultation on security issues and expand practical cooperation in several areas.[113] Since then, they have held regular bilateral 2+2 talks and trilateral strategic dialogue meetings with the United States. The bilateral relationship was upgraded in 2010 with the Acquisition and Cross-Servicing Agreement, a level of defence cooperation just below that of a treaty for a full military alliance. Australia and Japan also signed an economic partnership agreement and a defence technology treaty.[114] In 2013, the Japanese government created a National Security Council, released its first national security strategy and updated its national security doctrine. In 2012, Australia and Japan signed an Information Security Agreement to facilitate sharing classified information and in 2014 elevated their relationship to a 'special strategic partnership'.[115] In 2015, the Japanese government adopted legislation to expand the scope of activities of the Japanese Self-Defence Force, which would allow it to participate in overseas conflicts in support of collective self-defence or to help a friendly country under attack. Japan has also actively promoted its 'Free and Open Indo-Pacific' strategy and, along with the United States, Australia and India, is a member of the Quad.

Australia's relationship with Japan has deepened considerably in recent years. In 2021, the two states signed a Reciprocal Access Agreement, which guarantees the movement of each other's military forces within their respective territories. Then, in October 2022, they updated their 2007 Joint Declaration on Security Cooperation to include an ANZUS-like clause which provides that Canberra and Tokyo will 'consult together' if their territorial integrity or security is threatened. Japanese prime minister Fumio Kishida elaborated on the update by saying that the clause is confirmation of 'consultations and consideration of responses regarding contingencies' that could impact regional security.[116]

This reflects that while Japan's alliance with the United States is deep (the United States maintains twenty-three bases in Japan, which is also a port for significant military assets, such as the US Pacific Fleet),[117] Japan has been seeking to diversify its strategic relationships[118] in accordance with the US policy of integrated deterrence. Indeed, the Australian government now declares Japan to be 'Australia's closest partner in Asia'.[119]

WHAT SHOULD AUSTRALIA DO DIFFERENTLY?

The Western Pacific is where Australia will likely be forced to confront its most pressing foreign- and strategic-policy dilemmas. While all three of the region's flashpoints may bring Australia's dilemmas to a head, it is Taiwan that attracts the most attention in Australian debates. There is a creeping sense of inevitability that conflict will occur, even though China's grey zone tactics suggest that for the time being it prefers to wage a pressure campaign or war of attrition to wear down Taiwanese resistance rather than mounting a full-scale invasion.

But before we launch into the well-worn arguments about whether Australia should support the United States in the event of conflict over Taiwan, we must acknowledge the importance of recognising the agency and perspectives of the Taiwanese people. Taiwan is not an object to be fought over, but is home to twenty-three million people. This means Australia's strategic imagination needs to view Taiwan through more lenses than just the competition between the United States and China.

Opinion polls conducted in Taiwan suggest that most Taiwanese people are not in favour of Taiwan establishing closer political ties with China.[120] The polls also show that they agree Taiwan should become independent if it can maintain peaceful relations with China.[121] However, Taiwanese people are clear-eyed about the prospects of war and of receiving international support in the event of a conflict, with a majority of opinion-poll respondents agreeing that China will launch an armed attack on Taiwan in the future.[122] They are also sceptical about whether Taiwanese people would go to war for their independence if threatened by China,[123] whether Taiwan could successfully defend itself without assistance[124] and whether the United States would commit its military to defending Taiwan if China were to attack.[125] This means that while many Taiwanese would prefer independence, a majority favours maintaining the status quo.[126]

The Albanese government has signalled that it will maintain its policy of strategic ambiguity.[127] Given how many Taiwanese people have expressed a preference for maintaining the status quo, as well as how devastating the consequences of a war would be, the Australian government should resist being distracted by the drums of war that certain members of its national security community hear beating[128] and instead prioritise policies that can de-escalate tensions and mitigate the possibility of conflict. One way the government can more actively deter conflict is by assisting efforts to internationalise the issue and encouraging other states to cooperate on de-escalating tensions – for instance, by adding the issue to the agenda of trilateral, multilateral and minilateral dialogues such as the G20 and G7.[129]

The government could also contribute by designing and advocating for diplomatic crisis-management and conflict-avoidance mechanisms. For example, it could try to persuade Beijing to restart the cross-strait hotline[130] and it could advocate for the resumption of the China–US Military Maritime Consultative Agreement meetings, which were suspended after Pelosi's 2022 visit to Taiwan. Australia could also combine its efforts to promote new mechanisms with the efforts of regional partners that would be affected by a Taiwan conflict, such as South Korea, Japan, Indonesia and Singapore.[131]

The government could also do much more to directly support and engage with Taiwan and its people. Australia already has deep relations with Taiwan in terms of economic engagement, trade, education, knowledge and cultural exchange, and people-to-people links.[132] But these links could be expanded, as could high-level engagement between Australia and Taiwan, and support for increased Taiwanese

involvement in multilateral institutions. This could include continued support for Taiwan's push for observer status at the World Health
Assembly. Australia currently works with Taiwan through the Global
Cooperation and Training Framework, which hosts international
workshops in which Taiwan can share its knowledge and expertise
with other countries, sidestepping its limited diplomatic status.[133]
This approach could be used to progress discussions on topics such as
energy security, space, countering misinformation and cyber threats.[134]

But the risk of conflict over Taiwan remains. As China becomes
more aggressive, there is pressure on the US government to clarify
its position on Taiwan. This was demonstrated in January 2023 when
eighteen Republicans introduced a resolution to Congress calling for
the US government to recognise Taiwan as an independent state.[135]
This pressure is likely to crystallise in the lead-up to the 2024 presidential election. In the United States, public views on China are also
hardening, particularly following the February 2023 downing of a Chinese intelligence balloon that had spent days passing over US territory.

As we've noted, similar dynamics are evident in Australian national
security debates. And as we argue in Chapter 1, debates about whether
Australia would be technically required to aid the United States in
the event of war over Taiwan are effectively moot. Australia would
almost certainly support the United States in such a scenario. Their
'alliance halo' has generated deep and broad alignment[136] between
the two states. Australia wouldn't necessarily follow the United States
into war as a demonstration of loyalty[137] (although it has done so in
the past, supporting the United States in every conflict it has been
involved in since the ANZUS Treaty was signed in 1951) but because
it has difficulty imagining the Indo-Pacific region – and, indeed, the
world – without the United States as a great power, setting the rules
that determine how states interact. Australia's defence capability is also
so integrated with, and dependent on, the United States that it would
be almost impossible to disentangle. And while Australia hasn't yet
developed its fleet of nuclear-powered submarines using American and

British technology, the Australian Defence Force would find it difficult to imagine not fighting alongside its American counterparts as well. There are currently forty-five Australian personnel working inside the US Indo-Pacific Command or its component commands. Australia also relies heavily on the American intelligence it receives by virtue of being a member of the Five Eyes intelligence partnership.

Even if the government didn't choose to support the United States in the event of conflict over the Taiwan Strait, Australia would probably be pulled in nonetheless. US Marines and air power would likely operate from Australian bases,[138] and the Joint Defence Facility Pine Gap, near Alice Springs, would be a potential target for China's military, given that it would play a critical role in collecting signals intelligence and act as a relay station for early warning information on ballistic missile launches.

But the seeming inevitability of Australia following the United States into war should not preclude debates about whether this would be the right approach or the contribution Australia should make. Nor should it prevent us questioning the idea that war over Taiwan will be an unavoidable outcome of China's rise, especially given China's use of grey zone tactics designed to *avoid* provoking other states into conflict.

Some members of the Australian national security community emphasise the importance of protecting Taiwan because it is a fellow liberal democracy.[139] Australian public opinion seems to be swinging in the same direction. In the 2022 Lowy Institute Poll, 51 per cent of respondents favoured the use of Australian military forces 'if China invaded Taiwan and the United States decided to intervene', up from 43 per cent in 2019[140] and 37 per cent in 2013.[141] In contrast, other Australian defence thinkers are raising reservations and objections with increasing volume. They are sceptical about what substantive contribution Australia would make to a distant conflict with only indirect strategic importance and concerned about the costs such a conflict would impose.[142]

Much of the current debate in Australia, and elsewhere in the Western Pacific, does not consider the possible domestic costs of a conflict in the Taiwan Strait. Due to distance, it is unlikely Australia would make a major direct military contribution to such a conflict – it is much more likely that Australia would be called upon to secure sea lines of communication in its nearer region. However, this wouldn't necessarily be an easy task, and it could lead to a high number of defence casualties.

While much of the fighting would likely occur in air or maritime domains, a land war is not unthinkable should another flashpoint, such as the Korean Peninsula, become a proxy war for the conflict. Because the Australian Defence Force is small, conscription could be deemed necessary, as it was during the last major land war in Asia, the Vietnam War.

Any wide-scale conflict between China and the United States would have other domestic consequences: interruptions to global shipping and supply lines would make everyday life difficult for many Australians, particularly if its energy supply and critical imports such as medicines were interrupted. The effects of a nuclear escalation would be even more profound.

These risks highlight the importance of the government being transparent with the Australian people about how it understands Australia's obligations under the ANZUS Treaty, the reasons it would go to war to support the United States in the event of conflict over Taiwan and what kind of contribution Australia would make to such a war. There should be more public debate about the costs and benefits of going to war, and how these would differ according to the various contributions Australia could make. While there are reasons to keep a lid on these discussions – not least of all because of the signals they would send to the United States, China and Taiwan – it would be preferable to have them now, when heads are relatively cool, rather than in a time of crisis, when emotions are running high.

Australia also needs to openly discuss how other Asian states would respond to a conflict. Even some US allies have signalled a reluctance to get involved, with South Korea indicating it would not allow US bases on its territory to be staging points for the defence of Taiwan.[143] Among the Quad there is uncertainty about how India would respond in the event of war. India's stance on the Russian invasion of Ukraine signals that it would likely prioritise its own strategic interests, particularly its fraught relationship with China, over any loyalty to its Quad partners or the more amorphous idea of a 'community of democracies'.

Of course, not defending Taiwan would also have serious strategic consequences. If China were to successfully seize control of Taiwan – and that would be a big if, should Taiwan have US support – it would change the geostrategic landscape of Asia.[144] For one, it would put significant pressure on the United States. As General Douglas MacArthur observed in 1950, Taiwan is an 'unsinkable aircraft carrier and submarine tender' that could be used to threaten US bases in Japan and the Philippines.[145] That thinking has not changed: as the US Assistant Secretary of Defence for Indo-Pacific Security Affairs Ely Ratner has observed, Taiwan sits 'at a critical node within the first island chain, anchoring a network of US allies and partners'.[146] Given the centrality of a US-led regional order, such a blow to the United States' great power status would have meaningful strategic consequences for Australia.

A war in the East China Sea would have also have profound implications for Australia, and for similar reasons. Given its deepening strategic intimacy with Japan, Australia could well face pressure to support Japan in the event of conflict over Senkaku/Diaoyu. Australia has already come under some pressure to engage in joint military exercises with Japan in the East China Sea.[147] Since the United States is also a treaty ally of Japan, it's likely America would be involved in a Senkaku/Diaoyu conflict too.

While Australia does not currently conduct explicit surface Freedom of Navigation Operations (known as FONOPs) in the way the United States does, it regularly carries out regional presence deployments and exercises in and around the East China Sea. There is reason to think these practices are becoming more fraught, with reports in

July 2022 that HMAS *Parramatta* was closely tracked by the People's Liberation Army, which involved being followed by a Chinese nuclear-powered submarine, a warship and multiple aircraft, and was formally challenged on entering 'China's territorial waters' in the East China Sea.[148] The dangers of these incidents are also being amplified by an increase in the number of non-naval fishing and militia vessels in the region. For example, Chinese maritime militia vessels are increasingly testing Japan's tolerance to incursions into its exclusive economic zone. While the United States and China agreed to a Military Maritime Consultative Agreement in 1998 to improve communication between their militaries, and China and Japan have created a communication mechanism to reduce the risk of accidental clashes between their ships and aircraft, Australia is not a party to these arrangements and therefore has no formal mechanism to resolve such incidents.[149] This suggests that there may be some merit, now relations with China are thawing, for Australia to seek its own agreement with China on these matters.

Australia should exercise its strategic imagination to identify ways to de-escalate tensions between Japan and China in the East China Sea. One way to do this would be to work with other middle powers interested in the region, particularly Vietnam, the Philippines, South Korea and Indonesia, to create mechanisms for communication and dialogue that could pave the way to diplomatically clarify Japan and China's claims, identify their red lines and discuss the ramifications for breaching them. This could, in turn, lead to the development of crisis-management mechanisms, including diplomatic 'off-ramps' to mitigate potential escalation points and provide practical methods to deal with incidents.[150] This might involve collaborative discussions with regional powers on containment points and post-incident controls to ensure that the political and economic damage felt on both sides is minimal in the event of conflict.[151]

Conflict on the Korean Peninsula also remains a possibility, but you wouldn't necessarily know this from Australia's national security debate, which is primarily preoccupied with the potential conflict with China. This preoccupation has meant other pressing foreign- and strategic-policy challenges have been neglected. In the Western Pacific, this presents an opportunity for the government to reimagine its security, and broaden the horizons of its foreign- and strategic-policy lens to capture the full range of challenges that Australia faces and identify creative ways to respond to them.

One step should involve determining what makes Australia a unique international actor. Although not perfect, Australia is a relatively 'good' international citizen that generally observes the rule of law both internationally and at home. For the most part, it avoids taking unilateral actions and tries to work multilaterally, or at least, minilaterally. Drawing on this record and its identity as a middle power, Australia can promote the importance of international law to resolving disputes, attempt to deter states in the Western Pacific from taking unilateral actions and try to de-escalate any tensions that arise.

Australia should also recognise that while its military is too small to make a decisive contribution to any conflicts in the Western Pacific, it can be a smart international actor that employs all arms of statecraft – national, environmental, economic and human – to grapple with the region's challenges. This would involve Australia using tools of diplomacy to work multilaterally and minilaterally to encourage initiatives that would de-escalate tension and deter conflict.

Most importantly, Australia must avoid creating or feeding into self-fulfilling prophecies regarding the likelihood of conflict in the Western Pacific. This involves taking a long view when making its foreign- and strategic-policy choices, alive to the risk that decisions now will have consequences later – and may preclude alternative paths that would ultimately lead to better outcomes.

4

THE SOUTH CHINA SEA

When ABC television's *Utopia* shone its satirical lens on defence policy-making, it provided a sharp take on Australia's approach to the South China Sea. In one scene, a stressed out public servant named Tony grapples with the tensions inherent in Australia's thinking: while Beijing presents the biggest threat to maintaining an open trading route through the South China Sea, most of Australia's trade is with China. This raises an obvious question: why would China block its own trade? When Tony pithily sums up the situation, asking, 'So we want to defend our trade to China from China?', the defence leaders nod their heads in agreement. For lecturers in international relations, the clip provided entertaining teaching material on the importance of thinking critically about 'national interests'.

Nowhere is this truer than in the South China Sea. Claims are often made about the importance of this domain to Australia by those on both sides of politics. Former attorney-general and ambassador to the United Kingdom George Brandis once described the South China Sea as 'arguably *the most difficult issue* in the relationship between Australia and China'.[1] Labor's defence spokesperson (now federal defence minister) Richard Marles declared in 2020 that 'there is no sea which is more important to us than the South China Sea'.[2] Former Liberal defence minister Peter Dutton was even more strident, warning in 2022 that Australia and its allies would 'lose the next decade' unless it stood up to China in the South China Sea.[3] Australian politicians almost uniformly believe Australia has key interests in the sea and that those interests are threatened by China. At times, the South China Sea has been subsumed by broader political concerns around Chinese interference in Australian democracy. When former Labor senator Sam Dastyari and Liberal representative Gladys Liu attempted 'neutral' stances on the South China Sea, they were accused of having links to the Chinese Communist Party.[4] Yet there is little evidence that Beijing's efforts to influence Australian thinking on the South China Sea have had any impact in China's favour. If anything, the opposite is true.

The South China Sea is home to complex territorial and maritime disputes between China, Vietnam, Taiwan, Indonesia, Malaysia, the Philippines and Brunei. These disputes give rise to a range of security challenges, including the risk of incidents at sea causing wider-scale conflict between contesting claimants, and China's military installations on several of the features it claims, which could be used to limit freedom of navigation and overflight in the region.

Australia is not party to the territorial or maritime disputes in the South China Sea, nor to the Code of Conduct negotiations underway between China and the ten member states of the Association of Southeast Asian Nations (ASEAN), designed to establish a framework for managing them. Yet, politicians and analysts have at certain times presented the South China Sea as vital to Australia's strategic and economic interests. Why?

Utopia's send-up of Australia's South China Sea policy is funny but falls short in its simplified critique of Australia's strategic tensions and national interests. Australia does have legitimate stakes in the South China Sea, including ensuring open trade. A recent Defence-funded study found that Australia imports 90 per cent of its refined fuel, most of which comes from South Korea, Singapore, Japan, Malaysia and Taiwan via the seas of Southeast Asia. A blockade or conflict in the South China Sea would threaten supply chains for energy sources that are critical to Australia's economy and defence.[5]

While there is a lower risk of great power conflict in the South China Sea than in the Western Pacific, that risk can't be entirely discounted given the danger of incidents between claimants escalating. The United States, like Australia, is not geographically proximate to the South China Sea and makes no claims to land or sea in the domain. However, it has an ally (the Philippines) that is a claimant and has expressed a 'vital' interest in defending freedom of navigation.[6] As the waterways become increasingly crowded, unplanned encounters and unsafe manoeuvres also increase the risk that a conflict might be unintentionally sparked. Military-to-military incidents have recently occurred between Australia and China in the region, with Defence Minister Marles describing the release of a bundle of aluminium chaff by a Chinese J-16 fighter jet near an Australia P-8 surveillance aircraft in 2022 as 'very dangerous'.[7]

Another area of strategic concern relates more directly to Australia's territorial defence: whether the artificial bases built by China in the South China Sea could enable long-range missiles to reach the Australian mainland. While such an attack seems improbable, new technologies and a changing threat environment cast doubt on a key pillar of Australia's strategic imagination: that its isolated geography gives it 'time to prepare and space to exhaust potential adversaries'.[8]

Just as importantly for a middle-sized state such as Australia, the South China Sea disputes are widely viewed as a litmus test for China's intentions to rewrite the so-called rules-based order. It also reflects how China, the United States and Southeast Asian states seek to manage their relationships in an increasingly contested environment. The regional order, which has served Australia's regional peace and prosperity since World War II, is becoming increasingly destabilised and uncertain. China's maritime ambitions and assertions in the South China Sea constitute a threat to the United Nations Convention on the Law of the Sea (UNCLOS), the legitimacy of which is necessary for ensuring Australia's own vast and lucrative maritime entitlements. Yet, if China is trying to replace UNCLOS with an alternative vision of maritime order, it is not entirely clear what this order would look like.[9] The evidence suggests China is an *exceptionalist* rather than a revisionist power; as great powers are wont to do, Beijing would like to carve out an exception for itself in the South China Sea. The United States is no stranger to such exceptionalism itself. But while China's actions might destabilise the global maritime order, this is a different proposition to a wholescale revision of the rules set out in UNCLOS.

WHY HAS THE SOUTH CHINA SEA HISTORICALLY MATTERED TO AUSTRALIA?

The South China Sea has long been linked to Australia's security interests and alliance with the United States. During the Cold War, the maritime highways of Southeast Asia were viewed as particularly important for Australian policymakers. And Australia has been concerned about the Spratly Islands (which lie off the coasts of Malaysia, the Philippines and southern Vietnam) falling into Chinese hands and the potential militarisation of the sea since the 1950s.[10] The 1987 *Defence of Australia* white paper noted Australia's ongoing cooperation with its Southeast Asian partners in the Five Power Defence Arrangements – a multilateral security agreement between Australia, Malaysia, Singapore, New Zealand and the United Kingdom – to conduct surveillance of the South China Sea, including out of the Butterworth air base in Penang, Malaysia.[11] The *Defence White Paper 2013* and *2016 Defence White Paper* both presented the South China Sea as potentially 'destabilising' for regional security.[12]

Australia has only recently entered the testy political waters of the South China Sea disputes in a less-tentative fashion, following the rapid intensification of China's claims and assertions in the region after 2009. There are several reasons for this delay, including the risk-averse nature of Australian policymaking and the belief that the benefits of positive relations with China outweighed Australia's South China Sea interests.[13]

This is not to say that the seas were historically stable or free of conflict. In fact, the complex geography of the South China Sea has made it ripe for disputes between states. The semi-enclosed sea encompasses around 3 million square kilometres of maritime area and hundreds of land features, including islands, rocks, reefs, submerged shoals and low-lying elevations, which have collectively shaped the region's maritime politics. Contested claims over these often tiny land features have existed since the early twentieth century, occasionally leading to the use of force.[14]

In the 1974 Battle of the Paracel Islands, China was able to comprehensively extend its control over the entire Paracel Islands group in the South China Sea after an armed conflict between the Republic of Vietnam's Navy and the Chinese People's Liberation Army. Fourteen years later, a second Sino–Vietnamese skirmish broke out at Johnson South Reef in the nearby Spratly Islands chain, leaving sixty-four sailors dead and two Vietnamese ships sunk by Chinese naval frigates.

Today, six parties – China, Taiwan, the Philippines, Vietnam, Brunei and Malaysia – claim territorial ownership over some or all of the land features dotting the sea. Additionally, Indonesia has maritime contests with China in what it calls the North Natuna Sea, although it avoids being cast as a party to the South China Sea disputes, preferring to adopt a neutral position.[15]

The territorial sovereignty and maritime disputes in the region are often confused and incorrectly conflated in the media. While sovereignty over land features has implications for the division of maritime resources in the surrounding waters, they are distinct issues governed by two different regimes of international law. So, while Australia has been vocal about what it views as China's violation of UNCLOS in the South China Sea, like the United States it remains neutral on the issue of who owns which land features.[16]

Understanding how and why these tiny and mostly uninhabited land features matter in material terms requires grappling with a rather niche part of international law known as 'the regime of islands'. Under international law, possession of islands can provide states with lucrative maritime resources such as fish and hydrocarbons. According to UNCLOS, a land feature classified as an island is entitled to a full 200-nautical-mile exclusive economic zone. However, a land feature classified as a rock that can't sustain human habitation only gets a 12-nautical-mile territorial sea. If the land feature is a low-tide elevation, the maritime benefit is next to nothing: it is accorded a 500-metre safety zone. These disputes are as much about how land features are classified according to UNCLOS as about who owns them.

Territorial and maritime disputes have intensified over the past decade, with consequences for regional security – a key interest for Australia. This increase was partly due to a process that coastal states are required to undergo under UNCLOS: those that claim a continental shelf beyond 200 nautical miles from their coastline are required to submit those claims and justifying information to the Commission on the Limits of the Continental Shelf.[17] In May 2009, Malaysia and Vietnam made a joint submission regarding a portion of their continental shelf in the southern part of the South China Sea.[18] China rejected Malaysia and Vietnam's claims by submitting a note to the Commission, attaching a map depicting the now infamous 'nine-dash' or 'U-shaped' line. First published in 1947 by the Republic of China (Taiwanese) government, various incarnations of the line appear to represent China's claim to around 90 per cent of the South China Sea.

One of the central difficulties in resolving and managing the South China Sea disputes is that China is deliberately ambiguous about what it *actually* claims. Publicly, it claims 'indisputable sovereignty over the South China Sea Islands and the adjacent waters'.[19] The moderate Chinese legal view is that it claims sovereignty of the islands and rocks within the nine-dash line, historical sovereign rights to fishing and other marine resources and sovereign rights to resources in the seabed, including oil and gas.[20] The nine-dash line could therefore act like a maritime boundary. But the nine-dash line could also support a territorial claim to the South China Sea, operating more like a land border. Such a claim to full sovereign control over the maritime area would far transcend what coastal states are entitled to under international law. There is an underlying international legal principle that seas and oceans (beyond internal waters and territorial seas) are a 'global commons' and not subject to the total control of one state. Even in exclusive economic zones, navigating states have rights to transit that coastal states cannot violate. If the territorial interpretation of the nine-dash line is correct, then it could lead to the South China Sea becoming a 'Chinese lake' within which Beijing could deny the navigation rights of other states' warships and commercial vessels, including Australia's.

China has engaged in several destabilising activities in the South China Sea, including artificial island-building, naval militarisation and other militarisation activities, the use of grey zone tactics, whereby paramilitary actors defend national interests, and maritime safety incidents in the increasingly crowded waterways. China's actions have been described as 'salami slicing', as it has incrementally 'sliced' away the maritime entitlements of other states and subtly changed the balance of power through the construction of artificial islands and militarisation. Small actions built up to a much bigger whole, and over a matter of five years China substantially changed the material facts on the ground with little consequence. Such actions can fly under the radar until it's too late.

Beginning in 2013, China engaged in rapid, large-scale artificial island-building and militarisation in the Spratly Islands, constructing seven new islands and creating more than 2000 acres of new land.[21] China pledged not to militarise the islands, but three military-grade mid-ocean airfields quietly emerged in 2016. While other claimant states have also built up land, China's island-building has allowed it to substantially militarise the South China Sea because the islands serve as military outposts. This has raised debates about China's intentions: Is this militarisation defensive and meant to protect China's South China Sea claims? Or is it about pushing the United States out of the first island chain?

Since completing its artificial islands in the Spratly Islands in 2016, China has shifted its focus to advancing its 'maritime militia' of fishing vessels. While they are ostensibly engaged in fishing, these vessels 'operate alongside Chinese law enforcement and military to achieve political objectives in disputed waters'.[22] The Asia Maritime Transparency Initiative has tracked the substantial increase in Chinese fishing vessels in the South China Sea, finding nearly a hundred boats deployed near Philippine-occupied Thitu Island in 2018, and around two hundred at the unoccupied Whitsun Reef in 2021.[23] These vessels seek to enhance Beijing's control of the South China Sea by flooding the waters to prevent others from accessing their maritime rights and wearing down the other claimant states.

China has also engaged in 'white-hull' warfare in the South China Sea, using its coastguard for strategic and law-enforcement purposes. China appears to conceptualise most of the South China Sea as its maritime jurisdiction, which means its coastguards increasingly treat it as an area of domestic law enforcement. In 2021, its ambiguous China Coast Guard Law provoked concern across the region. Article 22 of the law permits the coastguard to employ 'all means necessary including the use of force' to stop foreigners infringing Chinese 'sovereignty, sovereign rights and jurisdictional rights'. And in April 2021, Beijing expanded the authority of the China Maritime Safety Administration to fine and expel foreign ships found to be potentially hazardous to marine traffic safety in China's 'jurisdictional waters', a term that has no basis in international law. These Chinese laws contribute to a growing pattern of China using operational, lawfare and administrative strategies to physically, normatively and legally *territorialise* the seas – that is, to bring them under the sovereign control of the state contrary to the 'free seas' precept – and intensify pressure on regional states with overlapping maritime claims.

In 2013, the Philippines initiated a case against China to test its claims to 'historic rights' within the nine-dash line. China protested the case and decided not to participate. In 2016, the arbitral tribunal found Beijing's claims were inconsistent with international law.[24] It also made the crucial finding that none of the land features subject to the arbitration could be legally classified as islands and, therefore, carried no entitlements to an exclusive economic zone or continental shelf. The ruling was rejected by Beijing. Since then, it has used various quasi-legal narratives to justify its dubious claims to the South China Sea, including the claim that some of the island groups form outlying archipelagos, which is not supported by international law. But Beijing's actions do not represent a wholesale revision of rules. While it wants to restrict other states' freedom of navigation rights in the South China Sea, it wants to retain those same rights for itself in other maritime domains. Rather, it seems that China seeks to manipulate international law by picking and choosing the provisions that support its interests in any given domain and ignoring the rules that don't. This ultimately undermines the universality of UNCLOS, something that Australia does not want.

THE RELEVANCE OF CONTEMPORARY SECURITY ISSUES TO AUSTRALIA'S SECURITY

The South China Sea disputes symbolise a rapidly transforming Asian security environment, defined primarily by the rise of China and the declining power of the United States. Contemporary security issues in the South China Sea are complex, multilayered and interrelated, involving ownership of land features, the delimitation of maritime boundaries, rights to marine resources, the strategic balance of power in the region and access to sea lines of communication and key trading choke points. While these security and resource interests often drive the disputes, they are also subject to maritime nationalism, as elites and citizens position ownership of land features and authority over maritime area as central to the exercise of their sovereignty.[25]

Australia, in its adoption of the 'Indo-Pacific' concept, increasingly recognises the regional and global nature of its maritime interests. So although it is not directly party to the territorial and maritime disputes in the South China Sea, it has stakes in the disputes' global and regional implications. Australian policymakers are concerned about five key issues in particular: first, how China's militarisation of the South China Sea affects Australia's core defence interests; second, how its naval build-up and modernisation tilt the regional balance of power further away from US primacy; third, the prospects of regional or great power conflict breaking out and whether Australia would be drawn in; fourth, the enduring legitimacy of the UNCLOS-centred maritime rules-based order; and, finally, commercial and military freedom of navigation through the South China Sea.

The vital defence interest of Australia – or any state – is its ability to protect its territory and population from external attack. Historically, an aspect of Australia's favourable geography was that it existed beyond the military reach of China and its anti-access sanctuary. But there are new questions about whether the militarisation of the South China Sea threatens Australia's ability to protect itself, exposing it to the potential of long-range missile attack.

China is not alone in the rapid expansion and modernisation of its navies and coastguards, nor in its acquisition of new capabilities, including a long-range missiles force and anti-ship missiles. However, China already has the world's largest coastguard, encompassing about 130 ships, together with seventy or so patrol vessels.[26] As mentioned previously, it is estimated that the People's Liberation Army Navy will grow to 460 ships by 2030.[27]

While at least some of China's artificial bases in the South China Sea have environmental and structural weaknesses, they might still enable long-range missiles to reach Australian territory. Submarines leaving South China Sea bases could be in striking range of Australia within days.[28] China's capacity to project power across vast distances is likely to become far greater than Japan's in World War II.[29]

While territorial defence is of paramount importance to defence planners, there is a far greater likelihood that Australian security interests in the South China Sea will be challenged by military conflict between the great powers.[30] Like many other regional states, Australia is concerned about what China's military modernisation means for the global balance of power and China's strategic competition with the United States.

Over the past decade, the Chinese leadership has made its ambitions to become a global maritime power clear. Its geography of expansive land boundaries and short coastlines has meant that China has traditionally focused on continental defence, but such an approach left it exposed to interventions by hostile foreign powers via the South and East China seas. The first and second island chains identified by Chinese defence planners shape how they view their maritime and continental security. Situated within the first island chain, the South China Sea is classified by China as a vital interest. It has established artificial islands in the region and equipped them with military installations to enhance its 'anti-access / area denial' (A2/AD) capabilities, which may be used to push US warships out of the area. The depths of the South China Sea may also enable China to use it as a submarine bastion for projecting force into other maritime areas, such as the Western Pacific or Indian Ocean.

However, US security interests in the domain are quite limited, which means the risk of a great power conflict in the South China Sea is relatively low. Nevertheless, it can't be discounted. While analysts have argued that a firmer US South China Sea policy is unwarranted because it might generate an increased risk of a high-intensity war with China,[31] the Biden administration has confirmed that the United States would stand with Philippine allies in 'upholding the rules-based international maritime order', and an armed attack on Philippine armed forces, public vessels or aircraft, including those of the coastguard in the South China Sea, would invoke US commitments under Article IV of the 1951 US Philippines Mutual Defense Treaty.[32] The defence of Taiwan and the Philippines may also rely upon access to the South China Sea.

What such a scenario would mean for Australia's commitments under ANZUS are questionable, although as we argue in Chapter 3 we think debates about whether Australia would support the United States in a war in the region are effectively moot. Indeed, given Australia's unimpeachable record of following the United States into war, Washington would likely anticipate Australian military support in the event of a maritime conflict in East Asia.[33] But it is unlikely that Southeast Asian states would uniformly accept an intervention from the United States, given it is not part of the region. Forcing the notoriously hedging Southeast Asian states – even those that traditionally trend towards Washington, such as Singapore and the Philippines – to 'choose' between the United States and China would be unwise. The United States has a mixed history in the region (the Philippines, after all, is a former US colony), and its inconsistencies have precipitated concerns about its reliability. More recently, a perhaps unfair criticism of the Obama administration was that it was unwilling or unable to assist smaller Southeast Asian powers against the salami-slicing tactics of China in the South China Sea. Ultimately these dynamics suggest that Australia should be cautious but not alarmed about the prospect of being dragged into a regional conflict in the South China Sea.

Australia shares a view with the United States that China's actions in the South China Sea threaten freedom of navigation and undermine a global maritime order based on the principle of free seas. If China were to gain strategic control of the South China Sea, it could seek to limit the transit of other states' warships or commercial vessels. Given Australia's strategic dependence on the US alliance, Australia views it as advantageous for both the Royal Australian Navy and the US Navy to have maximum room to move across the world's oceans and seas. Yet, Australian and US views on freedom of navigation do not necessarily align with those of Southeast Asian states. These views can be roughly classified as 'open seas' versus 'enclosed seas'. During UNCLOS negotiations in the 1970s and early 1980s, the most powerful navies – those of the United States and the Soviet Union – advocated a 12-nautical-mile territorial sea and a high seas corridor to permit their navies expansive freedom of navigation rights. But developing coastal states wanted greater control over their surrounding seas, including their maritime resources. The 200-nautical-mile exclusive economic zone was a compromise, creating a unique jurisdiction wherein coastal states would have sovereign rights to resources in this zone but maritime powers would maintain navigation rights akin to those in the high seas. UNCLOS also provides navigating states with rights of innocent passage through the territorial seas of coastal states, yet across Asia there is conflicting views on whether this right extends to warships. China supported the establishment of the exclusive economic zone but now attempts to restrict other states' freedom of navigation rights – for instance, by requesting that they obtain prior authorisation before transiting within China's territorial seas. Because there are different opinions on navigation rights, there is a risk that overly vocal expressions in favour of 'freedom of navigation' will be viewed by Southeast Asian states as supporting US rather than regional priorities.

Around a third of the world's trade passes through the South China Sea, including nearly two-thirds of Australia's exports by volume, including major coal, iron ore and liquefied natural gas exports. For this reason, the 2016 *Defence White Paper* makes it clear that it is in Australia's interests for commercial freedom of navigation to be maintained in the South China Sea,[34] particularly through key choke points such as the straits of Lombok, Sunda and Malacca, which are only hundreds of nautical miles from Australia rather than thousands. One estimate holds that Australia's non-Chinese trade by value in the South China Sea was only 6.6 per cent in 2016,[35] but free and open sea lines of communication are also vital to Australia's fuel security, and that of its key Northeast Asian economic partners, Japan and Korea. Nevertheless, Australia's national interests are tied less to commercial freedom of navigation and more to alliance politics and sustained advocacy for US presence and leadership in East Asia.[36]

As the world's largest trading nation,[37] China has just as much at stake as Australia or any other coastal state in keeping crucial South China Sea sea lines of communication open, if not more. Yet it is difficult to predict China's intentions. We should therefore look to its actions. China has yet to carry out any commercial blockades, but it has prevented commercial activities in the South China Sea: its paramilitary's harassment of fishers and survey ships could be interpreted as a violation of commercial freedom of navigation. Analysts have often assumed that if blockades were to occur the cost of circumventing the South China Sea would be significant, but evidence suggests it would depend on which and how many choke points were closed.[38]

Another way to measure the economic consequences of tensions in the South China Sea is to consider whether Australia's language on the subject has had ramifications for its bilateral trading relationship with China. Beijing has used trade sanctions to punish Australia's firmer stance on defending maritime norms and in 2020 it expressed displeasure at Australia's attitude to the South China Sea in its infamous 'fourteen grievances' document, which included an item about Australia being 'the first non-littoral country to make a statement on the South China Sea to the United Nations'.[39]

However, Australian trade in Asia has not been disrupted because China has sought to close maritime trading routes but rather because of deteriorating relations between China and Australia. In 2019, when one of China's biggest ports banned lucrative Australian coal imports, it was viewed in Australia as linked to broader issues in the bilateral relationship, such as foreign interference laws and visa revocations.[40] In 2020, under the guise of COVID-19 restrictions, China barred cargo vessels holding Australian goods from unloading in Chinese ports.[41] At the time, Beijing had also imposed a range of significant tariffs on Australian industries, aimed at punishing the Australian government for its anti-China policies and rhetoric.

Arguably, Australia's immediate economic interests – if they are indeed paramount – would be better served by being less vocal on contentious issues such as the South China Sea and more focused on improving diplomatic relations, which seems to be the basis of the Albanese government's toned down China rhetoric. But Australia's conception of its national interests in the South China Sea has not been shaped primarily by economics so much as security.

Other supply chains issues are likely to have much more substantial effects on Australia's security than those created by China, including issues posed by the pandemic or climate change. For example, international shipping companies were accused of being 'modern-day pirates' when they used the COVID-19 pandemic to justify setting high prices for shipping transportation in Australia, using a loophole that the Australian Competition and Consumer Commission wants repealed.[42] This increased the price of goods in Australia and created freight backlogs.

But the more substantive issue at stake in the South China Sea for Australia is the erosion of a maritime order based on norms and international law. Disputes in the South China Sea are fraying the rules-based order, which down the track may restrict the access of warships and commercial ships to the global maritime commons. Australia's long-standing position on the South China Sea is that maritime disputes should be resolved through international law. China's ambiguous assertions in the South China Sea and rejection of the 2016 arbitral tribunal ruling raise concerns that Beijing seeks to undermine a maritime order based on UNCLOS.

Threats to UNCLOS in domains such as the South China Sea challenge the UNCLOS-centred order that underwrites Australia's own maritime rights and entitlements. If a great power can unilaterally impose its will on other states in the maritime domain, this challenges the position of smaller and middle-sized countries such as Australia that are incapable of defending their maritime zones through military and constabulary capabilities alone. Australia would need to pour billions of dollars into defence capabilities to defend its maritime domains independently.[43] Instead, Australia depends on the durability of UNCLOS. The South China Sea is where its legitimacy is most challenged. China's actions in the South China Sea provide Australian politicians and policy planners with a tangible example to use in its own strategic narratives about how Beijing seeks to revise the maritime rules-based order that Canberra wishes to uphold.

Australia does have a stake in an order based on international law, particularly in the maritime domain. But the problem is how Australia uses narratives emphasising the importance of the ruled-based order to support policies that are unsuitable for a regional order in which US primacy no longer exists. Australian leaders have relied on the slippery notion that a US-led order and a rules-based order are essentially the same thing. Putting aside the numerous instances in which the United States has ignored or neglected the rules – for instance, the Iraq war, the withdrawal from the Trans-Pacific Partnership and the white-anting of the World Trade Organization – the fact remains that the United States has not ratified UNCLOS. While it claims to abide by the precepts of UNCLOS as customary international law, Washington exists beyond the international dispute-resolution mechanisms that enabled the Philippines to take China through an international arbitration process to assess excessive claims in the South China Sea. It is little wonder, then, that China draws upon US hypocrisy to defend its own refusal to participate in the arbitral tribunal, with varying degrees of success.

In the South China Sea, as much as any other maritime domain, the security challenges that states are required to manage are linked in complex ways. There is a tendency to try to split up 'traditional' or 'military' threats from 'emerging' or 'non-traditional' threats such as climate change and the COVID pandemic, but there is no clear separation between the strategic, environmental and human security challenges in the South China Sea. Large-scale artificial island-building, for instance, has significant environmental ramifications, creating pollution and damaging marine ecosystems. Journalist James Borton evocatively describes the South China Sea as an 'environmental crime scene'.[44] Studies have also demonstrated that climate change is intensifying the risk of fisheries conflict, as it affects the fish population, creates scarcity and affects the abilities of states to manage their fisheries.[45]

The collapse of fishing stocks in the South China Sea due to overfishing and climate change will have detrimental effects on food and job security in coastal Southeast Asian states. Catches from South

China Sea fisheries were estimated to be worth over US$15 billion in 2018, which helps explain why the boundaries of exclusive economic zone are so hotly contested.[46] Yet lucrative catches are unlikely to continue: climate change, marine plastic pollution, ocean acidification and coral bleaching are all putting stress on the marine ecosystem and encouraging fish species to migrate north. It has been predicted that even if the best-case scenario of low emissions and a 50 per cent decrease in fishing were achieved, we would still see the South China Sea lose US$6.5 billion by 2100.[47] The worst-case scenario would see over US$11 billion lost in fisheries revenues and over six million tonnes of fish biomass lost from the South China Sea ecosystem. There is little chance that the degradations in fish stocks can be reversed.[48]

The 'threat multiplier' effects of climate change in maritime Southeast Asia are significant: climate change contributes to changing migratory patterns of fish, population displacement, the destruction of important coral reefs and rising sea levels. In Southeast Asia's maritime domain it could also create simultaneous humanitarian crises that 'will greatly test… [Australia's] national capacities, commitments and resilience.'[49] On a purely instrumental level, this has effects on Australia's national interests. But more broadly, contributing to the prevention of such humanitarian, development and environment disasters should be central to how Australia imagines itself as a regional actor.

AUSTRALIA'S CURRENT POLICY APPROACH

Australia's policy incorporates diplomatic, legal and operational engagements in the South China Sea, including routine military presence operations, multilateral engagement, public diplomacy strategies and the modelling of international maritime dispute resolution processes.

Over recent years, the United States has encouraged Australia to step up in the South China Sea by engaging in Freedom of Navigation Operations. FONOPs are one part of a global freedom of navigation program the United States uses to defend its interests and counter maritime claims it deems not in accordance with international law. The most well-known aspect of a FONOP is operational: a warship is often sent to transit through oceans and seas in a way that deliberately and publicly challenges a coastal state's maritime claim if the United States sees it as excessive. This is a global program and the United States conducts FONOPs against claims made by friends and foes alike, including Japan, Korea and India in the broader Indo-Pacific and Vietnam in the South China Sea. The United States does not, however, conduct FONOPs against Australia, even though it makes maritime claims, including to historic bays and a dubious exclusive economic zone off the coast of the Australian Antarctic Territory, that the United States interprets as excessive and are publicly called out in its Navy's reference manual on maritime claims.

In Australian public and political discussions, FONOPs have become a critical threshold for testing Australia's resolve to push back against Beijing. 'America first' analysts have argued that Canberra should support US efforts to resist Beijing's assertiveness by engaging in US-style FONOPs.[50] Others have suggested that doing so is necessary for supporting the 'rules-based order'.[51] In the past, members of both the Coalition and Labor, such as Concetta Fierravanti-Wells and Stephen Conroy, have publicly supported Australian FONOPs. Australian discussions tend to refer very narrowly to FONOPs as warships sailing within 12 nautical miles of Chinese-claimed features in the South China Sea[52], and often fail to provide the broader context of FONOPs as specific to a unique US global program. Although the UK Royal Navy conducted a US-style FONOP in the South China Sea in 2018, other states have been reluctant to engage in such activities.

While Australia publicly respects the rights of other states to conduct these operations and reserves the right to employ them under international law in future, it currently views FONOPs as too risky and symbolic, and unnecessary for Australia's strategic interests. In his memoir, former prime minister Malcolm Turnbull explained Australia's position on FONOPs: they present unreasonable risks to Australian personnel and naval assets; they are potentially destabilising to the region; they could provoke economic retaliation from Beijing; and they would present Australia as too closely aligned to the United States. Most interestingly, Turnbull goes on to say that the United States may not come to Australia's aid if there was an incident:

> If one of our ships were to be rammed and disabled within the 12-mile limit by a Chinese vessel, we don't have the capacity to escalate. If the Americans backed us in, then the Chinese would back off. But if Washington hesitated or, for whatever reasons, decided not to or was unable immediately to intervene, then China would have achieved as enormous propaganda win, exposing the USA as a paper tiger not to be relied on by its allies.[53]

There have also been problems with the legal messaging of US FONOPs. After the USS *Lassen*'s FONOP in the Spratly Islands in October 2015, international law experts were confused as to whether the US Navy had conducted its transit according to the rules of 'innocent passage' near the Chinese-claimed Subi Reef. Innocent-passage transits are conducted within the territorial seas of coastal states. Warships must travel continuously and expeditiously, suspend military capabilities and avoid any activities that could be considered harmful to the coastal state's security. But an artificial island such as Subi Reef does not legally generate a territorial sea under UNCLOS. By conducting innocent passage, the United States may have unintentionally confirmed that a territorial sea exists.[54] The geographical complexity lends itself to legal complexity as well. Given this, Australia is right to avoid entangling itself in new forms of operational challenges. It has no formal global program for challenging excessive maritime claims as the United States does; instead, it conducts routine 'business as usual' operations to uphold freedom of navigation norms.

It is also reasonable for Australia to distance itself from activities too closely aligned with US interests and approaches to maritime security. Australia has its own toolbox of operational strategies it's used to step up its presence in the South China Sea in the past decade. In 2014, Australia had five ships operating in the South China Sea; by 2018, there were nine. Australia also created the Indo-Pacific Endeavour, the largest joint taskforce in over forty years, which transited through the South China Sea in most years since 2017. Australia's transits take place outside particularly contentious waters. Australian defence exercises in the South China Sea are typically bilateral or multilateral and include port visits, training and coordinated naval exercises with partners. In 2023, Australia became the second country after the United States to commit to joint patrols with the Philippines in the South China Sea. Over a period of five years, Canberra upgraded its defence partnerships with Southeast Asian states: Australia now enjoys comprehensive strategic partnership–status with Indonesia (2018), Malaysia (2021) and ASEAN (2021), and Strategic Partnership–status with Vietnam (2018) and the Philippines (2022). Of course, in 2014 Australia agreed to describe its relationship with China as a comprehensive strategic partnership, so the precise value of such arrangements is not always clear. Nevertheless, there is an important performative element to such arrangements: they signal to the bilateral partner and others in the international community that there is a level of trust between the parties and a commitment to cooperate on strategic issues. Joint statements with Vietnam, Indonesia, the Philippines and Malaysia have all expressed concern about developments in the South China Sea.[55]

Much of this cooperation is not new. Australia has been a member of the low-profile but durable Five Power Defence Arrangements with Malaysia, Singapore, New Zealand and the United Kingdom for over fifty years. The Royal Australian Air Force has maintained Operation Gateway, a program of maritime surveillance flights over the South China Sea, operating out of Malaysia's Butterworth air base, since the Cold War. This was originally established in response to the use of Vietnam's Cam Ranh Bay as a Soviet base, which Australia viewed as contrary to its regional security interests. Now, Australia's long-range maritime patrol aircraft conduct routine surveillance over the South China Sea. While

Australia refuses to conduct FONOPs at sea level, the Royal Australian Air Force conducts them in the airspace, occasionally invoking the ire of Chinese military. However, most of Australia's joint activities have tended to be with partners that are not Southeast Asian states.

In recent years, Australia's strategic imagination has primarily viewed the South China Sea through the lens of 'destabilising strategic competition'; it is concerned about China's intentions and capabilities as a rising power and how the evolving balance of power will affect the United States' leadership role in the regional order.[56]

Since the 2016 South China Sea arbitral tribunal ruling, Australian officials have been more vocal in calling upon China to halt destabilising activities, reinforcing Australia's support for freedom of navigation and overflight, and requesting that parties to the dispute (principally China) abide by the ruling. Australia's rules-based-order narratives intensified following China's refusal to abide by the ruling: the term 'rules-based order' was used fifty-six times in the *2016 Defence White Paper*, but only nine times in the *Defence White Paper 2013*. The government has continually reaffirmed its position that the ruling was final and binding on both parties, and that the parties must resolve disputes according to UNCLOS.[57]

Australian leaders have also supported maritime norms in the South China Sea though bilateral and multilateral forums, including ASEAN meetings, the East Asia Summit and other regional forums, advocating its interests in regional stability and dispute-resolution processes that conform to international law. Beijing has responded publicly and privately by accusing Australia of hypocrisy, pointing to its dispute with Timor-Leste over maritime boundaries and oil and gas resources in the Timor Sea.

The enforcement of the 2016 arbitral tribunal ruling has not been strongly advocated by either the Southeast Asian claimants or the international community. For a long time after the ruling, the Australian government was one of only eight governments to publicly support it, with eight opposed. But since 2022, following Russia's invasion of

Ukraine, and the Philippines' renewed advocacy of the ruling, sixteen other governments have publicly endorsed the ruling as legally binding.[58] In 2020, Australia clarified its legal position on the ruling by providing a note verbale to the United Nations, just a week after the United States. In it, Canberra explicitly rejected China's claim to 'historic rights' in the South China Sea and its 'Four Sha' (four sands) strategy, which involves the construction of straight archipelagic baselines around the land features in the Pratas, Paracel, Spratly and Macclesfield Bank groups in order to claim the maritime area within those baselines as part of China's exclusive economic zone and continental shelf.[59] But China's position does not accord with what UNCLOS says about which states can claim archipelagic status and on what basis.

While Australia has pushed back against China's dubious claims that its sovereignty over land features is 'widely recognised by the international community', it remains neutral on the issue of who owns the land features.[60] As mentioned, Australia does not take sides on competing *territorial* claims, a point that is often missed in popular commentary. When the media reported on Australia's 2020 note verbale to the United Nations, many outlets incorrectly stated that Australia considered China's territorial claims invalid. This is important to note because the historical record shows that states are much more likely to go to war over land than fishing resources. The fact that Australia remains neutral on issues of sovereignty indicates it wants its Southeast Asian partners to be able to access their legal maritime entitlements without intensifying the sovereignty disputes in the region.

Like the United States, Australia also made no comment on the logic underpinning the arbitral tribunal's classification of *natural* land features as islands, rocks, or low-lying or submerged elevations. Both Australia and the United States make exclusive economic zone claims on the back of land features that may not meet the necessary criteria to be classified as islands. Australia, for example, claims a 200-nautical-mile economic exclusion zone around the 'rocky and desolate' Heard Island and McDonald Islands in the Southern Ocean. If the arbitral tribunal's logic on island classification becomes the standard bearer in international law (and it may not), then the Heard Island and McDonald Islands are unlikely to meet the threshold for an exclusive economic zone.

WHAT SHOULD AUSTRALIA DO DIFFERENTLY?

Strategic competition is just one of many maritime security challenges in the South China Sea. Australia already has a relatively well-balanced South China Sea policy, but it could improve its policy in certain areas such as climate change, which presents significant maritime challenges in the domain. Thankfully, Albanese's Labor government has expressed a greater determination to address this issue than previous Coalition governments.

But while Australian officials in diplomacy and defence work assiduously with Southeast Asian partners on 'unconventional' maritime security challenges, some of the political discourse on the South China Sea, and freedom of navigation more broadly, continues to present a desirable concept of regional order as based on US primacy, even as the United States itself recognises such primacy no longer exists.[61] At the heart of these discourses is a paradox: a desire to fortify and cling to the old order while simultaneously grappling with the end of the United States' unipolar moment. Australia will need to maintain an independent, clear-eyed analysis of the intentions and ambitions of both the United States and China, as well as those of other relevant states, particularly in Southeast Asia. It must also ensure its policy settings support its key normative interest: that an UNCLOS-led maritime order will continue to underpin the legal entitlements of middle-sized and smaller states in the region beyond US primacy.

In Australia, the South China Sea is a symbol of a shifting balance of power that is destabilising the region. While Australia has been unwilling to damage its relationship with China in the defence of maritime norms in the South China Sea, its policymakers have at times adopted strident messaging, without going so far as to adopt US-style FONOPs. Consequently, Washington looks to Canberra to remain a steadfast regional ally as the Biden administration prioritises coalition-building through integrated deterrence to ensure 'a free and open' Indo-Pacific.[62]

As tensions in the area rise, there is a risk that Australia could be pushed to follow the United States into conflict. To prevent this, Australia needs to think creatively about how it can de-escalate tensions and position itself as a source of security, rather than instability, for its Southeast Asian partners. There are five ways it could work towards these goals.

First, Australia should continue to resist pressure to engage in FONOPs. In 2016, Labor's Opposition spokesperson on Defence said Australia should stop 'pretending' to conduct freedom-of-navigation exercises and take more concrete action in the South China Sea.[63] But the risks of this would outweigh the benefits. Some Southeast Asian countries view US-style FONOPs as destabilising, and realistically have done little to change China's behaviour. It would be better for Australia to continue its business-as-usual approach to operations in the South China Sea but with more engagement on maritime security challenges other than great power politics.

Second, Australia must be seen as working with Southeast Asian countries, not forcing them to choose between the United States and China. Australia should focus on elevating its relationships with Southeast Asian claimants and prioritising the broader set of maritime security challenges they are tackling. The maritime domain provides fertile ground for cooperation with states such as Indonesia, the Philippines and Vietnam, particularly on 'unconventional' challenges. This should involve increased diplomacy and defence cooperation.

The COVID-19 pandemic affected Southeast Asian states' defence spending and procurement, and this has had negative consequences for their naval and coastguard capabilities. Australia could prioritise maritime capacity-building by enhancing the sovereign capabilities of Southeast Asian states to police their maritime zones, defend their legal entitlements and maintain their independence from more powerful states, including China.[64] Such activities could improve the ability of navies and coastguards (or in Australia's case, its Maritime Border Command) to work together, building on existing initiatives, including the Defence Cooperation Program and the ASEAN–Australia Defence Postgraduate Scholarship Program, designed to build naval and defence capabilities through training, personnel and expert exchanges, dialogues and joint exercises. Moreover, such capacity-building activities could be coordinated with other regional non-claimant states, such as Japan. More could also be done to support Southeast Asian states in areas of maritime domain awareness, knowledge of law of the sea, expert exchange, and naval and coastguard training.

Australia often emphasises the 'centrality' of ASEAN, including in the management of regional disputes and the upholding of international rules and norms. But as ASEAN struggles to grapple with the multitude of the region's security challenges, including the South China Sea disputes and the Myanmar crisis, Australia has increasingly looked to so-called 'minilateral' security arrangements, such as AUKUS and the Quad, for solutions.

In 2017, China and the ASEAN states began negotiating a draft code of conduct in the South China Sea, excluding regional non-claimant states such as Australia. Australia's stated interests in the code of conduct are fourfold: any agreement should not prejudice the interests of third parties or the international legal rights of all states; it should not undermine the existing regional architecture; the principle of ASEAN centrality should be maintained; and claimant states should express a commitment to ceasing actions that could escalate tensions, including militarisation and island-building. Australian officials have engaged all parties to the code of conduct and advocated these interests in bilateral and multilateral forums. The government stance on whether the code of conduct should be legally binding depending on its conformity with UNCLOS, but it is unlikely that an UNCLOS-compliant code of conduct would be supported by China.

Third, Australia needs to recognise the different perspectives and agency of Southeast Asian states. Despite being a non-claimant in the South China Sea, Australia's public alignment with the United States and vocal opposition to China's maritime claims means its language has often been more forward-leaning and assertive than that of its Southeast Asian partners. While Vietnam might appreciate Australia's efforts to contribute to 'good order at sea', if Australia seeks to become more involved in armed deterrence in the South China Sea it could raise concerns among other Southeast Asian states. This has already occurred: Indonesia and Malaysia both expressed concern that Australia's planned acquisition of nuclear-powered submarines under AUKUS would contribute to a regional arms race. However, this was partially due to the Australian government's clumsy diplomacy surrounding the AUKUS announcement and failure to explain the rationale for how and why the submarines would enhance rather than destabilise regional security. This further highlights the importance of diplomacy in regional engagement, in and beyond maritime security.

Conducting joint patrols with Southeast Asian partners in the South China Sea, such as those recently committed to with Manila, can signal Australia's commitment to upholding UNCLOS and increase its ability to work cooperatively with key regional partners. While other claimant Southeast Asian states may be hesitant to engage in joint patrols in case they inflame tensions with China, Australia is right to leave the possibility open.

Fourth, Australia should encourage all states to be clear about their maritime claims and the basis upon which they are made. A good place to start would be to map conventional and emerging maritime security threats – such as environmental degradation, illegal fishing, piracy and pandemics – across the maritime domains of our region, understanding how complex threats intersect and affect Australia's trading, security and environmental interests. In doing so, Australia should be conscious that maritime domains are subject to different ordering dynamics – specific geographies, strategic cultures and regional rules. Australia must also be careful not to assume that China can or will use the same narratives and approaches across different maritime domains. The South China Sea is not necessarily a litmus test for invalid assertions in areas such as Antarctica or the Southern and Indian oceans, where Beijing's efforts to extend quasi-legal claims to 'historical title' or an offshore archipelago seem unlikely to be attempted.

Finally, Australia should promote an integrated approach to the South China Sea, employing all the diplomatic, economic and military instruments required to meet the domain's complex challenges. How to address security risks that proliferate outside the traditional domains of defence and security – in areas such as domestic politics, health and trade – is a crucial challenge for Australia.

The COVID-19 pandemic exacerbated a variety of transnational crimes in the South China Sea and elsewhere, most notably smuggling (of pandemic-related medical supplies, drugs, food and other items) and human trafficking. Big-ticket naval vessels such as submarines may help in raising maritime domain awareness – an important component of addressing blue crime – or be useful in conflict, but Australia needs to be more expansive in its thinking. Australia has the potential to demonstrate its middle-power commitment to Southeast Asia by leading the development of new rules and structures to deal with problems such as vaccine equity and access. Pandemics are not going away, and the institutional infrastructure needed to respond to them is sorely lacking. There is an opportunity to build this infrastructure through regional partnerships and leadership.

Tackling climate change and marine pollution in the South China Sea – vital to environmental and human security in the domain – is another non-traditional but urgent security predicament. The challenge in the South China Sea, and more generally, is for Australia to develop credible responses to climate change that can demonstrate to its neighbours a substantive commitment to reducing carbon emissions, beyond rhetoric.

5

THE SOUTH PACIFIC

On 24 March 2022, news the Australian government had been dreading exploded onto social media: Solomon Islands was close to signing a security agreement with China. For many in the government and national security community, this confirmed their anxieties about China developing a military presence in the region. Reports in Australia dramatically declared the agreement a 'precursor' to the construction of a 'home port' from which the People's Liberation Army Navy could operate.[1] Anxieties about China's naval presence in the Pacific had been building since April 2018, when rumours spread that China was in talks to build a military base in Vanuatu. These fears intensified when Solomon Islands and Kiribati switched their diplomatic allegiance from Taiwan to China in 2019, and China attempted soon afterwards to lease a World War II–era Japanese naval base in Solomon Islands and update strategically located airstrips in Kiribati.

The initial Australian media storm highlighted two enduring dynamics of Australia's South Pacific policy. The first is its anxiety about a potentially hostile power establishing a presence in the region from which it could threaten Australia or its sea lines of communication. This fear has motivated Australia's long-term pursuit of strategic denial, a policy that aims to restrict real or potential adversaries from pursuing their military objectives in the Pacific. The second dynamic is its persistent misunderstanding of South Pacific states and Australia's ability to exercise power over them. Underpinning both these dynamics are broader ones shaping Australia's overall foreign and strategic policy: a sense that its geography isolates it from its primary security guarantors and leaves it vulnerable to threats from within or through its near region.[2]

The geography of the South Pacific has been key to the government's security imaginary of the region: its sheer size makes it difficult for Australia to project force there. The South Pacific is often referred to as Australia's 'patch', 'neighbourhood', 'backyard' and, most recently, 'home',[3] but the domain is bigger than these terms suggest: the South Pacific occupies 15 per cent of the Earth's surface, and Pacific Island countries are spread over 30 million square kilometres. Crucially, 98 per cent of the South Pacific is ocean, as the combined landmass of the region's twenty-two states and territories is less than 600,000 square kilometres, 84 per cent of which is Papua New Guinea. The entire region has a combined population of only 11.2 million people, nearly nine million of whom are in Papua New Guinea.

As we've already described, Australia is linked to the South Pacific by the Timor Sea, the Arafura Sea, the Torres Strait and the Coral Sea. Consequently, successive defence white papers have focused on protecting Australia's air–sea gap in the north, sometimes described as a strategic 'moat'. But the reality of South Pacific geography has challenged Australia's security since before Federation, as have the conditions within and between Pacific Island countries: distances are great (even within countries), infrastructure is often poor, and terrain and weather conditions are difficult (and being made worse by climate change). Territorially small Pacific Island countries identify as 'big ocean countries', with 'stewardship' over a vast maritime Pacific.[4] Their stewardship faces a range of environmental and human-made threats, including rising sea levels; illegal, unreported and unregulated (IUU) fishing; deep-sea mining; and the vulnerability of the submarine cables that provide Pacific Island countries with crucial internet and communication access.

Although Australia has vast material resources in comparison to its South Pacific neighbours – it contributes 60 per cent of the region's development assistance and represents 94.5 per cent of its gross domestic product (GDP), 98 per cent of its defence and security spending and 60 per cent of its population – its ability to influence events in the region, including in the maritime domain, is increasingly constrained.

The government was reminded of this soon after the news of the Solomon Islands–China security agreement leaked. Responding to foreign criticism of the deal, Solomon Islands prime minister Manasseh Sogavare delivered a blisteringly defiant speech in his nation's parliament on 29 March 2022. He criticised Australia for its lack of action on climate change, despite the threat it poses to the region, and its media's calls for Canberra to 'invade' Solomon Islands and 'topple its government'.[5] Sogavare used an evocative image to justify Solomon Islands' agreement with China: 'When a helpless mouse is cornered by vicious cats, it will do anything to survive,' he said.[6]

Australian prime minister Scott Morrison's furious lobbying of Sogavare and other regional leaders, including PNG prime minister James Marape and Fijian prime minister Frank Bainimarama, did not persuade Solomon Islands to abandon the deal. Years earlier, Bainimarama had himself resisted Australian power, ignoring and sidestepping Australian pressure to return Fiji to democracy after his military coup of 2006. He didn't initiate elections until 2014, after he had amended the Fijian constitution to guarantee his party would win government. Marape also had form: in 2018, he accepted Australia's funding and construction of the Coral Sea Cable, which Australia undertook to prevent the involvement of Chinese multinational Huawei, but then contracted Huawei to build its domestic network.

There are many examples from over the decades of Australia seeking to exercise its power to achieve strategic denial in the South Pacific and failing as often as it succeeds. Australia's problems partly reside with its history of 'sub-imperialism', inspired by British imperialism and the US Monroe Doctrine,[7] and its ongoing failures to recognise Pacific agency and Pacific Island countries' legitimate security interests in and beyond the maritime domain. For instance, after former prime minister Kevin Rudd suggested that Australia should offer citizenship to Pacific Islanders in exchange for control of their fisheries, Bainimarama responded by asserting that Fiji 'can hardly tolerate such insensitive, neocolonial prescriptions'.[8]

With global geopolitics in flux and South Pacific states taking advantage of the strategic competition between the United States (and its allies) and China, Australia's ability to exercise its power to achieve its strategic interests in the South Pacific is more constrained than ever.

WHY HAS THE SOUTH PACIFIC HISTORICALLY MATTERED FOR AUSTRALIA?

The historian Neville Meaney once argued that Australian foreign policy can be succinctly summarised as 'the search for security in the Pacific'.[9] This is because of geography: most of Australia's main sea and air lanes of communication lie in the South Pacific.

The South Pacific was a concern of British colonialists long before 'Australia' even existed. When Captain Arthur Phillip landed in Botany Bay on 18 January 1788, his letters patent defined the territories over which he and his successors were to exercise jurisdiction as 'all the Islands adjacent in the Pacific Ocean'.[10]

However, the Australian colonies were a long way from Britain, and the French and Germans began to move into the South Pacific, while the Dutch moved westward, during the late nineteenth century. To deal with the encroachment of these potentially hostile forces, Prime Minister Edmund Barton commented in the first session of the Australian parliament that he hoped British New Guinea (also referred to as Papua) would one day 'be a territory, perhaps, a State of this Commonwealth'.[11] He also envisaged Australia acquiring Solomon Islands and the New Hebrides (now Vanuatu) to make a 'federation of the sea', given the perceived importance of acquiring territories 'from which the proximate danger may arise'.[12] But there was little public or political appetite for Barton's proposal, and though Australia acquired German New Guinea during World War I, its attention drifted from the region in the interwar period.

World War II quickly reminded Australia of its strategic geography. The Pacific War (1941–45) began with an attack on the famed US Pacific Fleet at Pearl Harbor. By January 1942, Rabaul, the capital of New Guinea, had fallen to Japan. Japan then raided Port Moresby and bombed Darwin in February 1942. By May of that same year, Japan's advance reached its southernmost point when its forces landed in Solomon Islands. The war was on Australia's doorstep, threatening US supply lines to Australia. For many Australian citizens, the threat of invasion felt existential. Thankfully, while Britain was unable to offer much assistance, another security guarantor came to its aid: the United States. Naval warfare proved to be a decisive factor in tipping the military balance in the Pacific in the Allies' favour. The Allies' effective amphibious operations and their success in naval battles such as the Battle of the Coral Sea and the Battle of Midway helped them prevent further expansion by the Japanese navy and regain lost territory.

After the war, Australia sought to bed down US support in the South Pacific through the ANZUS Treaty, which specifically identified the Pacific as the region in which the United States, New Zealand and Australia would respond to 'common danger'.[13] In 1951, Australia entered into the Radford–Collins Agreement, under which the Australian, US and NZ navies would share responsibility for protecting sea lines of communication in the South Pacific and Eastern Indian Ocean.

But after US president Richard Nixon announced his Guam Doctrine in 1969, the Australian government realised it would have to be more self-reliant when it came to defence. It re-evaluated the strategic geography of the South Pacific and became increasingly concerned that the Cold War–era decolonisation of Pacific Island countries had opened the region to Soviet and Libyan influence. The presence of Soviet fishing vessels in the Pacific was a particular concern.

The government responded to the perceived communist threat by encouraging South Pacific regionalism, believing that if a security community among Pacific leaders existed it would discourage the leaders from forming close relationships with potentially hostile powers. In 1971, the South Pacific Forum (now known as the Pacific Islands Forum, or PIF) was founded to foster cooperation between independent Pacific Island countries, Australia and New Zealand. Australia also encouraged the creation of the 1984 South Pacific Regional Trade and Economic Co-operation Agreement and developed an aid program and a defence cooperation program, the most important aspect of which was the Pacific Patrol Boat Program, under which it provided patrol boats to Pacific Island countries, supplemented by technical and operational support. The first boats were rolled out in 1987, following the first Fijian coup, which had highlighted Australia's need for a defence presence in the region, as well as the challenges posed by the region's maritime geography. Recognising the importance of the maritime to the broader national and economic security of Pacific Island countries, the Pacific Patrol Boat Program sought to help them protect and capitalise on the extensive maritime resources that could support national development and coastal livelihoods. Australia also supported Pacific interests in the negotiations preceding the 1982 United Nations Convention on the Law of the Sea (UNCLOS), advocating for the creation of exclusive economic zones, which provide Pacific Island countries with international rights to maritime resources, and the subsequent declaration of Pacific Island countries' maritime boundaries.

The 1987 *Defence of Australia* white paper argued that an unfriendly maritime power in the Southwest Pacific could inhibit freedom of navigation and threaten Australia's supply of military equipment and strategic matériel through and from the United States. It was no coincidence that the government adopted the strategic policy of the Defence of Australia in 1987, the year Fiji experienced two coups. The coups were followed closely by riots in Vanuatu, a secessionist conflict in New

Caledonia in 1988, a worsening security situation in the Bougainville region of Papua New Guinea and a riot by members of the PNG defence force in Port Moresby in 1989. These events made the government more aware of the difficulties the Australian Defence Force faced in projecting force in the region, especially the challenges it encountered when it attempted to evacuate Australians from Fiji. The 1991 *Force Structure Review* soberly acknowledged that although Australia would likely need to 'respond to regional requests', it had 'no single vessel capable of operating a number of helicopters simultaneously',[14] a vital capability given the maritime geography of the South Pacific.

However, despite the political instability in Fiji, Bougainville and Solomon Islands during the 1990s, a perception that the South Pacific wasn't a probable danger to Australia meant the government entered the 2000s resolved to avoid military intervention in the region except if its vital interests were threatened, in the case of a major humanitarian emergency[15] or if a Pacific Island country faced 'substantial external aggression'.[16] And while the Labor government outlined a new policy of 'constructive commitment' in 1988, whereby Australia resolved to deal with Pacific Island countries based on 'sovereign equality and mutual respect' and balance its bilateral relationships with 'effective regional co-operation',[17] its attention soon drifted from the region again.

This meant that although Australia cooperated with New Zealand and other Pacific Island countries to facilitate a peace process in Bougainville, it resisted pressure to respond to both the May 2000 civilian coup in Fiji and Solomon Islands prime minister Bartholomew Ulufa'alu's requests for assistance with deteriorating security. This reluctance was reflected in the Department of Foreign Affairs and Trade's 2003 white paper, which stated that 'Australia cannot presume to fix the problems of the South Pacific countries'.[18] However, this reluctance came under pressure after the terrorist attacks of 11 September 2001 saw fragile states emerge as perceived security threats. It then became untenable as the security situation in Solomon Islands declined.

Accordingly, Australia led the multilateral PIF-approved Regional Assistance Mission to Solomon Islands in 2003, as well as smaller interventions in Papua New Guinea and Nauru in 2004, with the intention of building the capacity of institutions of governance and security. This reflected a significant policy shift, with Prime Minister John Howard observing:

> There was a time not so long ago when sensitivities about alleged 'neo-colonialism' perhaps caused Australia to err on the side of passivity in our approach. Those days are behind us as we work constructively with others to address the challenges faced by our immediate neighbourhood.[19]

A defining feature of these interventions was their whole-of-government approach, which reflected the expansion of the government's security imaginary after 9/11 to recognise a range of non-traditional threats, such as poor governance, terrorism and transnational crime. This saw Australian police officers and public servants assigned directly to South Pacific government institutions for a combination of in-line and capacity-building work. However, military capability to deploy into the region was still prioritised, and in 2004 the government resolved to purchase two amphibious 27,500-tonne landing helicopter docks to assist its capability to conduct stabilisation operations.[20]

While Australia's interventions in Solomon Islands and Nauru were approved by the PIF and conducted multilaterally in cooperation with New Zealand and other Pacific Island countries, questions emerged about whether the interventions were strengthening the fragile states and achieving sustainable gains. Much instability was caused by deep-seated challenges relating to governance, economic development, societal cohesion and, ultimately, the nature and legitimacy of state institutions. While Australia provided some assistance to address these challenges, it was poorly equipped to facilitate locally driven socio-political adaptation and reconciliation. This meant the legacy of these interventions has been mixed and many of the benefits short-lived.

In 2006, Australia declined to take action to head off a military coup in Fiji. This was partly because Fiji had a very well-trained and effective military, facilitated by many years of training and support from Australia. In 2008, Australia sought to recalibrate its relationships in the South Pacific via the Port Moresby Declaration made by then prime minister Kevin Rudd. The declaration echoed the earlier policy of 'constructive commitment' by claiming that Australia wanted a 'new era of cooperation' with Pacific Island countries that respected their independence and worked with them based on 'partnership, mutual respect and mutual responsibility'.[21] Australia accordingly agreed to bilateral Partnerships for Development with several Pacific Island countries, created a seasonal worker program to facilitate labour mobility and took action on climate change, including by ratifying the Kyoto Protocol.

But concern about security in the South Pacific region remained on Australia's agenda, reflected in its 2012 national security strategy, which identified Australia's 'enduring interest in the security, stability and economic prosperity of the Pacific Islands region', home to 'both fragile and developing nations'.[22] The *Defence White Paper 2013* envisaged that the Australian Defence Force could be involved in humanitarian assistance and disaster relief, the evacuation of Australian citizens and stability operations, with enhanced amphibious capability considered important. It also committed Australia to replacing the Pacific Patrol Boat Program with the Pacific Maritime Security Program, which involved a more ambitious agenda to help Pacific Island countries police their extensive exclusive economic zones and prevent and deter IUU fishing.[23]

While the *2016 Defence White Paper* implicitly downgraded the strategic importance of the South Pacific by specifying that other regions and defence objectives had the same level of strategic import,[24] the South Pacific was not downgraded for long.

THE RELEVANCE OF CONTEMPORARY SECURITY ISSUES TO AUSTRALIA'S SECURITY

In April 2018, rumours that China was seeking to establish a military base in Vanuatu emerged, escalating Australia's strategic anxieties about the South Pacific. Suddenly, the long-held principle of strategic denial seemed to be in real danger. Prime Minister Malcolm Turnbull quickly declared that Australia 'would view with great concern the establishment of any foreign military bases in those Pacific Island countries and neighbours of ours'.[25]

Although the geopolitics of the region had become 'crowded and complex',[26] the government's strategic interests remained unchanged. But the government found its power to influence the South Pacific was constrained by the number of other players focusing on the region, which offered Pacific Island countries the opportunity to play off potential partners.

While Australia, New Zealand, the United States, the United Kingdom and France were anxious about the increasing presence of alterative partners in the region – including China, India, Indonesia and Taiwan – many Pacific Island countries had a different view. Although Pacific leaders recognise that the geopolitics of their region are changing, traditional security concerns are not generally their top priority. When given the opportunity to make a major statement about their concerns in the Boe Declaration of Regional Security, adopted at the 2018 PIF leaders' meeting, they looked beyond geopolitics to articulate their priorities as 'an expanded concept of security inclusive of human security' (encompassing humanitarian assistance and the protection of the rights, health and prosperity of Pacific people), 'environmental security' and 'regional cooperation in building resilience to disasters and climate change'.

Of these concerns, climate change is by far the most important for Pacific Island countries. As the Boe Declaration states, 'Climate change remains the single greatest threat to the livelihoods, security and wellbeing of the peoples of the Pacific'. Rising sea levels are an existential threat for Kiribati, the Marshall Islands, Tokelau and Tuvalu, which are either entirely or almost entirely made up of low-elevation atolls and reef features at risk of being eroded or inundated. In addition to posing human-security challenges, changes to coastlines or the complete submergence of islands or features will alter, and most likely severely diminish, Pacific Island countries' maritime zones and, with them, their ability to access, control and protect critical resources.

These maritime zones are vital to Pacific Island countries that depend on fisheries for employment, traditional food and livelihoods, and revenue from licences and access agreements. The Pacific Ocean provides approximately a third of the world's tuna catch, and the region's tuna fisheries are valued at around US$6 billion.[27] In smaller states such as Kiribati, Tuvalu and the Marshall Islands, fisheries provide one of their few non-aid sources of foreign income. As technology for locating and extracting minerals improves, seabed mining presents another potential source of revenue. But if the maritime boundaries of Pacific Island countries erode due to sea-level rise and the surrounding area becomes classified as high seas, it would give other actors greater opportunities to mine and exploit resources in these zones, which would no longer be protected maritime jurisdictions under UNCLOS. Pacific Island countries recognise these challenges and have been working since the early 2000s to clarify and declare the extent of their maritime jurisdictions through the Pacific Islands Regional Maritime Boundaries Programme, a partnership between the Pacific community and the Australian government. They have also been negotiating the delimitation of the estimated forty-eight maritime boundaries between them, with only thirteen left to be confirmed.

Like other states in the Indo-Pacific, Pacific Island countries must cope with deterring and responding to a range of emerging threats and transnational 'blue crimes', including IUU fishing, drug and arms trading and human trafficking. These threats are complex and intersect with other challenges such as climate change: increased piracy, climate displacement, poverty and overfishing are linked to climate-induced pollution, ocean warming and acidification, and changing migratory fish patterns and sustainability problems have encouraged IUU fishing, with slavery-like conditions found in the distant-water fleets navigating the South Pacific. Such governance issues require significant investments in resources, training and intergovernmental coordination. Regional cooperation on oceans governance, resource management and maritime patrol and surveillance has therefore been paramount, including through the Solomon Islands–based Forum Fisheries Agency and the Quadrilateral Defence Coordination Group of Australia, New Zealand, France and the United States.[28]

Climate change is also changing rainfall patterns, causing coral bleaching and ocean acidification, and generating more frequent and severe natural disasters, including cyclones. Cyclone Pam devastated Vanuatu in 2015; Cyclone Winston caused significant damage to Fiji in 2016; Cyclone Harold caused death and destruction across Vanuatu, Solomon Islands, Fiji and Tonga in April 2020; and Cyclones Judy and Kevin hit Vanuatu in March 2023. In January 2022, an underwater volcanic eruption triggered a tsunami in Tonga and caused considerable damage, including to a submarine cable.

The challenges created by natural disasters in the South Pacific were exacerbated by the COVID-19 pandemic. Although most Pacific Island countries managed to prevent the coronavirus entering their borders during 2020, it seeped into the islands in 2021. Its impact was most severe in Papua New Guinea and Solomon Islands, which had very low vaccination rates, due partly to vaccine hesitancy and partly to the difficulties of vaccinating populations spread across challenging geographies with limited state capacity. When Cyclone Harold hit in April 2020, the affected Pacific Island countries had closed their borders to limit entry of the virus, which meant assistance from Australia and other states was less hands-on than it might otherwise have been. The same challenge arose after the 2022 Tongan tsunami.

The COVID-19 pandemic wasn't just a crisis of health for the Pacific people: the economic consequences were devastating, particularly because the necessity of closing international borders and limiting internal movement exacerbated challenges such as uneven economic development, underemployment, underdeveloped public services, unequal gender relations, transnational crime and unrest over resource projects. It also harmed island economies that are highly dependent on trade and tourism. Climate change makes all these challenges worse, especially due to its impact on the productivity of the food gardens, rivers and small-scale artisanal fisheries that many Pacific people rely on for food security.

Political challenges also persist in the South Pacific. Although the Regional Assistance Mission to Solomon Islands, which ran from 2003 to 2017, restored stability to the country, incomplete reconciliation and the instrumentalisation of geopolitical competition by domestic political leaders means future instability remains a live risk there. And while 98 per cent of the population of the Bougainville region of Papua New Guinea voted in favour of independence in December 2019 (after a peacebuilding process resulted in them achieving autonomy in 2005), questions remain about if, and how, the transition to independence will occur.

A struggle is also ongoing in New Caledonia, where the indigenous Kanak population have long sought independence from French colonial rule. New Caledonia is not of immediate concern for Australia, but its independence would have strategic consequences, as it would likely see some drawdown of the French military presence (although many French forces may relocate to French Polynesia) and potential inroads by alternative powers, including China – a prospect not welcomed in Canberra. That would in turn have consequences for the geopolitical balance of the South Pacific and the level of support France would be able to provide in response to humanitarian crises.

Although many Pacific leaders downplay the issue, the South Pacific is becoming a microcosm of broader international strategic competition. At first blush, this competition is between the United States (and its allies and partners) and China. But that doesn't capture the complexity of the interests some powers have in the region or the diplomatic relations of many Pacific Island countries.

China is one power that has increased its presence in the South Pacific over the last fifteen years. In fact, it has been slowly building a diplomatic and economic presence since the early 1970s in the context of its competition with Taiwan for diplomatic recognition. While the intensity of that competition has ebbed and flowed, largely influenced by domestic Taiwanese politics, it has increased since 2018. And Beijing has had success, persuading both Solomon Islands and Kiribati to switch diplomatic recognition to China in 2019. Only four Pacific Island countries now recognise Taiwan.

But there is more to China's interest in the South Pacific. Although China built a satellite tracking station in Kiribati in 1997 (which was mothballed when Kiribati recognised Taiwan in 2003), until recently it had not displayed overtly strategic objectives in the region. The April 2018 rumours that China was in talks to build a military base in Vanuatu suggested that the situation had changed. Although both the Vanuatu and Chinese governments quickly rejected the rumours, they were taken seriously by the governments of Australia and its allies. Their concerns were exacerbated by reports in September 2019 that a Chinese company had sought to lease Tulagi, home to a former Japanese naval base, in Solomon Islands. The Solomon Islands government vetoed the lease, which had been agreed to by the provincial authorities. Then, in May 2021, China was reported to be funding the upgrade of an airstrip in Kiribati on Kanton, a remote coral atoll located near Hawaii that hosted military aircraft during World War II. The April 2022 news that Solomon Islands had signed a security agreement with China that may facilitate the presence of Chinese troops made many Australian national security analysts anxious that the strategic balance of the region was shifting in ways that could be dangerous for Australia.

For many Australian strategic thinkers, the memory of Japan's advance through the Pacific Islands during World War II remains vivid; Australia's longstanding policy of strategic denial seems to be under threat. This perception is enhanced by the Chinese government indicating that the South Pacific is part of its 'second and third island chains of defence'.[29] Although these chains are not precisely defined, most accounts include the Micronesian subregion in the second island chain, with Melanesia and part of Polynesia in the third.

China has made some obvious attempts to woo the region. President Xi Jinping went to Fiji in November 2014 and attended the Asia-Pacific Economic Cooperation (APEC) summit in Papua New Guinea in 2018. Multiple Pacific leaders have made diplomatic visits to Beijing, where they have been met with much pomp and ceremony. China has had its chequebook out, offering Pacific Island countries concesional loans for infrastructure projects, most recently under its Belt and Road Initiative (BRI). This triggered claims that China is engaged in 'debt-trap diplomacy', whereby it uses lending to advance its strategic objectives. Almost half of all Pacific Island countries are classified by the International Monetary Fund and Asian Development Bank as being at high risk of debt distress. But while China is the region's largest bilateral lender (holding approximately 12 per cent of all regional debt), its lending makes up less than half of the total debt held by any one Pacific Island country, except for Tonga.[30]

Chinese state-owned corporations have also undertaken major logging projects and developed fisheries enterprises across the region. They run the massive Ramu nickel and cobalt mines and the Frieda River copper mines in Papua New Guinea. As discussed in Chapter 2, 2020 reports that a Chinese company wanted to build an industrial fishing park on the island of Daru in Papua New Guinea raised concerns in Australia about China's interest in exploiting fishing resources in the Torres Strait and Pacific.

Beyond the potential strategic ramifications of China's growing economic presence in the South Pacific, there are implications for the

South Pacific's security – and consequently for Australia's. Competition between China and Taiwan for diplomatic recognition, as well as the alleged corruption of local politicians, was one factor behind the instability in Solomon Islands that necessitated the Regional Assistance Mission to Solomon Islands. It was also a factor in the 2006 riots in Solomon Islands and Tonga, which led to Australian and New Zealand stabilisation missions. And it contributed to the November 2021 riots in Honiara that necessitated an Australian, New Zealand, Fijian and Papua New Guinean stabilisation effort. Instability is often perceived as leaving certain Pacific Island countries vulnerable to being influenced by China in ways that undermine the interests of Australia and its allies and partners.

Reflecting their broader concern about China's increasing activism in the Indo-Pacific and globally, other powers have responded to China's manoeuvring in the South Pacific. Like Australia, Australia's longstanding ally, New Zealand, has sought to reset its international relations in the region, leaning heavily on its claimed 'Pacific identity'. Demography plays an important role in this identity, as one in five New Zealanders has Māori or Pasifika[31] heritage. New Zealand also has constitutional arrangements with several Polynesian states, giving it some level of control over the foreign affairs of the Cook Islands and Niue, and even more so over Tokelau.

The United States has long had a presence in the South Pacific, particularly in the Micronesian subregion, where it has a range of formal relationships, including compacts of free association with the Federated States of Micronesia, the Marshall Islands and Palau. American Samoa and Guam are also unincorporated US territories, and the Commonwealth of Northern Mariana Islands is a self-governing US territory. While the United States stepped back from the rest of the South Pacific after the Cold War, its withdrawal has been dramatically reversed over the last five years. It has opened new embassies in Solomon Islands and Tonga, enlarged its diplomatic presence in Fiji, Papua New Guinea and Samoa, and intends to open embassies in

Vanuatu and Kiribati. This reflects the United States' recognition that it had lost ground to China, and perhaps its perception that Australia hadn't done enough to counter China, in a valuable security frontier for projecting American naval power, particularly the Micronesian subregion, which is strategically important for conducting operations in the Western Pacific. The United States also maintains Joint Region Marianas, consisting of US Naval Base Guam and Andersen Air Force Base in Guam, and the Ronald Reagan Ballistic Missile Defense Test Site on Kwajalein Atoll in the Republic of Marshall Islands. In October 2020, Palau president Thomas Remengesau Jr invited the United States to establish a permanent military presence in Palau. The United States has also increased its military deployments in the South Pacific – for instance, it has expanded its base in Guam and its 'Shiprider' fisheries monitoring program.

The Trump administration kicked off the US push back into the region, creating a new director role for Oceanian and Indo-Pacific security in its National Security Council. In 2019, it adopted a 'Pacific Pledge of the Indo-Pacific Strategy' to enhance its regional relationships, and senior American officials have since visited the region more often, with Vice-President Mike Pence attending the 2018 APEC summit in Papua New Guinea, and Secretary of State Antony Blinken visiting Fiji in 2022. The United States has also sought to work with Australia to directly counter Chinese lending. It is part of the PNG Electrification Partnership, with Australia, Japan and New Zealand, which aims to increase the proportion of Papua New Guinea's population connected to electricity from 13 per cent to 70 per cent by 2030.

But as is often the case in US South Pacific policy, whether implementation will follow announcement is yet to be seen. In 2019 the United States joined with Australia and Japan to announce the Blue Dot Network, intended to evaluate and certify infrastructure projects. No tangible outcomes of this announcement have yet materialised. Similarly, Congress passed the *Better Utilization of Investments Leading to Development Act* in late 2018, which has led to few tangible outcomes. And although Democratic Hawaiian representative Ed Case has introduced the *Boosting Long-term Engagement in the Pacific Act* into Congress, it is yet to get past the committee stage. Moreover, while President Joe Biden hosted Pacific leaders at a summit in Washington in September 2022 (the first time such an event had taken place) few of the raft of funding announcements made have been ratified by Congress. And in May 2023, Secretary of State Antony Blinken met with Pacific leaders in Papua New Guinea (after Biden had to withdraw to participate in debt-ceiling negotiations in Washington), and Secretary of Defense Lloyd J. Austin signed a defence cooperation agreement with Papua New Guinea. But while Biden held another summit with Pacific leaders in September 2023, Solomon Islands prime minister Manasseh Sogavare declined to attend, saying the United States 'lecture you and lecture you' about 'how good they are', but 'nothing came up out of' the first summit.[32] After several delays, the US government has also renegotiated its compact of free association agreements with the Federated States of Micronesia, the Marshall Islands and Palau, which gives the United States the prerogative to operate military bases in, and make decisions about the external security of, the three Pacific Island countries. The pace of activity in Washington directed at the South Pacific suggests that, if there was ever a time that the United States would follow through on its commitments to the region, it is now.

And Australia wants the United States to follow through, reflecting its longstanding belief that it needs its security guarantor to be engaged in Asia and the Pacific. A stronger US presence would also align with Australia's pursuit of strategic denial. But there's a paradox in Australia's thinking: it wants to reassure Pacific Island countries that Canberra has learned from Australia's neo-colonial past and respects their sovereignty and autonomy. Yet it also seems clear that the most desirable policy setting for Australia is a Western-led sphere of influence.

Other Indo-Pacific nations are paying greater attention to the South Pacific. Since the 1970s, Japan has acted as an aid donor, trading partner and distant-water fishing nation. Like the United States, it has sharpened its focus on the domain over the last five years, motivated by its concerns about China's growing activism. India has also expressed greater strategic interest in the region as part of its Act East policy, as well as its deepening relations with Australia, the United States and Japan in the context of the Quad. Reflecting this, Prime Minister Narendra Modi travelled to Papua New Guinea in May 2023 and met with fourteen Pacific leaders for the third Forum for India–Pacific Islands Cooperation summit. Indonesia is also increasing its visible presence in the Pacific, having been accepted as an associate member of the Melanesian Spearhead Group.

Australia is looking to partner more with France in the region, as Paris retains control of several South Pacific territories. President Emmanuel Macron has suggested that France 'has great power in the Indo-Pacific region through its territories', which make it 'the second-largest maritime power in the world'.[33] The strategic importance of France was recognised by Australia in 2017 when the two countries formed a strategic partnership in the Pacific and Indian oceans, building on their agreements on defence cooperation and status of forces. That agreement, and subsequent ones (including on mutual logistics support), envisaged New Caledonia as a key regional base for military cooperation. However, France is an ambivalent actor in the region, as it has fiercely resisted calls to decolonise its territories and has previously conducted atmospheric nuclear testing there. This highlights a tension between how Australia should balance its interests and values: while France is seen as a valuable strategic partner, its stance on decolonisation contradicts Australia's stated respect for the sovereignty of Pacific Island countries (which is itself qualified, given the concerns Australia has long had about how self-determination movements in Papua New Guinea and Solomon Islands would fragment its neighbours). This tension is also evident with respect to the United States, which retains Guam and American Samoa as colonies.

The response of Pacific Island countries to the overtures and actions of these partners is equally important. Several prominent Pacific leaders have expressed concern about any implication that Pacific Island countries will eventually have to make strategic choices about their diplomatic and security relationships. For instance, previous PIF secretary-general Dame Meg Taylor said that she 'reject[ed] the terms of the dilemma which presents the Pacific with a choice between a China alternative and our traditional partners'.[34] While Australia and its partners perceive China's increasing presence as threatening, several key Pacific leaders do not share this perspective. In fact, some point to positive aspects of China's interest. According to Taylor, 'if there is one word that might resonate amongst all Forum members when it comes to China, that word is access. Access to markets, technology, financing, infrastructure. Access to a viable future.'[35] Several Pacific Island countries have developed 'tactical, shrewd and calculating approaches'[36] to exploit strategic competition to access aid, concessional loans, military assistance and international influence.

Yet not all Pacific leaders have the same view, as became obvious during Chinese foreign minister Wang Yi's tour of the region in May 2022. During his tour, Wang spruiked a draft communiqué and five-year action plan covering a range of security and development issues. Federated States of Micronesia president David Panuelo was quick to publicly reject the proposal. Ultimately, Samoan prime minister Fiamē Naomi Mata'afa led the regional pushback against the deal, on the grounds that it was unreasonable for China to expect it to be rushed through, as 'you cannot have regional agreement when the region hasn't met to discuss it'.[37] Perhaps uncoincidentally, Fiamē made these comments during a joint press conference with new Australian foreign minister Penny Wong, at which the two announced a new eight-year development partnership, as well as the donation of another Australian Guardian-class patrol boat under the Pacific Maritime Security Program.[38] However, Samoa also signed three bilateral economic and technical cooperation agreements with China during Wang's visit, highlighting the complexity of Pacific Island countries' approach to China.

In 2017, to provide a counternarrative to strategic competition and the Indo-Pacific concept, which was perceived to subsume Pacific countries within a broader region that did not resonate with them, PIF leaders articulated 'a long-term Forum foreign policy commitment to act as one "Blue Continent"'. The 2019 communiqué then set out the 'Blue Pacific Principles', emphasising 'regional priorities', a 'partnership approach' and 'collective outcomes and impact', among other things. A key element of the Blue Pacific concept is the assertion that Pacific Island countries should exercise 'stronger strategic autonomy' while 'understanding . . . the strategic value of our region' and 'maintain[ing] our solidarity in the face of those who seek to divide us'.[39] It also explicitly foregrounds the maritime nature of the South Pacific region, and draws on long-standing narratives that present South Pacific as a 'sea of islands', rather than 'islands in a vast sea'.[40] The Blue Pacific concept was consolidated in the 2050 *Strategy for the Blue Pacific Continent* endorsed by PIF leaders at their 2022 meeting.[41]

Tensions have arisen in the PIF due to Australia's and New Zealand's membership. Over the last twenty years, Australia and New Zealand have, at times, advocated for greater regional integration, but they have been met with limited enthusiasm from many of the island-state members. Australia's approach to climate change under its Coalition governments (2013–22) also frustrated the efforts of the PIF to present a collective position on climate change and the ambitions of Pacific Island countries to advance serious international action on the issue. Indeed, while the PIF was traditionally used as a caucusing group at the United Nations and at other international meetings, now the island member states caucus as the separate Pacific Small Island Developing States group and have pursued a more prominent collective diplomatic profile.[42]

While geostrategic competition offers opportunities for Pacific Island countries, it also poses challenges.[43] The most obvious risk is that competition becomes entrenched, with certain states aligning more closely with the United States and its traditional partners (including Australia), and others with China. This could undermine regional solidarity, including the fault line revealed by the controversy over PIF secretary-general Puna's appointment. Notably, all but one of Taiwan's remaining diplomatic partners in the South Pacific are in Micronesia. This is likely no accident, given their proximity to the Western Pacific. This may explain why Palau has invited the United States to establish a military base on its territory, and why China is seeking to upgrade an airstrip in Kiribati.

Strategic competition might also generate divisions, or exacerbate existing ones, within Pacific Island countries, and partners may compete for influence over them without adequately considering the consequences. The issue of diplomatic switching between China and Taiwan had a destabilising effect in Solomon Islands, where it was coopted into internal divisions between Malaita, its most populous province, and Guadalcanal, home to the capital, Honiara. These divisions had been critical to the conflict of the late 1990s that necessitated the Regional Assistance Mission to Solomon Islands. Former Malaita provincial governor Derek Suidani instrumentalised the switch to attack the national government, which he accused of corruption, and gain international assistance. Taiwan reportedly donated aid directly to the Malaita provincial government, initially without the knowledge of the national government, resulting in threats of a criminal investigation. The United States got involved in October 2020, announcing that US$25 million of its US$200 million of aid to the region would go directly to Malaita. These dynamics fed into conflict in November 2021, when riots broke out in Honiara, which necessitated a stabilisation deployment led by Australia, with assistance from New Zealand, Fiji and Papua New Guinea. Notably, Australia, New Zealand and Fiji's deployment was carried out under a bilateral security treaty between Australia and Solomon Islands, not under the imprimatur of the PIF. China later contributed six police advisers to train members of the Solomon Islands police force, generating unease in Australia and among its partners, especially as Australia had already spent several billion dollars between 2003 and 2017 on rebuilding and retraining the police force. More claims that China was interfering in Solomon Islands politics arose in February 2023, when Suidani was ousted as provincial governor following a no-confidence vote.

The rapid increase in aid and infrastructure funding from this range of partners also risks overwhelming the absorptive capacity of Pacific Island countries and resulting in poorly coordinated and unsustainable projects. While some loans are used for productive projects like improving water supply, roads, education and tuna canneries, many are spent on projects with little developmental value. And there is evidence that aid donated as part of diplomatic competition fuels corruption and violence.

AUSTRALIA'S CURRENT POLICY APPROACH

Australia has responded with alacrity to the churning geopolitical currents of the South Pacific by seeking to enhance its presence and relationships in the region.

At the 2017 PIF leaders' meeting, Prime Minister Turnbull signalled a major rethink of Australia's relations with the South Pacific when he committed Australia to 'step up' its engagement.[44] This reflected Australia's recognition that it had not followed through on its commitment to reset its relations with the South Pacific as laid out in the 2008 Port Moresby Declaration.

But Pacific Island countries had to wait a year for the next Australian prime minister, Scott Morrison, to flesh out what this would look like. In a major policy speech in November 2018, Morrison outlined that Australia's 'Pacific step-up' would include initiatives focused on enhancing development, security, and diplomatic and people-to-people links, particularly in maritime security and infrastructure projects. This built on Australia's provision of approximately half of all development aid to the region. The dedicated cross-agency Office of the Pacific was created in 2019 to oversee implementation of the step-up.

Notably, Australia created a $2-billion (later increased to $4-billion) Australian Infrastructure Financing Facility for the Pacific (AIFFP) – apparently to counter BRI lending – allocating an extra $1 billion to its export finance and insurance corporation, Export Finance Australia, to support investment. Australia has funded major infrastructure projects, including the PNG Electrification Partnership, the Coral Sea Cable and the redevelopment of the Fiji military's Blackrock Camp. In 2022, Australia funded Telstra to purchase Digicel Pacific, the South Pacific's largest private telco. This purchase and the latter two infrastructure projects were reported to directly counter Chinese offers.

The security aspects of the Pacific step-up have included the creation of the Australia Pacific Security College in Canberra, which aims to strengthen the capacity of Pacific security officials, and the Pacific Fusion Centre in Vanuatu, which promotes regional maritime domain awareness, important for dealing with and deterring transnational maritime crime, such as illegal fishing and drug smuggling. The government has also sought to formalise its security presence in the region, establishing a security treaty with Solomon Islands in 2017, the Fiji–Australia Vuvale Partnership (*vuvale* being the Fijian word for friendship) in 2019, a security agreement with Vanuatu in 2022 and a comprehensive strategic and economic partnership with Papua New Guinea in 2020 (with negotiations on a security treaty announced in 2022).

The maritime domain is a significant focus of the Pacific step-up, which reflects both Australia's and Pacific Island countries' strategic interests in protecting and exploiting their maritime resources. Australia has long played the leading role in maritime surveillance in the South Pacific, primarily through its Pacific Patrol Boat Program, which it replaced with the Pacific Maritime Security Program as part of its step-up. Under the new program, Australia has committed $2 billion for the provision of twenty-three Guardian-class patrol boats to twelve Pacific Island countries and Timor-Leste, beginning in 2018. While the boats are primarily intended for fisheries enforcement, they are also used for search and rescue, humanitarian assistance and medical evacuations. The local crews are trained in Australia, and technical and operational support is provided by the Navy's maritime surveillance and technical advisers. Australia is currently upgrading wharf infrastructure in thirteen Pacific countries to ensure they can safely operate and maintain the boats that will be delivered. Australia also often constructs accommodation for the boat crews and their families and provides fuel and maintenance services.

The government is redeveloping the Lombrum Naval Base on Manus Island in cooperation with Papau New Guinea and the United States. While this redevelopment is under the auspices of the Pacific Maritime Security Program, there is also a strategic rationale to refurbish Lombrum, as it sits on a natural harbour that is well located to provide forward support to Australian vessels operating in the Western Pacific. Involving the United States reflects the perceived importance of anchoring the United States in Australia's regional maritime security ambitions, in this case by maintaining an advantage in naval basing. The 2023 defence cooperation agreement between Papua New Guinea and the United States foreshadows a greater US military presence in the country, particularly in its maritime domain.

Recognising the importance of maritime domain awareness, both for Pacific Island countries and for itself, Australia provides aerial surveillance under the Pacific Maritime Security Program. The Australian Defence Force also conducts maritime surveillance patrols under Operation Solania, as do any Royal Australian Navy vessels operating in, or transiting through, the region. The Pacific Quad – the Quadrilateral Defence Coordination Group, comprising Australia, New Zealand, the United States and France – facilitates cooperation on air and maritime surveillance. The Australian Federal Police also provides maritime security assistance, including small craft to local police in some Pacific Island countries, as well as support to the Pacific Transnational Crime Coordination Centre and in-country transnational crime units.

The Pacific Maritime Security Program aids Pacific Island countries by improving their ability to secure their own maritime zones, but it also benefits Australia through the maritime surveillance intelligence it generates, particularly from its network of maritime surveillance and technical advisers. Australia faces a range of maritime security threats from or through the South Pacific, including irregular maritime arrivals, terrorism, transnational crime, smuggling and piracy, biosecurity risks, pollution and illegal exploitation of natural resources. The patrol boats give Australia a strategic presence in almost every Pacific Island country, which might explain why Japan and Taiwan have also donated patrol boats and the United States Coast Guard plans to deploy a cutter permanently in the region from 2024. The Pacific Maritime Security Program also facilitates regional cooperation and confidence-building, including through the Forum Fisheries Agency (to which Australia is a major donor), which coordinates policy advice and provides expertise and technical support to PIF members.

To further enhance its military presence in the region, in 2022 the government purchased a Pacific support vessel, ADV *Reliant*, to deliver Australian humanitarian and disaster relief. Indeed, Australia regularly provides this type of support to the region. Australia led the response to Cyclone Pam in Vanuatu in 2015; Cyclone Winston in Fiji in 2016; Cyclone Harold in Vanuatu, Solomon Islands, Fiji and Tonga in 2020; and the Tongan volcanic eruption and tsunami in 2022. Cyclone Winston was the first opportunity to deploy HMAS *Canberra*, one of two Canberra-class landing helicopter docks that it had commissioned in 2004 to serve as Australia's largest naval vessels. One of these ships – HMAS *Canberra* – carried approximately 880 personnel, engineering equipment, 60 tonnes of relief supplies and three MRH-90 helicopters to Fiji, demonstrating its use for narrowing the air–sea gap for regional humanitarian and disaster relief (HADR). Unfortunately, ADV *Reliant* can't support an embarked helicopter or independent operations by shallow-bottomed landing craft, despite both capabilities being important for maritime HADR operations. This was demonstrated during the 2022 response in Tonga, when both capabilities were crucial to bringing supplies ashore before the port and airport had been cleared of debris.[45]

The response to Cyclone Harold highlighted how the crowded and complex geopolitics of the South Pacific can complicate Australia's activities. Geopolitical competition played out in the humanitarian response when a plane chartered by a Chinese corporation that had donated supplies to Vanuatu was on the runway when a Royal Australian Air Force plane arrived with humanitarian supplies. Despite having received approval to land by the Vanuatu authorities, the RAAF plane was unable to do so. It flew back to Australia and returned the next day. The Australian media reported that there was 'growing concern within Defence about whether the hold-up was intentional to delay the Australian plane from landing'.[46]

The Tongan tsunami also demonstrated how crowded the humanitarian and disaster relief space is, as Australia worked alongside New Zealand, the United States, France, the United Kingdom, Japan, France and Fiji. Given the coordination challenges, a HADR International Coordination Cell was established at Australia's Joint Operations Command. Australia also coordinated with France and New Zealand under the 1992 France, Australia and New Zealand (FRANZ) Arrangement, which promotes trilateral cooperation in response to natural disasters and facilitates defence cooperation. Notably absent from the arrangement was China, which sought to make its humanitarian response felt, but without direct coordination with other partners. This raised questions about how personnel from Australia and its partners would work with, or at least alongside, Chinese personnel, on future humanitarian and disaster-relief missions, especially given they are mostly led by military forces. In early 2023, China launched a China–Pacific Island countries disaster management cooperation mechanism and the China–Pacific Island Countries Center for Disaster Risk Reduction Cooperation. It has also proposed a China–Pacific Island countries subcentre for marine disaster risk reduction cooperation.

These developments suggest China won't be seeking to cooperate with Australia and other partners anytime soon.

The Tongan tsunami also served as a reminder of the challenges Australia faces in the air–sea gap between itself and the South Pacific. Australia deployed one of its massive landing helicopter docks, HMAS *Adelaide*, with six hundred crew, but the ship was stranded on its arrival in Tonga by a major electrical power failure. Although the crew was able to restore essential functions relatively quickly, it took over a week for the *Adelaide* to become fully operational again. This raised questions about Australia's preparedness for responding to natural disasters and other crises in the region. The mission was also challenged by an outbreak of COVID-19 on the vessel, which meant that all assistance had to be conducted without direct contact with the Tongans.

WHAT SHOULD AUSTRALIA DO DIFFERENTLY?

When announcing the substance of Australia's Pacific step-up, Prime Minister Scott Morrison began by describing Australia and Pacific Island countries as being 'connected as members of a Pacific family'.[47] As well as reflecting Morrison's personal brand as a conservative Christian, using the family trope was a way to differentiate Australia from China in the South Pacific – an approach that has been used by Australian leaders before. Morrison used it again in 2019, when he made a veiled reference to China, saying: 'When you see yourselves as family, a relationship moves beyond a shallow transactional lens'.[48]

But it isn't yet clear what role Australia sees for itself in the Pacific family – and how Pacific Island countries see Australia. Is it a 'big brother',[49] 'uncle',[50] 'cousin'[51] or 'parent'?[52] And what does this mean for Australia's future maritime security policy?

The South Pacific is a large maritime domain – its islands, atolls and other features are spread across a vast ocean. This poses capability challenges that have been evident since before Federation, and while the two landing helicopter docks Australia rolled out in 2014 and 2015 have gone some way to bridging the air–sea gap, the difficulties that HMAS *Adelaide* faced in responding to the Tongan tsunami suggest that they are not foolproof. The Pacific Maritime Security Program boosts Australia's maritime surveillance capacity in the region, but as the maritime domain is becoming increasingly crowded Australia faces the prospect of shifting from being the region's flagship source of maritime surveillance support to becoming one of many.

This highlights the fact that Australia's ability to advance its maritime security interests in the strategically important South Pacific domain will depend on the perspectives and actions of the people who live on the islands. A lot will hinge on which of Australia's partners, allies or antagonists Pacific Island countries decide to welcome into the region – and what assistance they accept. Will Pacific Island countries continue to welcome Australia into their family – or will they seek a divorce? This question suggests that if Australia is to maintain its security it will needs to reimagine how it understands and engages with the South Pacific region.

First, Australia needs to better recognise that its policy of strategic denial in the South Pacific may no longer be viable. Since World War II, Australia has not faced the serious prospect of a potentially hostile power taking up residence in the region. The Solomon Islands–China security agreement may signal that the situation is changing. It is not yet clear whether the security agreement will lead to a Chinese naval base in the region, or even a military presence. But it does indicate that at least some Pacific Island countries are willing to overturn the unspoken geopolitical balance of the region by linking themselves more formally with China, against the objections of their traditional partners, Australia, New Zealand and the United States. The takeaway is that Australia must recognise that Pacific Island countries are sovereign states and their ability to play different powers off against each other is an attractive way for many of them to meet their almost infinite development needs. In this context, 'competing' with China on spending is not viable. Given the scale of their development needs, why would a Pacific Island country turn down funding unless the strings attached were too binding?

Australia should also recognise that while it has legitimate strategic anxieties about the increasing presence of China in the South Pacific, this view is not shared by all Pacific Island countries – especially those in the southern parts of the region that would not be in the direct firing line of a conflict between China and the United States. Many Pacific Island countries welcome China's interest, particularly as it keeps their traditional partners – several of which had been perceived to have neglected the region – on their toes.

Additionally, the government could better recognise that maritime security challenges are complex and do not always necessitate a conventional military response. While patrol boats and aerial surveillance play an important role, they need to be accompanied by developmental and diplomatic strategies that address the conditions that make some Pacific Island countries vulnerable to challenges such as transnational crime and IUU fishing. One area where Australia could play an important role is in helping Pacific Island countries to negotiate the challenges of forced labour on IUU fishing vessels through maritime domain awareness for identification purposes and judicial capacity-building to enable them to respond more effectively.

Chief among the conditions that make Pacific Island countries vulnerable to such challenges is climate change. Although the Albanese government has taken welcome steps to improve Australia's climate policy, there are concerns in the South Pacific that these are not yet sufficiently ambitious to address the existential threat of climate change that most Pacific Island countries face.

Another condition is underdevelopment and lack of economic opportunity. Australia has introduced labour-mobility programs, which are welcomed by Pacific Island countries looking for economic opportunities for growing and underemployed populations and popular with Australian horticultural producers desperate for workers. But reports of underpayment, exploitation and mistreatment of Pacific workers in Australia serve as a reminder of the racism of Australia's 'blackbirding' past, when Australia subjected Pacific Islanders to forced transportation and indentured labour.[53] Australia's policy of deporting Pacific people on 'character' grounds is perceived as the Australian government being tough on border security. But criminal deportations create havoc in the South Pacific, as they involve exporting criminal expertise and networks to the region, feeding into transnational crime.[54]

The Albanese government has signalled its intent to improve Australia's labour-mobility program, and in October 2023 it adopted legislation to create a scheme that will offer three thousand annual permanent migration places to citizens of Pacific Island countries. The government has also engaged in careful diplomacy, seeking to emphasise its interest in listening to the priorities and concerns of Pacific Island countries. But long-standing assumptions that Australia knows best for the Pacific will take time to break and, while Australia can be confident that its assistance is usually welcomed, there is still room for the government to develop greater humility about whether it has the answers to address the region's challenges and advance its interests. There is also room to find more ways to respect the autonomy and resilience of Pacific Island countries, including how they choose to shape their own futures in their relations with other powers and by supporting efforts at localisation, particularly of humanitarian and disaster response.

The Blue Pacific's emphasis on partnership highlights that Australia could also be a better team player, with both Pacific Island countries and other partners engaged in the South Pacific. This will again require some humility from Australia, including an acknowledgement that it doesn't have the power to compel Pacific Island countries to follow its lead and that other powers have a role to play in the region.

The Blue Pacific concept also emphasises the importance of regional cooperation and collective diplomacy to Pacific Island countries. As one of the only two non–island state members of the PIF, Australia is well-placed to use its position inside the tent to strengthen regional coordination on geopolitical and other security challenges. Australia's willingness to cooperate with partners to respond to the recent crises in Solomon Islands and Tonga is promising. Australia should do more to articulate how it will continue to cooperate on delivering better outcomes for the region and to smooth its own path. This could even involve seeking to cooperate with China in certain circumstances, recognising that China is in the South Pacific to stay and that working together may sometimes be the most effective way to protect Australia's interests, particularly if it allows Australia to ensure Chinese activities advance, rather than constrain, the sovereignty and development of Pacific Island countries.[55]

In addition to humility, Australia will also need to show greater empathy. This will involve recognising that structural and historical factors (such as the influence of globalised neoliberalism and the legacy of colonialism) have contributed to widespread economic disadvantage, underdeveloped public services and chronic infrastructure shortages in the region. In doing so, Australia must acknowledge the role it has played in these structures, particularly as the colonial power in Papua New Guinea and Nauru. A more empathetic approach would also help Australia to grasp the complexity of the security challenges that the region faces, recognising that being overly focused on security isn't always the best way to address these challenges or advance its own interests.

While Pacific Island countries are developing relationships with other actors, they continue to welcome Australia to their family meetings: its membership in the PIF is evidence of this. A reimagined approach to the Blue Pacific is within Australia's grasp – and with it the improvement in relations that is necessary to ensure its maritime security in the region.

6

THE INDIAN OCEAN

On 9 March 2014, Malaysian Airlines flight 370 disappeared off the radar en route from Malaysia to China, and with it 227 passengers and twelve crew members. The international search effort initially focused on the South China Sea, but investigators soon realised the plane had probably crashed into the Indian Ocean – the world's third-largest ocean, covering about one-fifth of the world's surface area. The task of leading the search fell to the Australian government, as the likely crash site was within its search-and-rescue region: an area in which Australia is responsible for responding to international security incidents as per UN International Maritime Organization recommendations.

At its height, the search for MH370 involved eight states: Australia, China, Japan, Malaysia, New Zealand, South Korea, the United Kingdom and the United States. The membership of the search team was telling: the only Indian Ocean littoral states taking part were Malaysia and Australia. It highlighted the gap in maritime capabilities of states with Indian Ocean frontiers. But even among participating states, tensions and lack of trust undermined cooperation. Insufficiencies in the region's cooperative architecture and habits of cooperation also challenged coordination.

The difficulties encountered during the search for MH370 exemplified those that have long faced maritime security efforts in the Indian Ocean region. Differences among its states, which are generally classified as falling within the land-based regions of South Asia, Africa, the

Middle East, Southeast Asia and Australasia, have undermined efforts to unite it in any meaningful way beyond geographical proximity. Unlike regions based around continents or closely linked islands, this region is defined by its waters – the Indian Ocean and all its associated tributary water bodies, including the Persian Gulf, the Red Sea, the Andaman Sea and the Strait of Malacca – which themselves divide.[1] The region covers more than 70 million square kilometres, and around three billion people (more than a third of the global population) live across more than forty-seven island, littoral and hinterland states that depend on access to these waters. These states include some of the world's smallest, least populous and most vulnerable, and also some of the most populous and highly developed. The region is characterised by extreme levels of cultural, political, economic and religious diversity, as well as an array of political statuses, including independent states and offshore territories. There are longstanding tensions between several Indian Ocean states, particularly India and Pakistan, and Iran and Iraq.

The Indian Ocean is home to some of the world's fastest growing economies, largely because they are resource-rich: it is estimated that 40 per cent of the world's offshore oil production comes from the Indian Ocean.[2] It is a crucial through point for global trade, and accounts for half the world's container traffic. In 2011, it was estimated that more than 80 per cent of maritime oil shipments transited through the Indian Ocean.[3] Yet many of these economic flows cross the Indian Ocean only to head out of the region, which means that 'the bottom-up commercial connections said to drive regional economic integration are limited'.[4]

The Indian Ocean also connects water and land through some of the world's most important maritime choke points,[5] the three most significant being the Strait of Hormuz between Iran and Oman, the narrow Strait of Malacca between Indonesia and Malaysia, and the Bab el-Mandeb Strait between Yemen, Djibouti and Eritrea. Despite these economic and geopolitical realities, the Indian Ocean's strategic

relevance has historically been underplayed in global-security discussions. Even as its strategic relevance becomes clearer, the focus tends
to remain on the so-called 'strategic triangle': the United States, China
and India.

While India has long aspired to be the dominant Indian Ocean
state and is the largest maritime power in the region, Australia barely
identifies as one. Yet it is Australia that has the longest Indian Ocean
coastline (14,000 kilometres), the largest search-and-rescue region, and
the largest maritime domain (almost 6 million square kilometres). Its
exclusive economic zone in the Indian Ocean is 3.88 million square
kilometres, and it also claims an extended continental shelf of over
2 million square kilometres.[6] Australia's lucrative offshore hydrocarbon
industry – worth approximately $25 billion annually – is concentrated
in the northeast Indian Ocean.[7]

Over 50 per cent of Australia's seaborne exports leave Indian Ocean
ports. It is estimated that $130-billion worth of goods are transported to
and from Australia through the Strait of Malacca.[8] Moreover, these sea
lanes are used to supply energy to Australia from the Middle East and
Africa – this constitutes around 40 per cent of Australia's crude oil for
processing. If these trade routes were cut off, Australia's energy security would be vulnerable; its only oil stockpile is in the United States.
This explains why Australia depends on maintaining open sea lanes in
the Indian Ocean for its trade and commerce.

Yet despite its vast Indian Ocean maritime jurisdiction, its economic and security interests in the region and the entreaties of WA
foreign and defence ministers over the last several decades to 'look
west', Australia has historically looked north and east instead. It 'often
forgets that it's a three-ocean country'.[9] While this tendency may be
changing – Defence Minister Richard Marles has declared that Australia's 'interests stretch across the entirety of the Indo-Pacific'[10] – an
enduring trend of the government's engagement in the Indian Ocean
region is its piecemeal and muddle-through approach. Although
approximately half of Australia's naval fleet is located on the Indian

Ocean coast, and Australia's Indian Ocean territories, such as Christmas Island and the Cocos (Keeling) Islands, are increasingly viewed as having strategic value, the government lacks a comprehensive Indian Ocean policy.

The government began defining Australia's region of strategic interest as the 'Indo-Pacific' in 2013, but the questions that have dogged that concept – the most fundamental being whether the 'Indo-Pacific' is a region at all – have played out in its policy approach. Essentially, the government has failed to conceptualise the Indian Ocean as an integrated maritime region; Australia focuses almost exclusively on the northeast Indian Ocean. This reflects the relevance of the northeast Indian Ocean to Australia's interests in the Pacific Ocean and South China Sea, and illustrates how the increased import of the Indian Ocean to the government's strategic imagination has been driven primarily by geopolitical concerns around the changing role of China. The expanded Indo-Pacific conceptualisation gained traction in Canberra because it was seen to provide a logic for bringing India into a strategic region to balance China. Indeed, the government's big policy innovation – the Quad security dialogue between Australia, the United States, Japan and India – is framed as having an Indo-Pacific focus but is primarily about countering China's influence over the region. Consequently, the government does not yet substantively conceptualise Australia as an Indian Ocean state.

WHY HAS THE INDIAN OCEAN HISTORICALLY MATTERED FOR AUSTRALIA?

Australia hasn't always been so preoccupied with its northern and eastern approaches. The policy of 'Commonwealth Defence' adopted by the government at Federation in 1901 saw it prioritise its major maritime link with the United Kingdom and the location of many British territories: the Indian Ocean and the Middle East. Until Britain's withdrawal from the Indian Ocean after the Suez Crisis in 1956, Australia's western sea lines of communication were effectively defended by the British navy.

While World War II focused the government's attention north-wards, after the war it refocused on the Indian Ocean. In its first major strategic statement following the war, the government identified the Middle East and Indian Ocean as coming before Southeast Asia and the Pacific in the hierarchy of its strategic interests.[11] This focus also reflected developing anxieties about the Soviet presence in the region.

But the pull to the north and east was strong, particularly after the ANZUS Treaty was signed in 1951. This reorientation saw the govern-ment's strategic policy transition to one of forward defence, and the Indian Ocean attracted much less strategic attention.

That changed once again in the 1960s, as the decline of British power in the Indian Ocean created space for other states, particularly the Soviet Union, to exercise greater influence in the region. Consequently, by 1964 the Australian government had concluded that the Indian Ocean area would likely 'assume greatest strategic significance in the next decade'.[12] It was particularly concerned the Soviet Union might 'develop and use overseas ports and facilities'[13] that could threaten Australia's sea and air lines of communication. Its solution was to encourage Britain to retain an interest in its island territories and the United States to establish a presence in the region. Australia's concerns aligned with those of the United States, which established its Naval Support Facility Diego Gar-cia on the Chagos Archipelago in the British Indian Ocean Territory in 1971, and later went on to develop bases in Bahrain and Singapore.

In parallel to these developments, Sri Lanka was attempting in 1971 to initiate an Indian Ocean 'zone of peace' to facilitate cooperation between the region's newly decolonised states.[14] Australia initially supported Sri Lanka's efforts, but they attracted little support from others and Can-berra's attention soon drifted from the region again. That same year, the Joint Committee on Foreign Affairs recommended that the Australian government focus more on the west in anticipation of a large increase in minerals exports from Western Australia.[15] The Committee was also concerned about the potentially destabilising effects of the Soviet Union's power projection in the region, as well as escalating tensions between India and Pakistan. Despite this, the Indian Ocean region was not identified as a core strategic interest in defence-planning documents.

Instead, the government was preoccupied during the early 1970s with the security of Southeast Asia and the South Pacific.[16] While the government was concerned about the Soviet presence in the Indian Ocean, particularly that of its naval forces in the Middle East, Africa and South Asia, it concluded that Soviet naval deployments did 'not pose a direct threat of attack upon Australia' as they did 'not in present circumstances foresee them being used to coerce independent countries in Southeast Asia', which was Australia's primary area of concern. However, the government did recognise that the Soviet Union had 'legitimate commercial interests in the region which could contribute to regional economic prosperity'[17] and that Soviet economic aid could play a positive role. Indeed, while it cautioned that Australia 'should do nothing to encourage it', it recognised that the Soviet Union's interest in naval traffic could bolster Soviet 'interest in international arrangements which would preserve freedom of navigation through key channels such as the Malacca, Sunda and Lombok Straits'.[18]

During the 1970s, the government began to express more interest in India's growing strategic role, particularly in the context of its development of nuclear technology. While India's rivalry with Pakistan was seen as limiting its potential for wider regional influence, the government identified India's influence among non-aligned states as potentially 'advantageous to Australian interests'.[19]

There was another attempt to draw the government's attention westwards in 1976, when a Senate Committee was commissioned to report on the region. By this time, over 50 per cent of total world trade by tonnage was passing through the Indian Ocean, although Australia's trade in the region only accounted for 13.5 per cent of total Australian trade.[20] Importantly, the Committee identified a 'dilemma' Australia faced in the Indian Ocean region:

We recognise the importance of the ANZUS Treaty and retain close ties with the United States. On the other hand, we seek good relations with the Indian Ocean littoral states many of which support the Zone of Peace concept or profess to be non-aligned and want the Ocean free of superpower presence. Therefore, Australia is faced with the contradiction of being aligned with the U.S., supporting its presence in the Indian Ocean and sharing military facilities in Australia while serving as a member of the United Nations Ad Hoc Committee seeking to establish the Indian Ocean as a Zone of Peace.[21]

The dilemma was similar in the South Pacific and Southeast Asia after many states emerged from colonisation in the 1960s and 1970s: how could Australia reconcile its interests, particularly its alliance with the United States, with the often contradictory interests and views of its neighbours?

In 1976, the government released its first defence white paper, which outlined its solution to the dilemma: self-reliance within an alliance framework.[22] But while Australia's complacent reliance on its 'great and powerful friend' the United States had been shaken by President Nixon's announcement of his Guam Doctrine in 1969, Australia still prioritised the US alliance. The alliance was seen as particularly important given the Soviet military build-up in the Indian Ocean, and because the government's ambitions about what security it could achieve on its own were limited to 'areas closer to home', including in relation to its maritime resources.[23] The government saw maintaining a military presence in the Indian Ocean – it based Royal Australian Air Force elements in Malaysia and Singapore, and Royal Australian Navy vessels in Singapore – as important to achieving this.

The mid-1980s saw a renaissance in the government's interest in the Indian Ocean, with the appointment of Western Australian Kim Beazley as Minister for Defence in 1984. Beazley had co-written a book in 1979 about the importance of the Indian Ocean region to Australia's – and particularly Western Australia's – economic and security interests.[24] Under Beazley's influence, the 1987 *Defence of Australia* white paper moved the government towards a 'two ocean' policy that looked west to the Indian Ocean, requiring 'a major portion of the Navy's surface and submarine fleet' to be based in Western Australia for 'the first time during peacetime'.[25] However, the white paper continued to define Australia's direct military interests as Southeast Asia and the South Pacific, with the eastern Indian Ocean an area of 'primary strategic interest' only.[26] Beazley remained in office until 1990, ensuring the government's continued strategic focus on its western frontier.

The government's interest in the Indian Ocean grew again after the Cold War, as new opportunities arose to deepen relationships with key partners, particularly India and South Africa. This followed decades of inconsistent and sometimes frosty relations between Australia and India, blamed on a lack of rapport between prime ministers Jawaharlal Nehru and Robert Menzies. But Canberra's approach to New Delhi mirrored its ambivalent approach to the Indian Ocean region more broadly.[27] It wasn't until the government of Malcolm Fraser (1975–83) that the relationship began to thaw.[28] Indian prime minister Rajiv Gandhi visited Australia in 1986, and Australian prime minister Bob Hawke reciprocated with a visit to India in 1989. A 1990 Senate Standing Committee inquiry subsequently recognised that India 'already is an important Asian power of the same general order as China', but that relations between Australia and India were 'underdeveloped'.[29] While the report did not think it conceivable that India would 'develop unfriendly intentions toward Australia', it did express concern about India's development of nuclear weaponry.[30] To enhance understanding of India, the government also funded several relationship-building and policy-development initiatives, including the creation of the Australia–India Council in 1992.

However, by the time the 1994 *Defending Australia* white paper was released, the government's strategic gaze was again turned firmly north and eastwards. Indeed, the paper's chapter on regional engagement focused primarily on Southeast Asia, Northeast Asia and the Southwest Pacific.[31] The discussion of South Asia consisted of only one paragraph, focused on India, with which Australia was described as having a 'modest defence relationship'.[32] Although the Hawke government adopted an 'Australia looks west' approach in 1994, this centred on economic linkages, and the government commissioned the Department of Foreign Affairs and Trade to produce a report about economic cooperation with India.[33]

The look-west policy nonetheless encouraged the government to foster Indian Ocean regionalism. Alongside India, South Africa and Mauritius, Australia established the Indian Ocean Rim Association for Regional Cooperation (IOR-ARC) in 1997. Australia hoped IOR-ARC could become an Indian Ocean version of the Asia-Pacific Economic Cooperation forum, but the diversity of interests among its members meant few others were enthusiastic. The IOR-ARC had, and still has, a loose institutional structure, guided by the principles of sovereignty, equality, territorial integrity, political independence, non-interference in internal affairs, peaceful coexistence, mutual benefit and consensus decision-making.[34] Other loosely constituted Indian Ocean associations include the Indian Ocean Naval Symposium (IONS), created in 2008, and the Bay of Bengal Initiative for Multi-Sectoral Technical and Economic Cooperation, created in 1997. Australia is a member of the former but not the latter.

After a change of government in 1996, Australia's attention again drifted from the Indian Ocean. The Howard government's enthusiasm for the IOR-ARC dwindled in 1999 after it became clear that voluntary trade liberalisation was not going to occur. Notably, the *Defence 2000* white paper did not even mention the Indian Ocean and only gave India minimal consideration, primarily in the context of potential competition with China, tensions with Pakistan and its development of nuclear weapons. Australia was once again looking north and eastwards.[35]

When there was another change of government in 2007, the Rudd and Gillard Labor governments followed the lead of Steven Smith, a Western Australian MP – and, variously, Minister for Foreign Affairs (2007–10), Minister for Trade (June–September 2010) and Minister for

Defence (2010–13) – who promoted an expansion of the government's strategic vision that stretched the 'Asia-Pacific' region 'from North Asia to the Eastern Indian Ocean'.[36] This vision paid specific attention to the Indian Ocean, which Defence said would have 'greater strategic significance in the period to 2030'[37] as a trading thoroughfare, home to ongoing or potential conflicts, location of transnational security issues and site of increasing strategic competition in the naval domain. The Indian Ocean was therefore placed 'within the ADF's primary operational environment'.[38] Again, India was singled out as an 'important partner' with which Australia would 'need to strengthen [its] defence relationship' and 'maritime security cooperation'.[39]

Under Smith's influence, the Australian Senate's Foreign Affairs, Defence and Trade References Committee conducted a review of the Indian Ocean rim's relevance for foreign, trade and defence policy. Reporting in 2013, the Committee recognised the importance of secure shipping lanes for Australia's economy and the energy security of both Australia and the wider region. It recommended that Australia promote the concept of the 'Indian Ocean rim' and endorse supporting regional institutional structures and mechanisms for the Indian Ocean rim countries.[40]

Then foreign minister Kevin Rudd embraced Smith's call to 'look west', arguing in 2011 that:

> We have long looked east across the Pacific to our longstanding allies, the United States. We have looked north, to the profound strategic and economic developments now taking place across East Asia. Equally now, Australia must look west, to the great challenges and opportunities that now present themselves across the Indian Ocean Region.[41]

The look-west perspective was evident in the Gillard government's *Defence White Paper 2013*, which redefined Australia's region of strategic interest as the Indo-Pacific: 'the arc extending from India through Southeast Asia to Northeast Asia, including the sea lines of communication on which the region depends,'[42] with 'Southeast Asia at its geographic centre'.[43] The concept again excluded the northwestern and southern Indian Ocean and East Africa.[44] The white paper justified the strategic shift to the Indo-Pacific based on 'China's continued rise as a global power, the increasing economic and strategic weight of East Asia, and the emergence over time of India as a global power'.[45] However, it acknowledged that the 'Indo-Pacific is still emerging as a system', and that, due to 'its diversity and broad sweep, its security architecture is, unsurprisingly, a series of sub-regions and arrangements rather than a unitary whole'.[46] A decade later, this characterisation remains salient.

Reflecting its widened strategic focus, the *Defence White Paper 2013* included a section specifically devoted to the Indian Ocean, where Australia's interests were identified as 'stable trade routes', peacebuilding and peacekeeping. The white paper recommended greater regional security cooperation, including through the IONS and IOR-ARC.[47] It emphasised the importance of the US alliance to Australia's interests, predicting that the United States would maintain its regional maritime superiority despite India's and China's rise, but cast India as a 'very important partner' for the future in 'building security in the Indian Ocean and broader Indo-Pacific region'.[48]

After a change of government in 2013, another Western Australian, Julie Bishop, assumed the role of Minister for Foreign Affairs and Trade and fellow Western Australian David Johnston became Minister for Defence. In 2014, Bishop reorientated Australia's foreign and trade policy under the principle of 'economic diplomacy'.[49] Bishop accordingly took an active role on Australia's behalf in the Indian Ocean Rim Association (IORA) (renamed from IOR-ARC in 2013) when Australia was chair from 2013 until 2015. She was instrumental in placing two cross-cutting themes on IORA's agenda: the 'blue economy' and women's economic empowerment. The blue-economy concept reflected a commitment to the sustainable and inclusive use of ocean resources to promote economic development, jobs and coastal livelihoods without damaging ocean ecology, an aim that had particular resonance for

Indian Ocean states. The government also sought to reinvigorate IONS when Australia took over as chair in 2014 and secured an agreement on the IONS Charter, which had languished since IONS was created in 2008.

The *2016 Defence White Paper* reaffirmed Australia's focus on the Indo-Pacific and continued its strategic shift towards the Indian Ocean, which it said had 'become an important focus for Australian strategic policy' because of 'vital trade and energy routes', offshore oil production and 'competition' between major powers.[50] It also recognised the 'benefits of practical defence engagement' revealed by Australia's cooperation with the United States, Japan, China, Malaysia, South Korea, New Zealand and the United Kingdom during the 2014 search for MH370, and pledged to strengthen Australia's ability to cooperate with regional partners,[51] citing the IONS and IORA as examples of where this could occur.[52] The white paper also recognised that India was 'an increasingly important economic and security partner' with shared 'interests in regional stability and order'.[53] This dovetailed with the Indian government's announcement of its SAGAR (Security and Growth for All in the Region) vision at the 2015 IORA meeting. The SAGAR initiative emphasises the importance of maritime security and cooperation and has provided the policy umbrella for India's increasingly active provision of maritime support in the Indian Ocean region.

THE RELEVANCE OF CONTEMPORARY SECURITY ISSUES TO AUSTRALIA'S SECURITY

When it was reported in 2015 that China was in negotiations to establish a military logistics base in Djibouti under the pretext of its 'international obligations', it seemed to justify the Australian government's westwards turn: the news suggested that China's economic initiatives in the region also had strategic objectives. This had been a concern for the Australian government since China announced its One Belt, One Road initiative in 2013, of which the twenty-first century Maritime Silk Road initiative was a part. Together, they became known as the Belt and Road Initiative (BRI). The Maritime Silk Road was intended to boost infrastructure connectivity throughout East Africa, the Indian Ocean, Southeast Asia and the South Pacific. In the years since, it has enabled China to create a network of military and commercial infrastructure stretching across Myanmar, Bangladesh, Sri Lanka and Pakistan. This 'String of Pearls' can connect to China's overland BRI infrastructure investments in Central Asia and provide China with the capacity for a substantial military presence in the region. Much of China's interest in the region stems from its 'Malacca dilemma': the risk that its adversaries could close off the Strait of Malacca and thereby cut off its vital energy supplies. To address this, it has sought creative solutions to circumvent the Strait, including its plans to build an overland pipeline through Pakistan as a component of the China–Pakistan Economic Corridor, as well as the Kra Canal through Thailand to connect the Gulf of Thailand with the Andaman Sea.

China has been building a naval presence elsewhere in the region as well. Along with other states, Australia has expressed concern about this development – but not always in a constructive way. In the lead-up to the 2022 Australian federal election, for instance, Defence Minister Peter Dutton inaccurately described a Chinese surveillance vessel transiting in Australia's exclusive economic zone off the coast of Western Australia as an 'act of aggression' (it was actually a permissible example of freedom of navigation, a key maritime principle that Australia strongly supports).[54]

Other events have prompted more reasonable concerns. In 2017, facing a debt crisis, the Sri Lankan government unsuccessfully asked Chinese, Japanese and Indian firms to lease Hambantota International Port, which had opened in 2010.[55] Instead, Beijing found an investor in CMPort, the parent company of which is the Chinese state-owned enterprise China Merchants Group. In a complex arrangement, the Sri Lankan Port Authority sold CMPort a 70 per cent stake in Hambantota for US$1.1 billion and agreed that CMPort would get to develop and operate the port for ninety-nine years.

This development compelled an Indian think tank to advance the concept of 'debt-trap diplomacy' to describe what it characterised as Beijing's plan to offer unsustainable infrastructure loans and then use the debt to seize strategic assets such as ports or airfields. While scholars have argued that debt-trap diplomacy is a 'myth' and a 'meme',[56] the August 2022 news that a Chinese survey ship had docked at Hambantota seemed to confirm fears that Hambantota Port, at least, could provide a home for a greater Chinese military presence in the region. Although China described the ship *Yuan Wang 5* as a scientific-research vessel, it is said to have also been used to track satellites and missiles.[57]

China also has access to ports or bases at Gwadar, Pakistan, and is intending to construct Kyaukphyu Port in Myanmar, possibly enabling it to add to its naval presence in the region. As a result, an increasing number of People's Liberation Army Navy warships and submarines now transit through the northern Indian Ocean, and over the last decade China has been transiting through, and conducting exercises and port visits in, the eastern Indian Ocean.

There have been reports that Chinese survey ships have been operating in the eastern Indian Ocean as well. They have been accused of disabling their Automatic Identification System broadcast when in Indonesian territorial waters and potentially mapping the seabed to gather useful data for operating submarines.[58]

China's Indian Ocean approach reflects the country's shift from 'offshore waters defence' to the 'open seas protection' policy announced in China's 2015 defence white paper.[59] The 'two oceans layout approach' calls for China to establish a presence in the Western Pacific and northern Indian oceans, outlined in China's authoritative military doctrinal text *The Science of Military Strategy*.[60]

In the western Indian Ocean, Russia has also expanded its military footprint. In 2020, it announced the establishment of a new naval base in Sudan, providing Moscow with strategic access to the Red Sea and the Bab el-Mandeb Strait strategic choke point. Smaller powers in the Indian Ocean are also diversifying their strategic partners by building relationships with states such as Turkey and Saudi Arabia.

These developments have concerned the Australian government and its partners and allies. China's Belt and Road Initiative has the potential to strengthen connectivity and regional integration across the Indian Ocean, linking small states through new ports, maritime infrastructure and shipping lanes, although it looks as if its pandemic economic woes have reduced its BRI spending, with evidence of delayed or abandoned projects.[61] Nevertheless, Australian governments have viewed China's growing presence in the Indian Ocean as threatening, primarily because they have been concerned that China could establish an anti-US bloc by influencing regional states to turn their backs on the rules-based order favoured by Australia. The rules set out under UNCLOS are vital for Australia in the Indian Ocean, where it relies on them to protect the sea-based and sub-sea resources in its exclusive economic zone. In 2021, the Indian Navy reported nearly four hundred incidents of IUU fishing in the area. It is also carefully monitoring the increased presence of Chinese fishing vessels, particularly in the northern Indian Ocean.[62] A recent CSIRO report identified IUU hotspot areas in the eastern Bay of Bengal and Andaman Sea, where poorly designed regulatory structures have enabled high levels of illegal fishing, especially in coastal fisheries.[63]

Australian has less ground for anxiety about a military threat posed by Chinese forces in the Indian Ocean region, even though their naval presence is enhanced by China's base in Djibouti and port access in Bangladesh, Myanmar, Pakistan and Sri Lanka, because Chinese forces would be vulnerable to the extensive presence of Indian, British and American forces. However, Chinese forces could still attempt to imperil Australia's sea lines of communication. There is also the suggestion that in the event of war China could strike first in the Indian Ocean to force the United States to shift some of its forces there from the Western Pacific.[64]

A more concerning possibility is that China could develop a coalition with Russia and Iran in the Indian Ocean region. The states have conducted the Maritime Security Belt exercise three times since 2019, with the aim of increasing cooperation between their navies. This could present a challenge to the United States' International Maritime Security Construct, created in July 2019 in the international waters of the Middle East region, including the Strait of Hormuz and Bab el-Mandeb Strait. Australia was a member of the International Maritime Security Construct in 2019 and 2020.

Despite the Australian government's concerns, its response to China's efforts in the Indian Ocean faces several constraints. As a middle power, it can't hope to compete against China either militarily or on infrastructure-funding on its own. Instead, the government needs to work with its allies and partners. However, the United States, which the government looks to first, is still developing a clear understanding of its role, interests and intentions in the Indian Ocean region. The United States' 2017 National Security Strategy adopted a definition of the 'Indo-Pacific' which stretched only from the 'west coast of India to the western shores of the United States'.[65] While the Biden administration has acknowledged the importance of the whole Indian Ocean, its 2022 Indo-Pacific Strategy only mentions the Indian Ocean once and does not mention the Bay of Bengal, Arabian Sea, Persian Gulf or Africa at all.[66] India and Japan have been encouraging the United States to expand its horizons west, but for now its leadership is limited.

The United States' ability to conceptualise a comprehensive military presence in the region is also undermined by the fact that while US Pacific Command became Indo-Pacific Command to emphasise the importance of the Indian Ocean, the command does not encompass a number of Indo-Pacific states, such as Afghanistan, Pakistan and various East African islands, which are instead the responsibility of US Central Command and US Africa Command.

While naval activities involving the US Navy in the Indian Ocean have increased, its permanent naval presence remains comparatively limited: it has more naval bases in Japan than in the entire Indian Ocean region, where its primary presence is the airbase at Diego Garcia in the contested UK territory of the Chagos Archipelago. American force posture – meaning the overall arrangement, strength and condition of readiness of its military – in the region is at least partly a consequence of geography: the Indian Ocean is less important as a defence buffer for attacks on the US mainland than the Western Pacific and Atlantic oceans. Australia, on the other hand, is unavoidably an Indian Ocean state.

The US Indo-Pacific strategy also lacks a comprehensive economic plan that could provide alternatives to China's Belt and Road Initiative, even though economic, rather than defence, policy 'is the only way to address the interrelated problems of development, pandemic recovery and adaptation to climate change – issues that plague policymakers throughout Asia and threaten to derail the region's peace and prosperity'.[67] But the US Indo-Pacific Economic Framework for Prosperity, launched in May 2022, contains a rather vague set of aspirations relating to creating consistent labour, environmental, trade and investment standards and hasn't been accompanied by big funding investments or greater access to the US market. This echoes earlier underwhelming US economic initiatives such as the Blue Dot Network, which promised to mobilise private-sector funding to infrastructure projects in developing and emerging economies but has failed to gain traction. In the Indian Ocean, many regional states are keenly interested in trade and infrastructure, and without greater US economic leadership and investment there are limits to what Australia can do to provide better economic and infrastructure options to smaller island states in the Indian Ocean region.

The United States' apparent reluctance to put its money where its mouth is in the Indian Ocean region exemplifies the longstanding dilemma generated by Australia's perception that it needs to rely on a security guarantor and the commitment and capabilities of that guarantor not being assured. This has encouraged the Australian government to seek out other partners, and India has become the most important of these. India is a key member of the Quad and, under its SAGAR initiative, has sought to develop its military presence in the region, including through naval access rights in Oman, bases in the Indian islands of Andaman and Nicobar, and in the Seychelles. India has also sought access to its partners' bases, including those of the United States at Diego Garcia, France at Réunion and Djibouti, and in Singapore and Indonesia.[68] Indeed, given its perception of itself as a regional leader, India can, at times, see a greater US naval presence in the region as potentially intruding on India's self-perceived status as a 'net security provider' and a 'preferred security partner' in the Indian Ocean.[69]

Alongside the risk of great power competition are an array of non-traditional maritime security concerns, many of which Australia shares with other Indian Ocean states. Shipping along choke points is currently more likely to be interrupted by non-state rather than state actors. In 2021, fifty of the eighty-two cases of piracy (robbery on the high seas) and sea robbery (robbery in a state's maritime jurisdiction) reported by the ReCAAP (Regional Cooperation Agreement on Combating Piracy and Armed Robbery Against Ships in Asia) occurred in the Singapore and Malacca Strait region.[70] Given its dependence on trade, the Australian government cares about piracy and sea robbery. Australia participates in the Combined Maritime Forces, a multinational maritime partnership, headquartered in Bahrain, that seeks to counter illicit non-state actors on the high seas under the command of a US Navy vice admiral and the deputy command of a UK Royal Navy commodore. The massive size of Australia's exclusive economic zone also means the government is concerned about IUU fishing, transnational crime, extremist terrorism, illegal incursions by vessels, marine pollution and 'unauthorised maritime arrivals'.[71] These challenges are interlinked. For example, IUU fishing threatens environmental conservation and sustainable fisheries and is worsened by warmer ocean temperatures, which place pressures on fish stocks and habitats.[72] Dealing with these maritime challenges often requires coordination between states, but states in the Indian Ocean region have very different capabilities to prevent and prosecute maritime crime, and regional coordinating institutions are underdeveloped.

The biggest security challenge facing the Indian Ocean is climate change. This is a particular risk for the low-lying island states of the Maldives and Seychelles, which are extremely vulnerable to sea-level rises. Ocean warming, acidification and coral bleaching are affecting national fishery sectors and changing the distribution patterns of fish species, with catches decreasing in Indonesian waters, the Red Sea, the Persian Gulf and the Bay of Bengal.[73] This is particularly challenging for the region's island states, as the fisheries sector is the backbone of the 'blue economy' concept – coastal communities rely on fishing for their food security, livelihoods and economic development. The region's island states are also especially vulnerable to natural disasters exacerbated by climate change, although larger low-lying Indian Ocean states, such as Bangladesh, are increasingly challenged by them as well. As a result, while Australia and the United States are primarily concerned about geopolitics, most island states that prioritise climate change have preferred to stay neutral on geopolitical matters or have expressed concern that rivalries between major powers will provoke a security dilemma that will ultimately 'create insecurity for others in the region'.[74]

Australia itself is not immune to the effects of climate change. Its maritime jurisdiction in the Indian Ocean is also affected by ocean warming, sea-level rise, flooding, coastal erosion, coral bleaching and ocean acidification. Studies have shown that Western Australia is susceptible to ocean warming, contributing to a decline in parts of the Great Southern Reef. In 2010, temperate kelp forests on Western Australia's reefs – worth $10 billion annually – disappeared.[75]

But the most politically salient non-traditional maritime security challenge for the government has been irregular migration, at least since the 2001 Tampa affair. The Tampa affair refers to events that occurred after the Australian Maritime Safety Authority directed the commander of Norwegian freighter MV *Tampa* to rescue hundreds of people in an overloaded Indonesian fishing boat trying to reach Australia to claim asylum. The Australian government refused to allow the *Tampa* to land the asylum seekers on Christmas Island and, under duress, the freighter's commander decided to enter Australian waters. The government responded by dispatching forty-five Special Air Service troops to board the ship and prevent it from sailing on to Christmas Island. It then negotiated to take the asylum seekers to Nauru and New Zealand. The Tampa affair, which became subsumed within the government's participation in the US-led war on terror, saw people seeking asylum who arrived by boat treated as a security challenge, rather than a humanitarian one.[76] This justified the use of Australia's maritime law enforcement agencies, especially Maritime Border Command and the Australian Defence Force (through Operation Sovereign Borders), to respond to so-called 'unauthorised maritime arrivals' for the next two decades. The government also excised Australia's Indian Ocean territories of Christmas Island and Ashmore Reef from Australia's 'migration zone' so people seeking asylum who landed there could not apply for refugee status under the *Migration Act*.

The Indian Ocean has been the focus of many such 'border protection' efforts, because most people seeking asylum who tried to reach Australia by sea were fleeing the conflict zones of Afghanistan, Iraq and Sri Lanka. It has been expensive: detaining people seeking asylum cost Australia over $2 billion in 2012–13, over $3 billion in 2013–14 and at least $1.2 billion in 2014–15.[77] Yet even at the peak of the influx, the number of people seeking asylum was comparatively low: in 2012, just 5175 people attempted to come to Australia via the sea, fewer than those arriving by plane (6316).[78] In contrast, Bangladesh currently hosts almost one million Rohingya refugees fleeing Myanmar. The Indian Ocean, rather than being overrun with irregular migrants, provides a natural buffer zone to Australia, allowing it to avoid its international responsibilities vis-a-vis international refugee law.

AUSTRALIA'S CURRENT POLICY APPROACH

With US priorities lying elsewhere, the Australian government has had to seek alternative partners in the Indian Ocean region. When Australia became concerned about the rising number of people seeking asylum trying to get to Australia by boat, for instance, the Australian and Indonesian governments co-hosted a Regional Ministerial Conference on People Smuggling, Trafficking in Persons and Related Transnational Crime in 2002. That conference crystallised into the Bali Process on People Smuggling, Trafficking in Persons and Related Transnational Crime, a forum which now has a membership that spans the Indian Ocean region and reaches into the South Pacific and Southeast Asia. The Bali Process aims to increase cooperation, including between law enforcement and border agencies, on a range of issues related to people smuggling. The government has also sought to tackle the issue through bilateral cooperation with Indonesia and Sri Lanka, gifting three vessels to Sri Lanka with the intention that they be used to intercept people-smuggling boats before they enter Australian waters.[79]

Achieving regional cooperation on other maritime security challenges has been difficult. Some regional agreements relating to fisheries management and the prevention of IUU fishing exist, including the 1996 Agreement for the Establishment of the Indian Ocean Tuna Commission and the 2012 Southern Indian Ocean Fisheries Agreement. The Indian Ocean Tuna Commission was established in 1993 to promote cooperation among its members to ensure the conservation and optimal use of tuna and tuna-like species. But the Commission lacks anything near the institutional mechanisms or member buy-in of the Forum Fisheries Agency in the South Pacific.

Establishing an effective regional cooperative response to strategic competition has been even more challenging. Australia has, at times, sought to bolster regional cooperative mechanisms, particularly the Indian Ocean Rim Association, which now has twenty-three member states and ten dialogue partners. However, greater regional cooperation within IORA is constrained by the diversity of its membership, regional geopolitics and tensions between nations and subregions. Iran's membership of IORA is one source of tension. Another is the wariness between India and China (the latter of which is an observer of IORA). Yet another is India's insistence that Pakistan be excluded, and South Africa's that Myanmar be blocked from joining.

These tensions have meant that IORA has tended to focus on relatively uncontroversial non-traditional security challenges. Its agenda has included sustainable development, economic and trade cooperation, and improvements to maritime infrastructure, security and governance. While IORA is not yet a forum for broaching more divisive issues such as strategic competition, it has been able to endure. It is now the only intergovernmental organisation that seeks to foster relations around the entire Indian Ocean region and has provided a platform for regional cooperation on non-traditional security matters.

In the absence of strong regional cooperation, the Australian government has turned to minilateral groupings to pursue its strategic interests. These include the Quad and a series of trilaterals: Australia–Japan–United States, Australia–India–Japan and Australia–India–Indonesia. While these groupings are dialogues rather than formal institutions, they are increasingly important forums for strategic coordination.

The Quad has attracted the most attention. It was first convened to coordinate responses to the 2004 Indian Ocean tsunami. Although the dialogue lapsed in 2008, informal discussions continued and the Quad was formally revived as an officials-level meeting in 2017 and then a ministerial-level meeting at the UN General Assembly in 2019. The Quad is frequently seen as a mechanism to dilute or constrain China's power. In 2019, US Secretary of State Mike Pompeo aided that perception, stating, 'We've reconvened the Quad . . . This will prove very important in the efforts ahead, ensuring that China retains only its proper place in the world.'[80] The perception has also been reinforced by the fact that the Quad's original manifestation quickly incorporated an attempt at joint military exercises in the form of Exercise Malabar, which started as a joint US–India exercise in 1992 but was temporarily expanded to include Australia, Japan and Singapore in 2007 (Japan became a permanent member in 2015, and Australia joined in 2020).

But while member states of the Quad and Australia's other new and enhanced strategic partnerships may (problematically) claim to share the same broad values – particularly support for democracy and the rule of law – whether they share the same *interests* is also not clear. Quad members have differing strategic geographies, threat perceptions and relationships with China, and therefore cannot be relied upon to perceive or respond to a threat in the same way – or even in a coordinated way. This matters, because if the Quad and Australia's other strategic partnerships become increasingly focused on defence and security issues, including joint military exercises without clear purposes, they may be (mis)perceived as quasi-military alliances. This poses risks to Australia and its partners, as they may find themselves making ambiguous political and military commitments that unintentionally draw them into future conflict. Of more concern, their actions may be interpreted as threatening by China, thereby exacerbating their strategic vulnerability.

Australia sees bilateralism as offering the most potential for advancing its interests in the Indian Ocean region, with its two most important relationships being with India and Indonesia, though neither relationship has been easy.

The government has been interested in building deeper relations with India – fellow Quad member and a major power – for the last decade. Indeed, with a population of 1.4 billion people, India can claim to be the world's largest democracy, which makes it an obvious partner for Australia. To build the relationship, Australia has made significant concessions, most notably in relation to India's possession of nuclear weapons. India, which is not a party to the Treaty on the Non-Proliferation of Nuclear Weapons, has conducted two nuclear tests: Pokhran-I in 1974 and Pokhran-II in 1998.

In the past, Australia was less willing to make such concessions. In 1998, within hours of the Pokhran-II test being carried out, Australian foreign affairs minister Alexander Downer called in the Indian High

Commissioner to convey the government's 'condemnation of the tests in the strongest possible terms'.[81] After Pokhran-II, the government escalated its response, cancelling ship and aircraft visits and suspending bilateral defence relations, non-humanitarian aid and ministerial- and senior-official-level visits. It had already banned the sale and export of uranium to India. Throughout the early 2000s, New Delhi viewed Canberra's unwillingness to supply uranium as indicative of its broader lack of commitment to developing the India–Australia relationship.[82]

But shared concern about China's increasing activism has helped Australia and India to find common ground on which to rebuild their relationship. After a long process, including the Gillard government's 2011 decision to reverse a ban on exports of uranium to India, the two states signed a nuclear cooperation agreement[83] in 2014 that permitted the sale of Australian uranium to India. This paved the way for warmer relations, and when Australia hosted the G20 summit in November 2014, Indian prime minister Narendra Modi addressed the Australian parliament during his visit. Modi and Australian prime minister Tony Abbott also agreed to a Framework for Security Cooperation, which built on the 2008 Joint Declaration on Security Cooperation[84] and provided for, among other things, annual summits between the two prime ministers and regular bilateral maritime exercises in the form of AUSINDEX, the biennial Indian Ocean–focused joint exercises that began in 2015.

Since then, bilateral relations between Australia and India have improved rapidly. During a virtual summit in June 2020, the two nations' prime ministers agreed to elevate the bilateral relationship from a strategic partnership (as agreed in 2009) to a comprehensive strategic partnership. The narrative suggests that Australia and India 'share the vision of a free, open, rules-based Indo-Pacific region supported by inclusive global and regional institutions that promote prosperous, stable and sovereign states on the basis of shared interests'.[85] Most relevantly, they also agreed to a Joint Declaration on a Shared Vision for Maritime Cooperation in the Indo-Pacific,[86] which identified their shared priorities as including freedom of navigation, terrorism, piracy, drugs and arms smuggling, irregular migration, people smuggling and human trafficking, unreported and unregulated fishing, and environmental challenges such as marine pollution and ocean acidification. It provided for the creation of the Australia–India Indo-Pacific Oceans Initiative Partnership to help develop the Indo-Pacific Oceans Initiative announced by India in November 2019,[87] an initiative for countries to work together to address common challenges in the Indo-Pacific region.[88] The two states have also begun to conduct more joint military exercises. As noted, Australia has been a permanent member of Exercise Malabar since 2020, and in 2023 it hosted the exercise for the first time. India has also joined Exercise Pitch Black, an Australian-led multi-national Air Force operation which brings together 3500 personal and 120 aircraft from eleven different countries.

To bolster defence and security cooperation, Australia is also seeking to build the economic dimension of its relationship with India, including by commissioning former DFAT secretary Peter Varghese to write the *India Economic Strategy to 2035* report in 2018. While talks on a Comprehensive Economic Cooperation Agreement between Australia and India had been launched in 2011, they were suspended in 2016. In 2021, it was announced that they were being relaunched and efforts to liberalise and deepen bilateral trade were progressing. The talks were successful and the Australia–India Comprehensive Economic Cooperation and Trade Agreement entered into force in December 2022. However, given Australia's emphasis on free market economics and New Delhi's protectionism, differences remain. While Australia is a part of the Regional Comprehensive Economic Partnership Agreement, designed to promote free trade, India has refused to sign on.

The Australian government has also sought to deepen people-to-people links with India. In March 2022, it announced the establishment of the Centre for Australia–India Relations, focused on scholarships and business and cultural ties. But these efforts also face challenges, with Australia needing to turn a blind eye to growing nationalism, the curtailment of civil liberties and declining democratic standards under the current Indian government.[89] These issues highlight the limits of the relationship and narratives of 'shared values'.

The government was reminded of the divergence between its own strategic outlook and regional relationships and India's in March 2022, when India abstained from voting on a UN resolution condemning Russian aggression against Ukraine and demanding the cessation of military operations. India doubled down on its position in April 2022, voting against removing Russia from the UN Human Rights Council. This move reflected India's historically close relationship with Russia and its reliance on Russia for defence matériel, despite recent arms deals with the United States. India also does not support some of the United States' naval operations in the western Indian Ocean, including those in the Persian Gulf aimed at Iran. And unlike the United States and Australia, New Delhi has sought to improve its relations with Tehran.[90]

In other areas of the Indian Ocean region, India's anti-colonial leadership conflicts with the Australian government's close relationships with the United States and United Kingdom. For example, the United States' Diego Garcia military base is in the British-claimed territory of the Chagos Archipelago. These islands came under British control in the nineteenth century as part of the colony of Mauritius. In 1965, in the lead-up to Mauritius's decolonisation, the United Kingdom detached Chagos from its Mauritius administration and named it the British Indian Ocean Territory. From 1967–73, the United Kingdom forcibly moved around 1500 Chagossians to Mauritius and Seychelles, and then prevented their return. Over time, Mauritius has challenged the lawfulness of the United Kingdom's actions. Although the United Kingdom compensated Mauritius in 1982, Mauritian officials claim the United Kingdom violated Mauritius's legal right to self-determination. Even though the International Court of Justice rejected UK sovereignty over the Chagos Archipelago in 2019, on the grounds that Mauritius's decolonisation was not lawfully completed, and the UN General Assembly voted in favour of strongly condemning British occupation of Chagos, the United Kingdom has refused to comply with the court's finding. This reflects the geostrategic importance of the Diego Garcia base, which provides US bombers with reach across the Indian Ocean. British officials have viewed the UK's possession of Chagos Archipelago as necessary for regional and global security and its relations with the United States and other partners, such as Australia. Notably, Australia sided against the UN General Assembly's motion condemning the United Kingdom while India voted in its favour, reflecting its anticolonial stance.

The Australian government has also sought to enhance its bilateral relations with other Indian Ocean states beyond India. For example, in 2021 Australia signed a Trade and Investment Framework Arrangement with Bangladesh and posted an Australian Defence Advisor to Dhaka. Australia is also hoping to improve bilateral relations in the Bay of Bengal by gaining observer status with the Bay of Bengal Initiative for Multi-Sectoral Technical and Economic Cooperation.[91] In February 2022, Australia announced the opening of a new high commission in the Maldives and a $36.5-million package over five years to improve regional cooperation on maritime shipping, disaster resilience and information sharing in the northeast Indian Ocean.

WHAT SHOULD AUSTRALIA DO DIFFERENTLY TO NAVIGATE THE INDIAN OCEAN?

Australia's attention to the Indian Ocean has ebbed and flowed, depending on how acutely it has identified its strategic or economic interests as being endangered. But Australia can no longer afford to give the Indian Ocean region such spasmodic attention. If Australia is going to ensure its security in and from the Indian Ocean, it needs to push the limits of its strategic imagination beyond the China threat. Australia must develop a holistic Indian Ocean strategy that recognises its place in the region, addresses the different types of maritime security challenges the region faces and engages more fully with the region's smaller island states.

Looking westwards isn't easy for Australia. For one thing, there are few Australians facing that direction: the west of Australia is sparsely populated and distant from Australia's capital and other major cities. Australia's ally the United States, to which Australia looks for strategic guidance (and protection), is in the opposite direction. And the states that make up the Indian Ocean region are disparate and their histories and identities very different to Australia's.

But the government has little choice other than to widen its strategic view to include its western frontier. China, now regarded as a strategic competitor, has gained ground in the Indian Ocean region. And the Indo-Pacific concept, of which Australia was an early and fervent proponent, places Australia squarely at the intersection between the Indian and Pacific oceans. This means the government must consider how to pursue security in the region.

Promisingly, Australia has recognised this need, with the *2020 Defence Strategic Update* prioritising Australia's 'immediate region', which it defines as including the northeast Indian Ocean, Southeast Asia and the Pacific Islands.[92] The 2023 *Defence Strategic Review* re-emphasised this, recognising that 'Australia is a significant Indian Ocean state with the longest Indian Ocean coastline and the region's largest search and rescue area'.[93] Australia's offshore territories in the region, Christmas Island and Cocos (Keeling) Islands, also have increasing strategic value, particularly the airfield and secure anchorages at the latter.

As the Australian government has sought to operationalise its Indo-Pacific strategic focus, the tempo of the Australia–India relationship has increased. But while this relationship is important, it is not a substitute for engaging with the entire Indo-Pacific region, particularly with potential partners such as Sri Lanka and Bangladesh. Because many Indian Ocean states are developing countries, there is scope for Australia to use development assistance and other economic tools of statecraft, such as investment, trade and labour mobility, to try to build relationships in the region, which would have flow-on effects for its security relationships. Australia has recently begun to do this work. The 2023 *Defence Strategic Review* also recommended expanding Australia's Defence Cooperation Program into the Indian Ocean region. Australia's attempts at multilateralism in the Indian Ocean region have been disappointing: regional states do not have sufficiently developed regional architecture to manage even a relatively uncontroversial security issue such as fisheries. However, this doesn't mean Australia should give up on regionalism in the Indian Ocean. Instead, it needs to replace its earlier intermittent – and, at times, transactional – attempts at engaging with regional institutions (particularly the Indian Ocean Rim Association) with sustained efforts at regional institution-building.

Australia also needs to be careful not to rely too heavily on the Quad. As a minilateral forum, the Quad could be viewed by smaller regional powers as exclusionary and/or an attempt by the four member states to impose their will on the rest of the region, much of which doesn't entirely share their concerns about China's rising influence. A largely unanswered question is how the Quad could involve other states and provide a source of regional leadership that is an alternative to Beijing by providing public goods and enhancing the sovereign capacities of states to enforce law in their maritime jurisdictions. So far, outcomes have not matched the rhetoric. The Quad's promise to produce one billion doses of COVID-19 vaccine for distribution across the Indo-Pacific underperformed (although it still provided 257 million doses) and its members made a 'quiet pivot away' from the program after six months, due to issues around logistics and indemnity.[94] Nevertheless, Quad leaders announced at their 2023 meeting that the program would evolve into a 'broader Quad Health Security Partnership' to 'strengthen our coordination and collaboration in support of health security in the Indo-Pacific'.[95]

A year earlier, at their 2022 summit, the Quad members announced the Indo-Pacific Partnership for Maritime Domain Awareness, which would encourage greater information sharing to develop a clearer picture of what is happening in (and beyond) the vast Indian Ocean region. Such awareness is vital for maritime law enforcement against maritime crimes such as IUU fishing, robbery and human trafficking at sea. However, more information is only useful if states also have the naval and coastguard equipment, personnel and training to identify and apprehend vessels and a domestic legal system that can effectively prosecute crimes and protect victims. Building these other aspects of sovereign capacity is another way Quad states could contribute to maritime security in the Indian Ocean Rim. Delivering will be the difficult part. There tends to be a gap between announcement and implementation when the United States is involved, as American spending must navigate contested Congressional approval.

Australia and many other states in the Indian Ocean region share several non-traditional security concerns, so the government should first seek to deepen regional cooperation to address these relatively uncontroversial challenges, such as maritime safety, humanitarian and disaster relief and transnational crime. To understand security dynamics in the Indian Ocean region and play a more substantive role in bridging the gap between smaller and bigger powers, Australia would be required to look beyond the cliched 'strategic triangle'. This could start at a minilateral level, with partners already engaged in strategic cooperation – such as India, the United States, Indonesia and France – and then gradually expand. France, for example, is an Indian Ocean state through its territories and a major player in the western Indian Ocean. The resumption of the Australia–France–India trilateral dialogues was announced in September 2022, following their suspension due to French concerns about AUKUS. There is also scope to enhance maritime security cooperation under the Indian Ocean Naval Symposium. Australia could contribute to mechanisms of coastguard collaboration to support the region, particularly as Indian Ocean states are primarily concerned about non-traditional maritime security challenges and 'white hull' cooperation is potentially less provocative than involving naval warships.

Once confident relationships and habits of cooperation are built, Australia could advance greater regional cooperation on other security issues. This is already happening. Australia has liaison officers at the Singapore-run Information Fusion Centre and the Indian-run Information Fusion Centre – Indian Ocean Region. Both centres are linked, as is the Regional Maritime Information Fusion Centre in Madagascar, funded by the European Union. There is potential to expand those linkages to the Pacific Fusion Centre that Australia funds in the South Pacific, connecting maritime domain-awareness information sharing between the four. This would also help add substance to the Indo-Pacific concept, which at an institutional level remains fragmented.

Given shared concern about IUU fishing in the Indian Ocean, the government could also consider expanding elements of its Pacific Maritime Security Program into the region. Australia should consider whether it is appropriate to donate the Guardian-class patrol boats it is rolling out in the South Pacific to certain states in the Indian Ocean region, such as Sri Lanka and the Maldives – to assist not just with irregular migration but also with those states' non-traditional maritime security challenges. This move would benefit the recipient states, which, like their South Pacific counterparts, depend on their fisheries resources for economic development and food security.

The government must also prioritise security initiatives that grapple with the consequences of climate change. Climate change is contributing to rising sea levels, which will have significant impacts on several Indian Ocean states. Increased salinity will result in crop failures, food security and water stress. Major coastal erosion will further degrade local ecosystems, biodiversity and food security. Climate change is also likely to amplify other non-traditional security challenges, such as health, water and energy insecurity. These insecurities may in turn exacerbate societal tensions, ultimately leading to conflict. The most dramatic consequence of climate change will be large-scale human displacement. Small island nations such as the Maldives and Seychelles are existentially threatened. Populous low-lying areas in the Bay of Bengal are also at extreme risk. Bangladesh is particularly vulnerable, with estimates that 4.1 million people had already been displaced by

2015, and that 13.3 million people could be displaced by 2050 if 18 per cent of the coastland of Bangladesh is inundated, as predicted.[96] Australia, which has typically placed a high premium on the security of its borders and stopping 'unauthorised maritime arrivals', will likely be challenged by how to respond to these necessary people flows. This might require some reimagining of its identity and role in the region.

Climate change is also expected to result in the increased frequency and severity of natural disasters, with each impact amplifying and compounding other effects. This means Australia will likely be called upon to engage in more humanitarian and disaster relief in the region. There may be merit in the government trying to coalesce a more institutionalised regional HADR mechanism. The Quad HADR Mechanism announced in 2022 is intended to coordinate Quad members' efforts but does not include space for other regional states to be involved. Both the Quad HADR Mechanism and the Indo-Pacific Partnership for Maritime Domain Awareness exemplify the tensions that the government faces when seeking to engage in the Indian Ocean region. While both initiatives include India, they essentially provide assistance *to*, rather than *in cooperation with*, the region, and there is a risk they could undermine nascent regional cooperation within existing mechanisms.

The government needs to balance its broader interests – particularly its alliance with the United States – against its regional interests, and those of its partners, in the Indian Ocean region. While it faces this challenge across its three oceans, it is particularly difficult in the Indian Ocean, where Australia and the United States have different priorities. While the government's Indo-Pacific concept specifies that its primary area of strategic interest is the northeast Indian Ocean, the United States has been focused on the Persian Gulf, reflecting its wars in Iraq and Afghanistan, as well as its substantial military presence there. The United States has moved to deepen its relationship with India, including through its involvement with the Quad, but it has primarily done so to encourage India to take the lead in the Indian Ocean region.

These tensions highlight the need for Australia to reimagine its engagement with the Indian Ocean region. Australia will need to be more confident to act without a US safety net. It will need to cooperate more within multilateral and minilateral mechanisms. And it will need to be realistic about the challenges it faces in its important bilateral relationships with India and Indonesia.

7

THE SOUTHERN OCEAN

After six years and eleven rounds of negotiations, on 2 June 1988 the Convention on the Regulation of Antarctic Mineral Resource Activities was adopted and opened for signature. The ratification of the convention looked like a done deal, and Australian officials strongly advised its leaders that signing and ratifying it would be the best diplomatic course.[1] But Australian prime minister Bob Hawke faced a political problem: civil-society organisations such as Greenpeace had mounted a persuasive domestic and international campaign to convince the government to reject the convention and pursue a permanent mining ban in Antarctica instead. Reading the political tea leaves, Hawke defied official advice and walked away from the convention, upsetting the careful negotiations. Doing so cemented his environmental legacy. Hawke and Australian officials, along with France and its prime minister, Michel Rocard, went on to play an important role in convincing other invested parties to pursue a more ambitious conservation agreement. Their diplomatic leadership ultimately led to the 1991 Protocol on Environmental Protection to the Antarctic Treaty (or the Madrid Protocol), which indefinitely prohibited exploitation of mineral reserves and mining in Antarctica (for non-scientific purposes).

Historically, Australia has been a leader in international cooperation around Antarctica and the Southern Ocean, especially in the area of environmental conservation. In 1959, Australia helped establish the landmark Antarctic Treaty, which has underpinned peace and stability in the region for over six decades. The treaty facilitated a cooperative approach to scientific and environmental advancements by 'freezing' sovereignty claims to the icy continent, including Australia's. The Antarctic Treaty was a novel, creative and pragmatic solution to the problem of what to do with a contested but uninhabited ice mass. It defied the international trend of carving up the world's territory into sovereign states and created a new form of cooperative international governance within a specific geographic region that belonged to no one state.

While sovereignty claims are 'on ice', Australia's interests in the Southern Ocean are nonetheless significant. The Southern Ocean is Australia's third ocean, and it abuts its south coast.[2] Depending on how it's defined, the Southern Ocean covers over 20 million square kilometres and represents approximately 15 per cent of the Earth's ocean area. It is difficult to separate the Southern Ocean from Antarctica given that it encircles the continent – and was formerly known as the Antarctic Ocean.

When states ratified the Antarctic Treaty and agreed to freeze sovereignty claims to the Antarctic, this had consequences for their future abilities to make claims under UNCLOS over the maritime area. The global order is based on the (not fully realised) ideal that the world's territory is divided into clearly delineated sovereign states, and UNCLOS also sets out a maritime zoning system based on this Westphalian ideal. But in the 'post-sovereign' arena of Antarctica, the lack of clarity around sovereignty creates issues around maritime zoning in the areas adjacent to Antarctic territory. This is not an inconsequential issue in the Southern Ocean: maritime areas viewed by some states as their exclusive economic zone can be classified by others as the 'high seas'.

Australia claims 42 per cent of the Antarctic continent as its sovereign territory. This claim is recognised by few states. It also has uncontested sovereignty over some islands in the Antarctic region, and legitimately claims offshore waters adjacent to them. Its total Antarctic and sub-Antarctic maritime claims – both legitimate and contested – total more than five million square kilometres, around 30 per cent of its entire marine jurisdiction, including exclusive economic zones and continental shelves directly off Tasmania's coast and Australia's southern mainland.[3]

Protecting a maritime jurisdiction is a challenging task for a middle power, and nowhere is the difficulty greater than in the treacherous, icy waters of the Southern Ocean. While one of the key dilemmas for Australia's broader strategic thinking has been the challenge of imagining a regional order not based on the United States as a great power, in the Southern Ocean it is a reluctance to imagine a future where the Antarctic Treaty System (the treaty and its related agreements and arrangements) no longer effectively creates order.

While Australia's foreign and strategic policy is often characterised as in permanent lock step with the United States, the Southern Ocean reveals their different interests, approaches and interpretations of UNCLOS. The Antarctic rules-based order is under challenge, and according to some reports, Australia's southern flank is set to become a zone of great power competition.[4] Rising powers such as China and Russia are increasingly interested in exploiting natural resources and military advantages in the region. There are growing concerns that the international law and cooperative treaty regimes that have underscored peace and security in the Antarctic are splintering, and that the region is experiencing a lack of trust and common purpose. A growing number of tourists, as well as confrontations between ships such as whaling vessels, environmental-rights activists, illegal fishing vessels, and naval and coastguard ships add to the hazards.[5]

Yet if Australia's strategic imagination is only just beginning to look west to the Indian Ocean, it remains largely blind to emerging threats from the south. Neither the 2020 *Defence Strategic Update* nor the 2023 *Defence Strategic Review* mention the Southern Ocean or Antarctica. Australia's security leaders have adopted a 'business-as-usual' approach to collective governance in the Southern Ocean, despite the looming range of traditional and non-traditional security challenges that threaten Australia's interests in the region. Australia's strategic complacency towards to the south is perhaps best reflected by the fact that its Indo-Pacific concept excludes the Southern Ocean altogether.

The key tension in Australia's Southern Ocean engagements is between its identity as a leader of innovative and cooperative global governance mechanisms on one hand, and the territorial and maritime sovereignty claims it makes on the other. How can the government maintain the position that the region is the cooperative 'common heritage of mankind', as envisaged by the Antarctic Treaty, while unilaterally pursuing its 42-per-cent stake in Antarctica? The increasingly 'activist' behaviour of several consultative parties to the Antarctic Treaty System – including China and Russia – means Australia may not be able to sit on the fence for much longer, particularly as material and territorial interests in strategic and resource competition intensify.

What does strategic competition mean for Australia's sovereign and maritime interests? Is there likely to be a new 'scramble for Antarctica'? And if so, how it will affect Australia's security interests? Such questions influence Australia's ability to continue hedging, defending its own sovereignty claims and a potentially excessive exclusive economic zone while maintaining the Antarctic Treaty System and advancing common environmental, conservation and non-militarisation objectives. The Southern Ocean therefore provides an interesting case study for broader debates about the government's strategic imagination and its capacity to respond to emergent national and international security threats.

WHY HAS THE SOUTHERN OCEAN HISTORICALLY MATTERED FOR AUSTRALIA?

The history of Antarctica and the Southern Ocean has typically been seen through the lens of exploration and discovery. Captain James Cook of Britain's Royal Navy explored the Southern Ocean in the eighteenth century, naming South Georgia Island and the South Sandwich Islands in 1775. But who was first to land in Antarctica is disputed among polar historians.[6] While the last four decades of the nineteenth century were a period of exploration, mapping and naming, particularly by Europeans and Americans, the 'heroic age' of Antarctic exploration from 1898 to 1916 produced stories that consolidated an image of the Antarctic region as a domain of adventure and discovery.

Unlike many other colonised territories, Antarctica had no indigenous human population to dispossess, although early discoverers did find the continent and surrounding waters teeming with wildlife – from albatrosses and penguins to whales, fish and krill. Antarctica's geography made it difficult to colonise. It is treacherous to even travel to Antarctica, let alone populate it. Generally, states developed sovereign claims by demonstrating their acquisition of territory by physical occupation, discovery, transfer of a legal title, treaties and/or conquest.[7] But the legitimacy of such claims is subject to historical debate – how does one define 'discovery', for example?

Despite its geography, Antarctica has not escaped empire-building efforts. Today, there are seven states that make territorial claims in Antarctica: Argentina, Australia, Chile, France, New Zealand, Norway and the United Kingdom. Australia's claim – the Australian Antarctic Territory (AAT) – is the largest, at 42 per cent of the total Antarctic landmass. How did Australia come to develop this claim? Partly it was based on those made by the United Kingdom from the nineteenth century onwards. During the 1920s, via a 'selfless policy', Britain encouraged Australia to take over a large portion of the continent.[8] In 1933, the *Australian Antarctic Territory Acceptance Act* transferred authority of most of the territory south of the 60th degree of latitude and between the 160th degree of east longitude and the 45th degree of east longitude from Britain to Australia.[9] In 1954, the *Australian Antarctic Territory Act* sought to extend Australian law over the area.[10]

Australia's claim is also based on the activities of its explorers. Douglas Mawson, for instance, led the Australasian Antarctic Expedition between 1911 and 1914, which resulted in multiple discoveries. And in 1928, Australian aviator Hubert Wilkins began exploring

Antarctica using aircraft, opening up new possibilities by mapping the territory from above.[11] But this history of exploration and discovery – and the creation of research bases on the territory – has not guaranteed the acceptance of ownership claims. Claimant states were unable to 'politically and economically "colonise" the territory to a standard required for international recognition of sovereignty'.[12] While Australia, France, New Zealand, Norway and the United Kingdom recognise one another's mutual claims, other states do not.

Geopolitics plays a role in this non-recognition. After World War II, the United States and the Soviet Union would not accept the sovereignty claims of the seven Antarctic claimant states. As the world's two superpowers, they were both keen to establish a strategic foothold in Antarctica and possibly put forward their own territorial and maritime claims.[13] In this environment, a 'new political settlement' emerged: the Antarctic Treaty, signed in December 1959 by the seven claimant states plus the United States, the Soviet Union, Japan, Belgium and South Africa.[14]

By negotiating the Antarctic Treaty, Australia was an important player in the formation of a new style of collective governance. It passed the *Antarctic Treaty Act* into domestic law in 1960. The treaty characterised the Antarctic region as an arena of peace, conservation and science, and prohibited the establishment of military bases, weapons testing or military manoeuvres within it. The aim was to manage geopolitical tensions during the Cold War but also to provide transparency around the activities of claimant states. That this treaty was negotiated during the Cold War was significant. As both superpowers wished to preserve their right to make a claim, the treaty was designed to suspend, but not resolve, the issue of sovereignty. Article IV of the treaty stipulated:

> No acts or activities taking place while the present Treaty is in force shall constitute a basis for asserting, supporting or denying a claim to territorial sovereignty in Antarctica or create any rights of sovereignty

in Antarctica. No new claim, or enlargement of an existing claim, to territorial sovereignty in Antarctica shall be asserted while the present Treaty is in force.

Therefore, only activities that took place *before* the Antarctic Treaty came into force can be used by Australia to bolster its sovereignty claims.[15]

These prohibitions have undoubtedly worked in Australia's interests: it has maintained its territorial claim to nearly half of the continent without needing to defend it against more powerful states. Australia hosted the first meeting of the Antarctic Treaty Consultative Parties in 1961. By 2023, the Antarctic Treaty had grown from twelve to fifty-six members, of which twenty-nine are consultative parties that possess a vote at Antarctic Treaty Consultative Meetings.

The establishment of the Antarctic Treaty had implications for the Southern Ocean. As UNCLOS was not adopted until 1982, the Antarctic Treaty had to address the issue of maritime rights. Article VI declared that:

the provisions of the present Treaty shall apply to the area south of 60° South Latitude, including all ice shelves, but nothing in the present Treaty shall prejudice or in any way affect the rights, or the exercise of the rights, of any State under international law with regard to the *high seas* within that area. [italics not in original]

However, the Antarctic Treaty failed to clarify which Antarctic waters could be classified as 'high seas'.[16] In some areas of the Southern Ocean, where ownership of islands is not contested, some states (including Australia) make relatively uncontroversial claims to maritime area. But as UNCLOS tends to assume that sovereignty issues are settled, the absence of coastal states in the Antarctic region has prompted conflicting ideas over maritime zoning in the parts of the Southern Ocean adjacent to the Antarctic continent.[17]

The United States' position on Antarctic waters is that maritime rights run 'with the land' and 'no zones of offshore jurisdiction may be extended seaward from Antarctica'.[18] Other non-claimants have adopted the position that no maritime jurisdictional zones exist below 60-degrees south latitude from Antarctic Territory, so long as the Antarctic Treaty is in operation. Australia, in contrast, claims a territorial sea, an exclusive economic zone and a continental shelf in areas adjacent to the Australian Antarctic Territory. In 1994, Australia formally declared an Antarctic exclusive economic zone of 2 million square kilometres off the coast of the Australian Antarctic Territory in the Southern Ocean. While this is controversial, Australia is not the only state to make this kind of maritime claim.

In 2004, Australia requested that the Commission on the Limits of the Continental Shelf – the key international body that adjudicates claims to the seabed and its resources – not consider or adjudicate Australia's claim to the offshore waters adjacent to the Australian Antarctic Territory. Nevertheless, its continental-shelf submission showed that Australia considers the outer limits of its extended continental shelf in the region of the Australian Antarctic Territory to enclose an area of up to 686,821 square kilometres beyond 200 nautical miles from the territorial sea baseline.[19] By submitting maps with its territorial and maritime claims while also asking the Commission not to rule on the validity of its Antarctic continental shelf claim, Australia sought to articulate those claims internationally without undermining its credibility as a supporter of the Antarctic Treaty. In contrast, Antarctic states New Zealand and United Kingdom reserved their right to make a submission in future.

In May 2012, Australia made the Seas and Submerged Lands (Limits of Continental Shelf) Proclamation, which limited its seabed claims in sub-Antarctic waters to the areas around Heard Island and McDonald Islands and Macquarie Island, which lie outside the Antarctic Treaty area and over which sovereignty is uncontested. While the proclamation did not include Australia's continental-shelf claims,[20] these are represented in other official government documents. For instance, a

2014 Australian Senate report contained a geoscience map of Australia's claimed area, and a 2019 Geoscience Australia report also outlined the extent of Australia's continental-shelf claim.

The Convention on the Conservation of Antarctic Marine Living Resources (CCAMLR) emerged from the Antarctic Treaty as 'the foundation for marine resource conservation in the Southern Ocean'.[21] The Convention came into force in 1982 to address intense fishing and overexploitation of fishing stocks recognised since the 1960s (although there was a longer and darker history of exploitation in the Southern Ocean in whaling and seal harvesting).[22] It was designed to support the sustainable use of marine living resources in the Southern Ocean using science, cooperation and a system of 'surveillance, enforcements and market controls'.[23]

Australia can legitimately claim an environmental leadership role within the CCAMLR: the Convention was drafted at a conference in Canberra in 1980, and the Commission for the Conservation of Antarctic Marine Living Resources held its first meeting in Hobart in 1982. It has since met annually in Hobart, where the Secretariat is located. Australia also acts as the Convention's depositary. Australia's stated goal within the CCAMLR is to ensure the conservation of the marine living resources within the Southern Ocean, promote itself 'as a responsible manager and sustainable harvester of Antarctic marine living resources' and ensure its continuing influence through active engagement.[24] Along with other party states, it recently restated the original vision of the CCAMLR in the face of sustainability challenges posed by other states.

Indeed, Australia's policies relating to the Southern Ocean, and the Antarctic region more generally, have tended to be defined in terms of its environmental leadership. As mentioned at the outset of this chapter, Australian leaders played an important role in advocating the Madrid Protocol, adopted in 1991. Under Article 7 of the Protocol, 'any activity relating to mineral resources, other than scientific research', is prohibited. But Article 25 makes it possible to review these terms in a review window that opens in 2048. This provision is often poorly understood as an 'expiry' date – but the Protocol does not have a termination date. The standard required for change is so high that it seems unlikely enough states would agree to alter the mining ban.

Taken as a bundle, these agreements (and others) are known as the Antarctic Treaty System (although there are many others that also contribute to what scholars describe as the 'regime complex' of Antarctic governance). While UNCLOS is the guiding framework for oceans governance, maritime domains also have their own rules, norms, cultures and political history that shape engagement and prospects for interstate cooperation within these regions. This is true in the Southern Ocean, which remains subject to this unique 'regime complex' that mostly developed in the second half of the twentieth century. The negotiations of the third United Nations Conference on the Law of the Sea coincided with negotiations for the CCAMLR.

In 1983, a debate on Antarctica in the United Nations was initiated by developing countries to extend UNCLOS's 'common heritage of mankind' principle to Antarctica. Under the principle, certain areas are not subject to sovereign appropriation and must remain free from exploitation by states and corporations. The resources would instead belong to 'mankind as a whole' (UNCLOS, Article 37). Malaysia led efforts to advocate for a regime that was 'truly universal in character and committed to serving the interest of the entire international community'.[25] This reflected concerns that particular states – including Australia – had been able to effectively colonise Antarctica and had excluded other states from having a role in governing the southern continent. However, more and more states have since been engaged in Antarctic governance, and even Malaysia joined the Antarctic Treaty in 2011, despite its previous concerns that Western states had used the Treaty to dominate the governance of Antarctica.

The Antarctic Treaty System continues to suit Australia's interests, as policy documents have acknowledged. Yet, there are serious questions about pressures on the system caused by strategic competition and how these affect Australia's maritime security interests in the

Southern Ocean. Despite Australia's historical legacy of leadership in Antarctic and Southern Ocean governance, there are concerns that its role is declining due to strategic complacency and a lack of investment.

THE RELEVANCE OF CONTEMPORARY SECURITY ISSUES TO AUSTRALIA'S SECURITY

A major security challenge for Australia is ensuring that the Antarctic Treaty System continues to govern the Antarctic region, including the Southern Ocean, in an increasingly contested political environment. The remoteness and inhabitability of Antarctica as a strategic theatre encouraged the comfortable assumption that no military threat could be directed at Australia from the Southern Ocean or Antarctica. However, this assumption is changing. Current debates centre on the extent to which the Antarctic Treaty System is being undermined by rising powers that seek to revise its key norms, rules and values. While it seems unlikely that the Antarctic region will become a hotbed of great power conflict, particularly given geographical realities and the higher stakes of other territorial and maritime disputes, there are security issues that exist in the grey zone as new powers jostle for influence.

Geopolitical challenges are intensifying in the Antarctic region as more actors become involved in Antarctic decision-making. Today, an additional forty-three states have acceded to the Antarctic Treaty. Seventeen additional consultative parties now contribute to collective decision-making about Antarctic governance at Antarctic Treaty Consultative Meetings (ATCMs) and twenty-six member states and the European Union now make decisions at CCAMLR meetings. There are more than eighty research stations from thirty countries on the Antarctic continent, although some of them operate on a seasonal basis and some operate year-round. The Australian Antarctic Division has three year-round research stations in Antarctica (Mawson, Davis and Casey) as well as the Macquarie Island station in the sub-Antarctic. While the growth in stations could be viewed as democratising Antarctic space, it will also put pressure on the Antarctic Treaty System if contesting powers use research and science to contest key values and norms such as non-militarisation and conservation.

Much attention has been placed on China's rising interest in the region. China joined the Antarctic Treaty in 1983 and has substantially increased its activities in the region in the twenty-first century, including in areas such as tourism and fishing. China now has four bases in Antarctica and a fifth on the way, including in the Australian Antarctic Territory. There are signs that Russia is also seeking to increase its Antarctic activities and presence; other states, such as India, France and the United Kingdom, have interests in Antarctica as well.

Some analysts have compared the interests and activities of China in Antarctica with its interests and activities in the Arctic or South China Sea. However, unlike the South China Sea, Antarctica is not a site of claimed Chinese territory – at least not yet.[26] China's interests in Antarctica are not vital, as they are in the South and East China seas. Still, there are fears that the South China Sea is a litmus test for China's intentions vis-a-vis the global maritime order in other strategic maritime domains, including Antarctica. However, this tendency to extrapolate dominant trends in one domain and apply them to others often fails to provide an accurate view of the internal geopolitical climates of each region.[27] The Antarctic region has its own unique complex regime and geographic realities that complicate cross-regional comparisons.

Nevertheless, there are legitimate concerns that the Antarctic environment – literally and politically – is conducive to grey zone activities that might strategically benefit inimical powers. The Antarctic Treaty itself established something of a grey zone, insofar as sovereignty of Antarctica remains unsettled, legal loopholes allow for different interpretations to arise, and monitoring and enforcement are complicated by geography and a lack of resources, which means the treaty doesn't prevent strategic competition but instead facilitates it.[28] While south of 60-degrees latitude is demilitarised due to the treaty, the prohibition of military activities raises questions about whether certain scientific or research activities and dual-use technology might provide a smoke-screen for military activities, including hydrographic mapping or the distortion – via GPS 'spoofing' – of fishing vessels' locations to avoid their detection.[29] International satellite systems have proliferated in Antarctica, including from the United States, China, the European Union and Russia, with implications for Australian defence.[30]

Another challenge is resource competition. While mining is banned, there are concerns this moratorium will be loosened as states are forced to diversify energy supplies (as noted, altering the ban will be difficult – but so too might be enforcing it). Antarctica and the Southern Ocean are known to possess oil and gas reserves in addition to other valuable mineral resources. In 2012, the Russian delegation submitted a paper to the thirty-fifth Antarctic Treaty Consultative Meeting which mentioned their scientists' interest in the 'structure, geological evolution and potential mineral resources of the Antarctic lithosphere'.[31] Given Australia's extensive continental-shelf claim in the Southern Ocean and long-term interest in preventing mining, efforts by states to extract resources from the Southern Ocean seabed – either in or around Australia's claimed seabed – would constitute a violation of Australia's claimed maritime and sovereignty interests. It is unclear what – beyond diplomatic outcry – Australia could do to prevent, or punish, this action. However, while concerns about resource competition exist, it is not yet commercially viable – and is technically very difficult – to extract minerals and other resources from the seabed in the Antarctic region.

Fisheries governance also presents a challenge. Fishing activity is regulated by the CCAMLR in its geographic scope, whereby fishing is allowed but must have a limited impact on ecosystems. Australia also has its own fishing zone in the Southern Ocean. Popular fish species are Patagonian and Antarctic toothfish, mackerel icefish and Antarctic krill. Australia's management and monitoring of IUU fishing is a significant issue, and its *2016 Defence White Paper* expressed concern about fisheries in the Southern Ocean being targeted by illegal distant-water fishing fleets.[32]

The presence of Chinese fishing vessels in the region corresponds with a growing concern in Australia about China's expanding footprint in Antarctica. Fishing can be a means of occupying space, which meets 'geopolitical as well economic goals by asserting power and securing future access.'[33] China's fishing interests relate not just to the size of the catch but also to its broader maritime agenda, as 'Antarctic fishing showcases China's quest for freedom in the "global commons".'[34]

There is concern that future contests between states would likely centre on fisheries, rather than minerals.[35] Contests will become keener as unsustainable fishing practices and food insecurity in areas such as the South China Sea push fishers into new waters. But too sharp a focus on the actions of powerful authoritarian states may encourage Australia to overlook the potential for corporations or other non-state actors to exploit the waters or seabed of the Antarctic region. More-over, amid the reporting on China's interest in the Southern Ocean, there is a story not often told about the reduction in rates of illegal fishing over the past two decades. This has largely been due to enhanced international coordination and cooperative measures such as licensing, monitoring, vessel inspections and an IUU fishing vessel list.

Australia's other great challenge in the Southern Ocean is climate change. The Southern Ocean is warming at a more rapid rate than the global average and is the most important ocean for absorbing heat.[36] This will affect the Southern Ocean's ecology, including its habitability for Antarctic krill, and erode Antarctic ice shelves and glaciers, in some areas irrevocably. This is likely to force Australia to alter its business-as-usual approach when it comes to the Antarctic Treaty System. Antarctica's Thwaites Glacier – known as the 'Doomsday Glacier' – is over 190,000 square kilometres in mass. It is at serious risk of shattering, leading to irreversible changes to sea-level rise across the planet. According to a recent study, global sea levels would rise by 65 centimetres over a hundred years if it melted completely.[37] Thwaites Glacier also acts as a natural dam: if it were to break off it could produce an additional three-metre rise as more ice entered the sea, with serious implications for coastal communities in Australia.[38]

There are a range of other so-called 'non-traditional' security issues that currently, or will in future, present challenges for Australia in this maritime domain. Australia's area of search-and-rescue responsibility under the International Convention on Maritime Search and Rescue is around 8.5 million square kilometres of ocean below 60-degrees south latitude: nearly half of the ocean. As the role of non-state actors and corporations grows in the Southern Ocean, so too do issues around shipping safety, which is important when considering Australia's responsibilities. Accidents, fires, collisions and loss of vessel power are all examples of maritime shipping safety.[39] A key interest for Australia, then, is ensuring that users of Southern Ocean sea lanes fulfil their international maritime safety responsibilities.

The extent to which states are committed to the norms and values of the Antarctic Treaty System is an important question for Australia's maritime security interests in the Southern Ocean. The Antarctic Treaty System's inclusive approach to membership and observership has put pressure on norms such as consensus decision-making, maintaining sustainable fisheries, the effectiveness and legitimacy of marine protected areas and broader conservation and anti-mining goals. Like other maritime regions, the Southern Ocean demonstrates that rules or norms are not always interpreted in the same ways, even by states that proclaim themselves to be 'like-minded'.

AUSTRALIA'S CURRENT POLICY APPROACH

Over the past decade, successive Australian Antarctic strategic plans in 2013 and 2016, and an update in 2022, have reaffirmed the importance of both the Antarctic Treaty System and Australia's investment in science and research to maintain its place as 'a leading Antarctic nation', and Hobart as the world's primary 'Antarctic gateway'.[40] The

2016 whole-of-government *Australian Antarctic Strategy and 20-Year Action Plan Update* emphasised both 'strategic and scientific interests' in Antarctica, including the preservation of sovereign rights over adjacent offshore areas in the Southern Ocean.[41] The 2022 *Action Plan Update* also provided for an investment ($800 million dollars) in Australia's 'strategic science' capability.[42]

The *2016 Defence White Paper* said that the Australian Antarctic Territory faced 'no credible risk' that would require a military response over the next few decades. The white paper went on to say that it was in Australia's interests to 'work with like-minded countries to prevent any militarisation of Antarctica which could threaten Australia's sovereignty over the Australian Antarctic Territory and its sovereign rights over its offshore waters'.[43] It only briefly mentioned Southern Ocean fisheries and the deployment of Australian Defence Force personnel, as part of Operation Sovereign Borders, to 'support maritime resource protection operations' in this area.[44] Defence's role was otherwise conceptualised as providing 'niche support' to the operations of the Australian Antarctic Division (within the Department of Climate Change, Energy, the Environment and Water), in line with prohibitions on militarisation. As noted, neither the *2020 Defence Strategic Update* nor the 2023 *Defence Strategic Review* mention the Southern Ocean, reflecting a sense that military threats to Australia's population are unlikely to emerge from the region.

While Defence may pay little attention to the Southern Ocean, the Department of Foreign Affairs and Trade – the domain of diplomacy – does. The *2017 Foreign Policy White Paper* committed $2.2 billion to protecting Australia's Antarctic interests through scientific research, a resupply icebreaker vessel and new aviation access and overland transport capabilities.[45] Of this, Australia allocated $1.9 billion to constructing a new icebreaker, the RSV *Nuyina*, in a package covering the design, build and its thirty-year operational and maintenance life span, 'representing the single biggest investment in the history of Australia's Antarctic program'.[46] These plans experienced some setbacks. After the Nuyina was delivered in 2021, its first voyage to the Antarctic was delayed due to faults. It was later removed from service due to further faults and did not return to service until April 2023.[47]

In 2018, the government also announced plans for the Davis aerodrome project, including establishing an airport and the first paved runway in Antarctica. But in 2021, Environment Minister Sussan Ley scuppered the plan due to concerns about the environmental impact and costs, and, possibly, in response to public pressure from Antarctic experts who had argued the project was less about science and more about 'flag-waving' in the context of China and Russia's rising influence.[48]

While governments have been concerned about the intentions of other states in the Antarctic region, Defence strategic-planning documents make very little mention of potential militarisation or emerging grey zone threats and unconventional challenges that could threaten Australia's security interests in the Antarctic and Southern oceans. There doesn't seem to be enough effort to link Antarctic and Southern Ocean planning and Defence planning. Consequently, the Australian Defence Force 'has little capacity to operate' in the Southern Ocean.[49] Australia risks sidelining the Antarctic region – a unique environment, both geographically and politico-legally – in its strategic imagination.

Current debates have presented Australia as facing a choice: continue to rely on the Antarctic Treaty System for security or prepare for a scenario in which the Antarctic Treaty System no longer plays an ordering role and new capabilities and strategy might be needed if Australia is to step up and defend its territorial and maritime interests in the region.

Australia's naval-procurement programs have rarely considered the difficult operating environment of the Southern Ocean, yet the Royal Australian Navy's capacity to operate there is limited – an issue that multiple parliamentary reports and analyses have identified over the years.[50] This difficulty was highlighted when an Antarctic cargo ship chartered to replace Nuyina had to return to Hobart in February 2023 after running aground at Mawson Station.[51]

While the Australian Border Force cutter *Ocean Shield* can operate in the Southern Ocean to address civil maritime security issues such as IUU fishing, there have been long periods – years – in which Australian vessels have not patrolled the Southern Ocean. This has been due to competing priorities, particularly in northern seas that are more susceptible to IUU fishing. One government report noted that Australia has relied on French patrols to tackle illegal fishing for decades, leading to accusations that it is 'freeloading'.[52] Because the Australian Defence Force and Australian Border Force have limited surface capacity to operate in the Southern Ocean search-and-rescue zones, Australia also calls on other states to assist with its role of coordinating these activities.[53] In 2014, the Foreign Affairs, Defence and Trade References Committee recommended Australia recommence maritime patrolling in the Southern Ocean, suggesting it use the *Ocean Shield* to conduct a minimum of two forty-day patrols in 2014–15 and 2015–16.[54]

As these examples indicate, Australia does not necessarily act like the state with the largest claim to Antarctica and its surrounding waters. While it has three year-round stations in East Antarctica, its presence across Antarctica is less than that of other states. China, as we've mentioned, is currently building a fifth station in the Ross Sea.

Those who are in favour of prioritising the cooperative ideals of the Antarctic Treaty[55] emphasise Australia's role as an environmental leader in the region. But this highlights some of the tensions between the Morrison government's absence of domestic climate-change policy and Australia's international image projection in its key maritime domains. Historically, Australia has demonstrated its 'good international citizenship' credentials by protecting the Southern Ocean – through the mining ban, for instance, but also through advocating for marine protected areas under the auspices of the CCAMLR. A key focus of Australia's approach has been conservation.

The world's first international marine protected area – the South Orkney Islands Southern Shelf Marine Protected Area – was established in 2009 under the CCMALR. In 2016, an agreement was reached through the CCMALR process to create the world's largest marine park, covering 1.55 million square kilometres, in the Ross Sea. Fishing was banned in a 'no-take zone' covering over 70 per cent of the marine park for thirty-five years, with some limited exceptions for fishing krill and toothfish. Australia has also supported marine protected areas in the East Antarctic seas, Weddell Sea and Antarctic Peninsula, recognising the importance of these governance systems for sustainability, biodiversity, and ocean and ecosystem resilience, particularly in the face of climate change.[56]

However, not all efforts have been successful, and only about five per cent of the Southern Ocean is protected. In 2017, Australia, France and the European Union tried to establish a marine protected area off the coast of East Antarctica, which would have spanned almost one million square kilometres, but it was scuppered by China and Russia due to concerns about the limitations it would put on fishing. In the Southern Ocean, where the battle is primarily over Antarctic krill, China has been pushing the boundaries on Atlantic Treaty System practice by exploiting fisheries. But it is not just China: Russia and South Korea have also protested fishing limits in the Ross Sea Region Marine Protected Area and Russia has contested the meaning of the term 'conservation'. As the number of state actors invested in Antarctic politics grows, Australia needs to ensure it is adequately resourced to continue the leadership role it has played in the region for over seven decades, especially when key norms, such as conservation, are likely to come under challenge by increasingly influential states.

One potential problem with Australia's current policy approach is that its maritime claims may become a source of contention because they are not fully recognised – and neither are its sovereignty claims to the Australian Antarctic Territory. While the map of the Australian Antarctic Territory in the 2017 *Foreign Policy White Paper* does not include Australia's exclusive economic zone or continental shelf claims, the white paper asserts Australia's sovereign rights over the offshore areas adjacent to the Australian Antarctic Territory. A document produced by Geoscience Australia in 2009 also declared that Australia's 'confirmed' marine jurisdiction (exclusive economic zone) off the Australian Antarctic Territory was over two million square kilometres. Australia's declaration of an exclusive economic zone is largely viewed as a contravention of the second clause of Article IV of the Antarctic Treaty, which prohibits states from new actions or activities that 'constitute a basis for supporting or denying territorial sovereignty claims'. Australia's continental-shelf and exclusive economic zone claims are not recognised by most of the international community and are explicitly rejected by its key regional partners, including the supposedly like-minded Quad states, the United States, Japan and India.

Australia has only sought to enforce exclusive economic zone law against Australian nationals as a way to maintain its claim without undermining the Antarctic Treaty. This has not been without its difficulties. In 2015, the Federal Court of Australia found the Japanese whaling company Kyodo had breached Australian domestic law in the Australian Whale Sanctuary, a protected area. However, Japan considers this area of the Southern Ocean as high seas, not an Australian jurisdiction. In line with Australia's efforts to designate the jurisdiction as applying to Australian nationals only, the Australian attorney-general even submitted to the court that a finding of jurisdiction in this case would potentially destabilise the Antarctic Treaty. However, in 2015 an Australian court found that Kyodo continued to kill whales in the Australian Whale Sanctuary, and a federal court fined it $1 million.

While this might be considered a conservation win for whales in the Southern Ocean, it reflects a problem with how Australia has sought to differentiate its international and domestic jurisdictions to maintain its sovereign and maritime claim. It also highlights the issue of whether 'like-minded' states actually have the same views on key norms in the Antarctic and Southern Ocean. Australia has long applied pressure to Japan about its whaling in the Southern Ocean: in 2014, the International Court of Justice ruled against Japan in a case initiated by

Australia which alleged that Japan used a scientific-research program to mask a commercial whaling venture in the Southern Ocean. Japan has since withdrawn its membership of the International Whaling Commission and now explicitly engages in commercial hunting within its own exclusive economic zone, but not in the Southern Ocean.

While these two episodes are examples of Australia's commitment to conservation leadership in the Antarctic region, Australia has largely adopted a 'normative hedging' strategy to Antarctic continental-shelf claims as well as the exclusive economic zone.[57] In some marine areas in the Southern Ocean, Australia's jurisdiction is uncontested, including its exclusive economic zone around Heard Island and McDonald Islands and Macquarie Island (part of Tasmania). After the Russian fishing vessel *Volga* was apprehended by the Royal Australian Navy for illegally fishing in Australia's exclusive economic zone adjacent to Heard Island and McDonald Islands in 2002, an international legal judgement found the islands were entitled to generating an exclusive economic zone. Concerns have been raised, though, about whether Heard Island and McDonald Islands meet the definition of an island under UNCLOS, especially following the 2016 South China Sea arbitration. Such a classification is necessary for the legitimacy of the exclusive economic zone.

The absence of recognition of territorial and maritime boundaries in the Southern Ocean region raises uncertainties about who is responsible for determining what activities are 'illegal' and which states are responsible for deterring and prosecuting such crimes. In such a maritime 'grey zone', claimant states such as Australia perform and narrate their sovereignty and maritime claims to international audiences in a variety of ways. But a central problem arises: do Australia's jurisdictional claims – viewed as excessive by its key allies and partners – undermine the maritime rules-based order that Canberra seeks to defend in the Southern Ocean? The tendency towards seizing sovereignty puts at risk the Antarctic and Southern Ocean region as a global space of cooperation.

WHAT SHOULD AUSTRALIA DO DIFFERENTLY?

The Southern Ocean highlights the integrated nature of contemporary security challenges and the need for genuine whole-of-government planning of oceans management and maritime security. Ultimately, Australia's Antarctic budget needs to reflect its aspirations in Antarctica, because 'we won't have an Antarctic strategy unless we commit the resources.'[58]

Australia should increase its leadership and presence in the Antarctic region. Failure to do so will enable rising maritime powers to increase their footprint and influence. Not only that, but the government also needs to explain the importance of the Antarctic region to the Australian public, as it will never be adequately resourced if citizens do not realise what is at stake, including how Australia's environmental stewardship and Antarctic diplomacy contribute more broadly to its international relationships and image projection. In one sense, maritime domain awareness is more than understanding what's going on in the seas: it is also lifting awareness among Australians about its Southern Ocean claims and interests.

Australia has been a key architect of the Antarctic Treaty System and a diplomatic leader in the governance of the Southern Ocean and Antarctic region. The Antarctic Treaty System has underpinned the stability of Australia's territorial and maritime interests, but its success has also meant the government has tended to neglect the region. Emerging challenges mean Australia should seek to grow its presence in Antarctica and the Southern Ocean, re-engage with its historical leadership role in the diplomatic and legal dimensions of managing the region and develop a greater domestic sense of Australia as a custodian of the Southern Ocean. Australia's strategic orientation towards the Indo-Pacific has narrowed both its geographic focus and how it conceives of itself as a middle power in a global context. Reacquainting itself with the core traditions of middle-power diplomacy would be a good place to start in reimagining Antarctic and Southern Ocean policy.

The Southern Ocean highlights larger issues at the heart of Australia's strategic imagination: What values does Australia advocate on the international stage? How does it conceive its international role and what national image does it seek to project? Is it a middle power with a role in advancing global norms and cooperating on common interests? Or is it a 'sub-imperial' power that is too narrowly focused on supporting its own interests, which it interprets though the dominant frames of the US alliance and threats posed by China? An emphasis on the latter would likely be problematic given the fact that Australia and the United States have conflicting views on territorial and maritime claims in the Antarctic region.

Australia's presence in, and leadership of, Antarctica is crucial for maintaining and advancing its maritime claims in the Southern Ocean. One radical option is for Australia to drop its 42 per cent stake to Antarctica and commit fully to cooperative governance, but that is both unlikely and undesirable, particularly given the prospect of which claimants might fill the vacuum it would create. If Australia were to fail to maintain its territorial claim, it would also lose over two million square kilometres of exclusive economic zone and continental shelf it currently (although ambiguously) claims.

Australia's maritime security in the Southern Ocean cannot be divorced from the strategic manoeuvring occurring on the continent. Some see Australia's existing approach as problematically prioritising the Antarctic Treaty System over the Australian Antarctic Territory. But the Antarctic Treaty System has enabled Australia to maintain its Australian Antarctic Territory claim without needing to defend it. Australia should recommit to the Antarctic Treaty and seek to persuade other states to do the same.[59]

There are emerging geopolitical challenges that Australia cannot afford to overlook, but there are also risks in advancing Australia's military interests in the Southern Ocean, particularly if this could undermine the Antarctic Treaty's non-militarisation principles that have served Australia's interests so well. Australia does not need warfighting capabilities in the Southern Ocean, but it does need presence, leadership and coordination to protect and conserve the marine environment and ensure maritime safety through search-and-rescue operations. Defence has a role to play in supporting whole-of-government approaches to civil maritime security, including through surveillance and maritime domain awareness. Australia should invest in new maritime patrol resources, especially if such resources could be used to strengthen monitoring and transparency. This approach should be less about provoking strategic competition through 'gunboat diplomacy' and more about recognising that coastguard ships may be less provocative than warships in enabling states to advance maritime security interests.[60] Australia could contribute further to shaming states and non-state actors that are not doing the right thing in the Southern Ocean according to the norms set out in the Antarctic Treaty System.

At the same time, Australia should avoid letting strategic competition hinder all forms of cooperation in the Southern Ocean. Rather than seeing the Antarctic as an area of exploitable resources that require the assertion and defence of conventional property rights, Australia should lean into a greater sense of guardianship of the region, building different frames for understanding the relationship between states and their maritime environments. More investment in scientific-research initiatives, the Australian Antarctic Division and patrolling resources is necessary to support the renewal of its Antarctic leadership.[61] Conducting research in areas of mutual interest with Russia and China, such as climate change, may offset risks of grey zone activity through knowledge-sharing and by holding these states more accountable, at least in the court of public opinion.[62]

Australia also needs much more investment in promoting inclusive approaches to regional diplomacy to combat traditional and nontraditional security challenges and ensuring it has the sovereign capacities to acquit its responsibilities. While Australia has been leading 'fishing diplomacy' through the creation of marine protected areas, it may need to counter narratives from sceptical states that these areas are more about extending Australia's sovereignty and control than about conservation. An emphasis on diplomacy, including public diplomacy, should continue to centre Australia's leading role in the custodianship of the maritime environment rather than a focus on 'colonial' ambitions to defend its territorial stake.

An Australian Senate report in 2014 sagely recommended that Australia include the Southern Ocean in its multilateral and bilateral diplomatic discussions with other states, especially its Asian neighbours, as well as seek new agreements with partners to cooperate in patrol and deterrence activities.[63] There are Asian states active in Antarctica: Japan and the Soviet Union were two of the twelve original signatories to the Antarctic Treaty, followed by China and India in 1983 and South Korea in 1986. Malaysia, once a critic, acceded to the treaty in 2011, as did North Korea in 1987 and Pakistan in 2012. Russia, India, China, South Korea and Japan have multiple seasonal or year-round bases in the Antarctic region. Cooperating more with Asian partners in the Southern Ocean and incorporating the Southern Ocean into regional diplomacy efforts could reaffirm Australia's historical role as an Antarctic leader and norm-setter.

A central challenge for maritime order in the Antarctic region is that the maritime domain is itself essentially a legal 'grey zone' in which maritime claims cannot be fully recognised or denied. The UNCLOS-zoning regime struggles to establish maritime order in the context of dominant Antarctic Treaty System governing instruments. The Antarctic region also provides another example of the issues involved in applying fixed notions of Westphalian territorial sovereignty to determining maritime zones, particularly as climate change is altering, and will continue to alter, land through sea-level rise. The Kyodo case demonstrated the unintended consequences of ambiguous claims to maritime area, which may arise again if Australia continues to 'normatively hedge'. While the Antarctic Treaty System sought to accommodate the interests of both claimant and non-claimant states by setting aside the resolution of sovereign claims, claimant states have simultaneously pursued their sovereignty interests and committed to global governance arrangements and cooperative endeavours.[64] The pervasive myth that territorial claim-making has been 'frozen' under the Antarctic Treaty does not grapple with growing strategic competition in the region. Confronting this issue with claimant and non-claimant states may become necessary to create a more stable situation in the maritime zoning in the waters adjacent to the continent.

A common policy recommendation is that Australia should do more with like-minded states such as Japan, the United States and India in the Southern Ocean, and it could indeed do more to engage collaboratively on new infrastructure with Antarctic Treaty partners, including the year-round air access that the Davis aerodrome project was supposed to provide.[65] But these states have different interests and interpretations of the law of the sea as it applies to the Antarctic maritime region. The Antarctic Treaty itself was negotiated because the United States (and the Soviet Union) was unwilling to abandon its right to make Antarctic claims. In the unlikely event that Australia faced conflict over its territorial or maritime claims in Antarctica, it is unclear whether Canberra could rely on US support, given that the two states do not necessarily share interests in the region and it is geographically distant from the United States. As technological advancements allow for greater colonisation and exploitation of Antarctic resources, and as energy insecurity increases and resources become scarcer as a result of climate change, conflict over who owns what in the Antarctic region may come to a head. It is imperative that Australia works collaboratively with regional states on these issues without relying solely on the US alliance to ensure its interests. The French arrangement of taking the lead on cooperative maritime patrols is often cited as a model for international coordination in patrol and deterrence in the Southern Ocean.[66] The lesson here is that Australian leaders should be more aware of, and sensitive to, the existing relationship patterns that contribute to Australia's security across the maritime domains adjacent to its territory.

CONCLUSION

We embarked on writing this book because it is important to think through the assumptions and arguments that dominate Australian national security debates. In doing so, we have identified new possibilities and perspectives, and some potentially challenging ideas, to enrich existing debates. This doesn't involve imagining away very real challenges or realities, but it does mean resisting – or at least questioning – the approaches to security that narrow future options and potentially lead Australian closer to conflict.

We have focused our analysis on the maritime domain, viewing Australia's regional and maritime security as intertwined. We have traced the ways in which traditional and non-traditional security challenges are diverse, interlinked and complex, particularly in crucial maritime domains. We have argued that an integrated approach to statecraft, combining and maximising diplomatic, economic and military instruments, is required to meet these complex challenges.

We have analysed examples of how Australia has demonstrated its global leadership credentials – for instance, by establishing and abiding by international norms, institutions and laws in areas such as the Southern Ocean – and we have identified areas where the government should make more ambitious and tangible improvements, such as to its climate policy, if it is to maintain its status as a regional leader.

While we were encouraged by the 2023 *Defence Strategic Review* advocating a 'whole-of-government and whole-of-nation' approach to Australia's security,[1] we remain concerned that the Albanese Labor government has continued the approach of its Coalition predecessors since taking office in May 2022 and has prioritised a *defence-led* approach to Australia's security. As we argue in this book's introduction, the *Defence Strategic Review* should have been part of an integrated national security strategy that was able to survey the full range of security challenges Australia is currently facing and will face in future. That strategy could then have identified all of the tools of statecraft that Australia needs to address them. As a member of the PIF, Australia committed itself under the 2018 Boe Declaration to developing a national security strategy. It has assisted several of its fellow members to develop theirs, but is yet to show signs of developing its own.

We are also wary of how central Australia's alliance with the United States is to its defence planning, although it is not surprising. After decades of defence procurement and efforts to cultivate interoperability and, more recently, 'interchangeability', Australia has become deeply enmeshed in the US defence establishment. In 1988, international relations scholar Coral Bell famously described Australia as the United States' 'dependent ally'. Nearly four decades later, Australia seems inclined to continue this dependence and indeed to encourage it through the capability to be acquired under the *Defence Strategic Review*. It seems Australia's search for security through its relations with 'great and powerful friends' is hardwired.

Australia's alliance with the United States extends well beyond a traditional alliance against military threats.[2] It is now a far deeper alignment that stretches into the political, economic and cultural spheres and comes with both political and psychological implications.[3] This alignment may be the best way to secure Australia's future: many in the national security community argue that the nature of Australia's strategic environment makes the alliance inevitable. But there is insufficient acknowledgement of how the habits of cooperation developed between Australians and Americans over the lifetime of the alliance influence

Australian national security thinkers. Neuroscience tells us that habits can make our lives easier and more efficient: they allow us to act without thinking. While we are not making a judgement about whether the US alliance is a good or bad habit, we think it's important to notice that habits can stop us from thinking about what we are doing and may thus prevent us from questioning what we are doing and recognising other possible actions.[4]

And the alliance would be an expensive habit to break: estimates suggest Australia would have to boost its defence spending by at least 4 per cent of its GDP annually – more than the cost of nuclear-powered submarines spread over three decades – to become fully self-reliant in its defence.[5] (Although such estimates are calculated on the assumption that Australia would continue and not recalibrate its current strategic policy.)

Whichever way you look at it, the US alliance is a highly consequential habit that needs to be examined regularly. There needs to be more consideration of how Australia can allow itself the most expansive range of strategic options possible and maintain the latitude it has had in the past to independently pursue its own interests. And the examination of that habit needs to be conducted via public and political debate, with greater transparency around decision-making processes. Beyond anodyne assurances that the Australia–US alliance and Australia's development of nuclear-powered submarines under AUKUS respect and are vital to 'securing Australia's sovereignty',[6] the Australian public is entitled to well-developed answers to basic questions such as: To what extent are Australia's interests and activities now inextricably enmeshed with the United States? How will Australia's strategic options be constrained if conflict arises in East Asia and the United States expects Australian support? Given that the *Defence Strategic Review* admits the United States is no longer a unipolar power in Australia's region, what risks are there for Australia if it is perceived to be creating, or feeding into, self-fulfilling prophecies regarding the likelihood of a conflict between the United States and China? How will Australia respond to a more unstable and unpredictable United States, if Donald Trump – or someone of his ilk – is president?

And the unanswered multibillion-dollar question is: how will nuclear-powered submarines, specifically, secure and defend Australia's people, territory and infrastructure? While the 2023 Lowy Institute Poll showed that 67 per cent of Australians are either strongly or somewhat in favour of the plan to acquire the submarines, the number of those who strongly support the plan dropped seven points to 26 per cent following the announcement of the $368-billion price tag. Put another way, a majority of those polled were in the ambivalent 'somewhat in favour, somewhat against' camp.[7] Nearly half say the additional capability provided by nuclear-powered submarines is not worth the cost.

Australia's ingrained dependence on its powerful friends is highlighted by the AUKUS security partnership with the United States and the United Kingdom that will ostensibly provide Australia with these submarines. During a February 2023 speech, Albanese argued that 'AUKUS is about much more than nuclear submarines, or even technological interoperability. AUKUS is about the future. It further formalises the common values and the shared interest that our three nations have in preserving peace and upholding the rules and institutions that secure our region and our world'.[8]

Albanese's reference to the importance of the 'common values' underpinning the AUKUS partnership was revealing, as it highlighted that one of the reasons Australia continues to look to its old allies for support: a sense of their having a shared worldview. This sense often causes Australia to look for security over the seas and beyond the states that surround it to the distant horizons of Europe and North America.

It was never wise for Australia to overlook its region and, as strategic competition intensifies, it is now unsustainable. Reversing this habit will require Australia to reimagine how it understands and engages with its near region. To do so, we argue that Australia needs to conceptualise its security beyond the settler-colonial state, recognising that it is a multicultural nation with a strong Indigenous history and a future that needs to be focused on its neighbourhood. To do this, it needs to cultivate greater awareness of how structural and historical factors – including its status as a coloniser – have contributed to the socioeconomic and security challenges facing communities both at home and in its region. And more could be done to listen to indigenous voices, both within and beyond Australia. This would require Australia to be empathetically aware that its security might not neatly align with the interests of others, that it doesn't always have the answers and that it may have things to learn from its neighbours.

In Southeast Asia, there is fertile ground for Australia to cooperate with states such as Indonesia, the Philippines and Vietnam, particularly to improve their maritime domain awareness and law-enforcement capabilities. In doing so, Australia needs to be careful it is seen by Southeast Asian states as a partner rather than a potential source of instability. It also needs to push past the idea that the only reason it should assist Southeast Asian states with their maritime security is because if it doesn't China will. These narratives of great power competition do not play well in Southeast Asia or the Pacific.

Australia also needs to be clear-eyed about its rhetorical commitment to the rules-based order. This is essentially code for a desire to return to an era of US primacy in our region (and beyond it). Australia needs to seriously consider how many of our Indo-Pacific neighbours would be willing to go to the wall to preserve a rules-based order based on US primacy. Yes, US primacy in Asia facilitated an era of stability and economic growth, which many states have appreciated. But how confident can Australia be that many of our Southeast Asian and Pacific neighbours will choose 'our' side in the event of any conflict between the United States and China? We are reminded of the gung-ho World War I officer who confidently went over the top of his trench, wrongly assuming his troops were behind him, and was consequently shot to pieces. We shouldn't be too confident about our support in Southeast Asia and the Pacific – and even in Northeast Asia. Much has been made by Australian national security analysts of the recent warming of the relationship between Japan and Korea, but they don't account for the fact that South Korean president Yoon Suk Yeol is a political outsider and the apparent rapprochement may not outlast his term. This example also highlights the risk of confirmation bias when analysing Australia's security – uncritically latching onto information or events that support commonly held beliefs.

We have advocated for an expanded concept of national security that encompasses securing the economic livelihoods and safety of coastal communities under threat from climate change. Australia and many of its immediate neighbours across the Indian and Pacific oceans and in Southeast Asia face similar challenges from climate change and the over-exploitation of maritime resources. A lack of capacity in such areas as maritime domain surveillance and intelligence across vast oceanic distances underscores just how important maritime security cooperation is with regional states.

We also argue that the *Defence Strategic Review*'s emphasis on deterrence is sound but needs to be accompanied by reassurances about its intentions. This is where diplomacy will be just as important in shoring up Australia's regional relationships and security interests. Canberra cannot assume that other states across Asia and the Pacific will accept that its policies of deterrence are designed to contribute to 'global security and stability'.[9] Indeed, Australia's neighbours may interpret its efforts at deterrence as militarisation, which destabilises, rather than contributes to, regional security. In Southeast Asia, Indonesian and Malaysian officials were vocal about their concerns that AUKUS was precipitating a regional arms race and undermining the global nuclear non-proliferation regime. In the South Pacific, leaders expressed their dismay that Australia had planned to develop nuclear-powered submarines without consulting them, given that the region is proudly nuclear-free under the 1986 Treaty of Rarotonga (to which Australia is a party). While Australian leaders and officials were quick to point out that developing the submarines won't technically infringe on the Treaty of Rarotonga or the 1968 Nuclear Non-Proliferation

Treaty, the perception that their development is against the spirit of both was enough. The perception that the submarines are overkill was also important, raising questions about why Australia thinks it needs such a capability.

The diplomatic fallout from the AUKUS announcement illustrates how much diplomacy and soft power matter. Since taking office in 2022, the Albanese Labor government has done a lot to invest in both. As Defence Minister Richard Marles remarked in a speech on 9 February 2023: 'We should never forget that Australia's frontline is diplomacy. Our primary effort it to use our diplomacy to reduce tensions and create pathways to peace.'[10] Marles also recognised that 'Australia's partnerships provide a critical advantage in advancing our national interests', as by 'pooling resources and combining strengths, we can shape our future, reduce our vulnerability to coercion and help deter conflict'.

This is a reminder that military deterrence is not enough to guarantee Australia's security. Military deterrence can trigger an arms race if potential adversaries feel threatened by one another's deterrence efforts. And many intractable issues can't be solved by threatening military retaliation. Instead, their root structural and historical causes must be reckoned with. Nor does the threat of military retaliation necessarily deter all potential adversaries. In some circumstances, such threats may in fact aid an adversary's cause if they help rally domestic support or are perceived to be disproportionate and thus attract international condemnation. This again highlights the importance of broadening our imagination when considering the range of statecraft tools Australia can use to pursue its foreign and strategic policy and rethinking how Australia understands itself and acts on the global stage.

AN AUSTRALIAN MARITIME SECURITY STRATEGY?

Both the AUKUS partnership and the 2023 *Defence Strategic Review* indicate that Australia is no longer 'seablind': the priorities outlined by the

Defence Strategic Review suggest that Australia is seeking to both deter and prepare for conflicts in maritime, air and littoral domains, reflecting its strategic geography and that of the broader Indo-Pacific region. The *Defence Strategic Review* also de-emphasises the land forces so integral to operations in Afghanistan and Iraq, suggesting that Australia can no longer afford – if it ever could – to become bogged down in faraway wars. Therefore, the *Defence Strategic Review* makes clear, the maritime matters to Australia. Its privileging of the maritime, air and archipelagic geography of Australia's near neighbourhood is consistent with the broader shift in Australia's regional outlook over the past decade. It rightly argues that the Navy should be 'optimised' for operations in Australia's immediate region and for securing crucial sea lines of communication.

But despite this emphasis on the maritime in Australia's defence planning, Australia lacks a comprehensive, holistic and whole-of-government approach to complex maritime security challenges. According to the *Defence Strategic Review*, the rise of major-power competition in the Indo-Pacific means the Royal Australian Navy will need to have a greater focus on conventional security challenges and change the way it operates within broader maritime security operations. This raises new questions about what the Navy's role is, or should be, alongside other maritime security stakeholders such as the Australian Border Force and Australian Federal Police. Unconventional and complex maritime security challenges are only likely to increase across Australia's maritime jurisdictions, putting more pressure on its maritime security governance arrangements.

As we've shown, the maritime domain illustrates the fragmented nature of Australia's security strategy more generally. In maritime security alone, Australia has over twenty relevant agencies and national security interests, spanning multiple seas and oceans.[11] Australia's civil maritime security strategy released in April 2022 deliberately excluded military operations by Defence and was instead designed to advance and protect 'Australia's interests by actively managing nonmilitary risk to Australia and Australia's maritime Domain'. But as we argue in our introduction, it doesn't make sense for Australia to maintain a separate approach to maritime security. While not necessarily new, so-called grey zone tactics are effective precisely because conventional, military-led approaches struggle to defend state interests against them. The *Defence Strategic Review* is right: Australia needs a joined-up strategy, including for securing its vast maritime domain, which is likely to be exposed to more maritime security challenges as the seas around it become increasingly contested.

Asia's more demanding geopolitical environment has compelled states in the region to rethink their approaches to maritime security, and the world's oceans and seas have increasingly become a site of geo-strategic competition. The 1998 Oceans Policy was an effort to develop a more comprehensive approach to these issues, but it failed because of political will. The changing nature of Australia's security environment means revisiting such a proposal makes strategic sense.

As we've demonstrated, conventional maritime security issues intersect with unconventional challenges across the maritime domains which are crucial to Australian interests in different ways. Considering Australia is a maritime nation, the Royal Australian Navy remains 'overlooked and under-resourced'.[12] The Navy's fleet of eleven to twelve major surface combatant ships, for instance, is insufficient for the swiftly changing regional maritime environment. Even in less contested times, fleet structure reviews advocated for the fleet to be increased to sixteen to twenty warships.[13] However, increasing Australia's defence capabilities is just one aspect of conceptualising Australia's security. For a start, maritime strategy should be driving Australia's investment in maritime capabilities. The AUKUS partnership, which prioritises the development of nuclear-powered submarines, is an example of the opposite: capability-led strategy. Additionally, Australia should adopt a whole-of-government approach that clearly defines maritime security. Such an approach should explain how the various arms of government – the Australian Defence Force, the Department of Foreign Affairs and Trade, constabulary, the various maritime agencies – will work together to defend Australia's vast maritime national security interests. Through this process, Australia may even reconsider its business-as-usual approach to maritime security governance, given the nature of contemporary challenges. It could reassess the debates about what benefits an Australian coastguard might offer, for instance. There's not enough solid evidence about the costs and limitations of a coastguard to recommend it, but this is an area for further research and discussion.

Given Australia's reliance on maritime trade and the changing nature of threat in and from its maritime security environment, ensuring robust supply chains is important for its economy and defence. In times of crisis, where critical supply chains may be disrupted, Australia must also be able to access its maritime assets. Australia's non-naval and peacetime maritime interests – especially in shipping – require investment, as the COVID-19 pandemic demonstrated. Australian shipping relies heavily on foreign-flagged ships. The Australian-flagged fleet consists of just fifteen vessels, and less than 1 per cent of Australia's trade is carried by Australian ships. As part of the Albanese Labor government's renewed focus on sovereign resilience, in October 2022 it established a Maritime Strategic Fleet Taskforce to consider how a fleet of up to twelve Australian-flagged and Australian-crewed ships could be established. While the shipping industry criticised the plan, a sovereign fleet of foreign vessels could support strategic interests in times of conflict – as occurred during World War II – or in other crises (natural or humanitarian disasters, for instance). However, a sustainable pool of Australian-flagged vessels would require more than the twelve vessels originally envisioned, and crewing these vessels would be a real challenge. Ultimately, the government needs to be clearer about what it wants this fleet to do. Developing a holistic national security strategy could allow the government to consider the kinds of roles that a strategic fleet could play across a range of humanitarian, environmental and conflict scenarios.

The kinds of trade Australia depends upon also matters. Not all goods traded are of equal strategic value. Fuel is critical. Australia's energy policy settings have made securing sea lines of communication a matter that has direct consequences for Australia's sovereign resilience and defence capabilities. The first issue is that Australia relies heavily on imported refined fuel – around 90 per cent comes from overseas and nearly 50 per cent of its refined petroleum from Japan and South Korea alone. Such supplies are vital domestically and for the economy, but also for providing the aviation fuel the Australian Defence Force needs for operations, particularly in a conflict scenario. Australia needs oil supply lines to be open from the Middle East and Southeast Asia to North Asia, as the refined oil transits back south through northern choke points. If those routes were to become blocked or unsafe, it could affect the Australian Defence Force's ability to defend Australia.[14]

This is linked to a second issue, that of Australia's dwindling refining capacity. During the pandemic, Australia lost oil refineries because they could not economically compete with Asian 'mega-refineries'. Just two were left behind, and they have been encouraged to stay open until 2030 with a 'Hail Mary' package of $2.3 billion.[15]

A third problem is that Australia's domestic fuel stockpile is low: it has around fifty-eight days of emergency fuel, less than two-thirds of the International Energy Agency's requirement of ninety days' worth. If vital trade routes were cut off, Australia's energy security would be vulnerable; its only other oil stockpile is in the United States. The Albanese Labor government has said it would look at Australia's onshore fuel storage, but Australia has been non-compliant with International Energy Agency's requirements for over a decade.

Finally, Australia's economy (and defence) continues to rely heavily on fossil fuels rather than renewable sources of energy. Defence Minister Marles rightly highlights the importance of the maritime 'rules of the road' to Australia's interests. In the short term, solving this problem will require boosting domestic stockpiles and cooperating with other states to ensure that sea lines of communication remain open. Over the longer term, Australia's sovereignty is inextricably bound with its energy security, and replacing imported fuel with more renewable energy sources should therefore be viewed as a strategic imperative.

REIMAGINING AUSTRALIA'S
SECURITY POLICY

While we are encouraged by the Albanese government's moves in the right direction on matters of Australia's security, particularly in the maritime domain, we want to end this book by reflecting on the questions we asked ourselves to guide our reimagining of Australia's security.

First, we asked what it would look like if Australia's strategic and foreign policy were to move beyond a siloed approach towards a holistic approach that coordinates and integrates all arms of statecraft to grapple with the complexity of interrelated security threats. The answer is: we don't know – our analysis of Australia's six key maritime domains has demonstrated that such a holistic approach does not yet exist in any substantive way. The closest it has come is in the South Pacific, where the government created a cross-agency Office of the Pacific in 2019 to improve coordination of Australia's Pacific 'step-up' policy and its delivery. While the Office of the Pacific has not been formally reviewed yet, according to anecdotal indications it initially struggled to herd the wide range of government agencies active in the region but is well-led and now hitting its stride.

Second, we asked how a more nuanced – and contingent – understanding of the range of security opportunities and threats that Australia faces could reshape its strategic and foreign policymaking. As we have shown, such an understanding would recognise that defence, diplomacy and development need to be deeply interrelated, because the threats they seek to address and opportunities they want to harness are themselves deeply intertwined. It is, for instance, impossible to discuss Australia's defence planning requirements in the South Pacific, north seas or Southern Ocean without grappling with the challenges of climate change. Similarly, it is nonsensical to discuss military contingencies without acknowledging how they are influenced by development in Southeast Asia, the South Pacific or the Indian Ocean.

Third, we asked how Australia could be a regional partner that is confident in its strengths, and ambitious on foreign and strategic policy, but humble about its limitations. As we have shown, this is something that Australia has struggled to do, although there are signs this may be changing, particularly in the South Pacific, where Australian leaders have deliberately changed their language to reflect a humbler approach (although this change has not necessarily filtered out to all Australian actors). There is still a lot of scope for Australia to learn from its neighbours and from its own people. For instance, there is much Australia can learn from Torres Strait Islanders about protecting and conserving the north seas.

Fourth, we asked how Australia could be a determined regional player that pursues its national interests while also being empathetic when its interests don't neatly align with those of others. We were particularly interested in whether Australia could accept that its neighbours and regional partners do not necessarily share its threat perceptions, nor its view of the best ways to achieve security. As we have discussed, this is another challenge Australia has struggled with, particularly in the South Pacific, where China's increasingly visible presence has generated significant anxiety. Australia has legitimate strategic interests in the South Pacific that justify this anxiety, but at times its emphasis on these concerns has been counterproductive because it has generated securitised and militarised responses that have heightened Pacific Island countries' sense of insecurity.

Fifth, we asked whether Australia can rethink its understanding of current geopolitical fluctuations in competitive terms to instead identify opportunities for greater cooperation and look for multilateral responses to shared challenges, drawing the largest possible number of partners into cooperative initiatives. The government has sought to deepen Australia's cooperative engagements over the last decade, and the pace of those efforts continues to increase. But there is one state with which, on current Australian strategic understandings, cooperation now seems impossible: China. This isn't all Australia's fault – China has changed its behaviour under the leadership of Xi Jinping, and its diplomatic style, which is assertive at times, hasn't necessarily made cooperation an attractive option. While we welcome the Albanese government's efforts to reset Australia's relationship with China, and see China's release of detained Australian journalist Cheng Lei in October 2023 as a positive sign that relations are thawing, we are concerned that a certain fatalism has seeped into the Australian national security community when it comes to China. The problem with the growing tendency to frame China as Australia's 'enemy' is that it closes off opportunities to think differently and, perhaps, identify areas in which cooperation might still be possible. If anything, Cheng's release points to how diplomacy can achieve tangible human rights outcomes. We are of the view that Australia should always seek to diffuse competition with cooperation – even if it doesn't work, it is surely better to try, especially as some challenges, such as climate change, require cooperative responses.

Sixth, we asked how a more relational and situational understanding of the way states and actors interact could change Australia's understanding of its security. As we have discussed, there is a tendency within Australian national security debates to understand the Indo-Pacific order as a hierarchy, assuming that the most militarily powerful states, the United States and China, can shape the regional order. But this interpretation is based on a short-term and transactional understanding of how states relate to one another. Understanding states' relationships over the long-term, during which relative power ebbs and flows, means that, instead of viewing every 'win' or 'loss' through a narrow transactional lens, Australia could recognise that building and maintaining good relationships takes time and involves compromise.

Seventh, one of Australia's key dilemmas centres on values, particularly around how to advance human rights globally. The 'principle versus pragmatism' framing that is common in Australian foreign policy debates is often unhelpful, and particularly tricky to manage in Asia and the Pacific, where most states are neither liberal nor democratic. For instance, the shared democratic values of Quad members tend to be overstated, and consequently the real differences in their values and interests can be overlooked. The organising principle of Australia's Indo-Pacific engagement should not be to rally democracies around a set of values, because many neighbouring states do not share these values and elites in the region do not buy into these narratives.

The human-rights rhetoric of Australia's national security community is also too often instrumentalised by China critics, who use it to develop a dominant threat narrative around China. These same critics are often willing to ignore rights violations or troubling legal developments in other states (particularly India and Indonesia) if they hope those states will help to constrain China's rise.

We are not arguing that Australia should downplay its values or turn a blind eye to human-rights violations. But Australia needs to be more self-aware about its own democratic and human-rights record. For instance, since the war on terror there has been a creeping tendency to seek to limit civil liberties and freedoms using national security justifications. Australia has also used national security justifications to avoid its obligations under the 1961 Refugee Convention, including through processing and seeking to resettle refugees in the South Pacific. Australia needs to recognise that its own failings – and those of its allies and partners – open it up to accusations of hypocrisy and hectoring, and undermine the rules-based order on which its foreign and strategic policy is based.

And there are other ways Australia can promote human rights beyond 'megaphone diplomacy'. First, Australia can engage more fully with international and civil-society groups that are invested in promoting human rights and civil liberties, often on the ground, in affected communities. Second, academics, think tanks and experts should feel free to take critical stances on human-rights abuses wherever they occur, even if this means unsettling a bilateral relationship. Third, Australia can use multilateral forums to promote a global human rights agenda and ensure that it consistently complies with international human-rights law. Fourth, politicians and national security advocates should avoid using human-rights discourse only in the context of geo-politics – universal principles should be applied universally.

Guided by the questions we asked ourselves, we have argued that Australia should reimagine its understanding of itself as a regional actor and consequently develop a coherent national security strategy, working with old and new allies and partners to shape the regional order in ways that ensure Australia's security. To achieve this, Australia needs an updated national security strategy, accompanied by a dedicated maritime security strategy, that seeks to address the full range of security challenges and opportunities faced by Australia and deploys the full range of tools required to address them.

We encourage the Australian government to expand its imagination and ambitions, and to be cautious about the roadblocks that lie ahead. For instance, while we welcome the government's commitment to implementing a First Nations foreign policy, we share the caution expressed by First Nations scholars such as James Blackwell that First Nations people are 'too often treated as subjects, not participants' in these processes.[16] As Blackwell observes, 'The point of First Nations foreign policy is to change the way we think about the national interest, the nation's relationships and responsibilities, and even the way we think about our country.'[17] But how such a rethink will be reconciled with other aspects of Australian policy, such as defence, remains unclear.

This highlights the perennial challenge for Australian security policy: the institutional and ideological gap between the Department of Defence and the Department of Foreign Affairs and Trade. Both will need to work together in much deeper and more integrated ways to address the complex, multifaceted and interrelated security challenges that Australia faces. The difficulties of integrating the development practitioners of AusAID into the Department of Foreign Affairs and Trade suggests the task will not be an easy one.

The Australian national security community does not often reflect enough on the assumptions that guide its securitisation of perceived threats or the subjective nature of its debates, which are influenced by the assumptions and interpretations of security actors, their backgrounds, institutional locations and interests. We are members of that community and have inevitably brought our own assumptions to this book. Importantly, unlike many in that community, we are academics first and foremost. This means one of our core beliefs is that all assumptions and interpretations are contingent and must be challenged by questions about whose ends they serve and what they seek to erase. We have tried to challenge ourselves in this way while writing our book.

We acknowledge that calls for change – in our case, to reimagine Australia's security – can be easily dismissed as impractical, idealistic and naive. We are comfortable with this, because Australia's security is too important to be allowed to rely on unchallenged assumptions or sentimental attachments to old orders. This book is our attempt to challenge that reliance. We hope it is the first of many.

ACKNOWLEDGEMENTS

This book had its genesis in March 2020, when a group of academics and think-tank analysts were invited to Russell Offices, the home of Australia's Department of Defence, for a day-long discussion of Australia's future strategic options. When one of the speakers was asked who represented Australia's ideal 'strategic personality', his response was 'Crocodile Dundee – confident and with a big knife'.

To be fair to the speaker, he was thinking on his feet. But the idea that Australia's way of viewing, interpreting and behaving in the world should be exemplified by a boorish hard drinker who solves problems with a knife sat uncomfortably with us. It seemed to reflect a stereotype of Australians that was unflattering when the film came out in 1986 and was even less desirable and accurate today.

So, before Joanne got up to present in the next session, some of the women participants decided to propose an alternative strategic personality: the Ngaragu woman, champion tennis player and National Indigenous Tennis Ambassador Ashleigh Barty.

The conversation we started that day led to an op-ed in *The Interpreter* about what an Australian strategic personality modelled on Barty would look like, and, ultimately, to this book.

This book has also been the product of many discussions we have had with other academics, think-tankers and practitioners over our careers. We are both fortunate to have many wonderful colleagues within Australia's international relations academic community. We especially thank our friends and colleagues who provided us advice and feedback on the book, including Troy Lee-Brown, Elizabeth Buchanan, Peter Dean and Brendan Taylor.

Having time to write has also been important, and Joanne is grateful to the Australian Research Council and the Department of Defence, as their funding for other projects has enabled and enriched her research. The University of Adelaide also provided funding for research assistance from Adela Alfonsi, Jack Butcher and Corey O'Dwyer.

Bec is grateful to the Department of Foreign Affairs and Trade for funding that has facilitated important maritime research and exchanges across the region. Bec would especially like to thank past and present La Trobe Asia staff – Kate Clayton, Matt Smith, Rei Fortes and Diana Heatherich – and colleagues in the School of Humanities and Social Sciences for all their support along the way. Kate, in particular, provided research assistance for this book.

We have enjoyed working with the team at La Trobe University Press / Black Inc., including Chris Feik, Kate Hatch and Emeritus Professor Robert Manne, and have appreciated their wise editorial advice and steadfast support.

Most importantly, Joanne thanks her husband, Ross, and her three children, Tom, Sam and Ben, for their love and support.

Bec would like to thank her husband, Lincoln, for his unwavering patience and encouragement.

NOTES

INTRODUCTION

1   Peter Dodds McCormick, 'Advance Australia Fair', Australian national anthem, 1878.

2   'Cultural Diversity: Census', Australian Bureau of Statistics, 28 July 2022, www.abs. gov.au/statistics/people/people-and-communities/cultural-diversity-census/2021.

3   'Trade and Investment at a Glance 2021', Department of Foreign Affairs and Trade, 2021, www.dfat.gov.au/publications/trade-and-investment/ trade-and-investment-glance-2021#two-way-trade.

4   In 2021, total Australian investment in the United States was $837,359 million, in the United Kingdom it was $507,440 million and in the European Union it was $327,428 million. The next largest destination was Japan, at $139,567 million, followed by New Zealand at $130,451 million: 'Trade and Investment at a Glance 2021'.

5   Ibid. In 2021, total investment from the United States was $983,742 million, from the United Kingdom $686,115 million and from the European Union $683,868 million. The next largest source of investment was Japan, with $241,091 million.

6   Commonwealth of Australia, *National Defence: Defence Strategic Review*, Canberra: Commonwealth of Australia, 2023, pp. 32, 7.

7   Richard Marles, 'National Defence Statement 2023', Canberra: Commonwealth of Australia, 2023, p. 5.

8   Daniel Hurst and Julian Borger, 'AUKUS: Nuclear Submarines Deal Will Cost Australia up to $368bn', *The Guardian*, 14 March 2023.

9   Commonwealth of Australia, *National Defence: Defence Strategic Review*, p. 8.

10   The early reporting of AUKUS suggested that Australia would operate its new submarines in seas far from home. By contrast, the 2023 *National Defence: Defence Strategic Review* emphasises their contribution to a strategy of 'deterrence through denial' (p. 32), which essentially means the deterrence, much closer to home, of military action against its territory and population. The key problem is that the government has never clearly explained the purpose and benefits of the submarines.

11   Commonwealth of Australia, *National Defence: Defence Strategic Review*, p. 33.

12   Marles, 'National Defence Statement 2023', p. 6.

13   Department of Defence, *Defence White Paper 2013*, Canberra: Department of Defence, 2013; Department of Defence, *2016 Defence White Paper*; Department of Defence, *2020 Defence Strategic Update*, Canberra: Department of Defence, 2020; Commonwealth of Australia, *National Defence: Defence Strategic Review*, p. 9.

14   Department of Home Affairs, *Australian Government Civil Maritime Security Strategy*, Canberra: Commonwealth of Australia, 2021, p. 3.

15   Penny Wong, 'An Enduring Partnership in an Era of Change', Speech, Centre for Grand Strategy, King's College, London, 31 January 2023.

16   Jacquelin Magnay, 'Heat on Wong Over "Colonial" Speech', *The Australian*, 1 February 2023.

17   Lawrence Bamblett, 'Before Australia', in Bridget Brooklyn et al. (eds), *Australia on the World Stage: History, Politics, and International Relations*, Abingdon: Routledge, 2023.

18   Ariana B.J. Lambrides et al, 'Changing Use of Lizard Island Over the Past 4000 Years and Implications for Understanding Indigenous Offshore Island Use on the Great Barrier Reef', *Queensland Archaeological Research* 23 (2020), p. 47.

19   James Blackwell, 'First Nations and Australia: Walking Together or Walking Alone?', in Brooklyn et al. (eds), *Australia on the World Stage*.

20   Lyndall Ryan et al., 'Colonial Frontier Massacres in Australia, 1788–1930', The Centre for 21st Century Humanities, University of Newcastle, 2017, https://c21ch.newcastle.edu.au/colonialmassacres.

21   Alexis Moran, 'What You Need to Know About the Frontier Wars', *NITV*, 19 September 2022. While the Frontier Wars are now widely acknowledged, truth-telling, reconciliation and reparations have not yet occurred.

22   Department of Defence, *2016 Defence White Paper*, pp. 68–69.

23   Ibid., p. 69.

24   Richard Marles, 'Securing Australia's Sovereignty', Statement to Australian Parliament, 9 February 2023.

25   Rosie Lewis, 'Gender Equality Envoy Stephanie Copus Campbell Attacks "Offensive" Remarks', *The Australian*, 14 February 2023.

26   Valerie Hudson, Bonnie Ballif-Spanvill, Mary Caprioli and Chad F. Emmett, *Sex and World Peace*, New York: Columbia University Press, 2014.

27   See for example, Greg Sheridan, 'Worst and Strangest Speech of Penny Wong's Life', *The Australian*, 14 February 2023.

28   Barry Buzan, Jaap de Wilde and Ole Waever, *Security: A New Framework for Analysis Analysis*, Boulder: Lynne Rienner, 1998.

CHAPTER 1

1   Andrew Carr, *Winning the Peace: Australia's Campaign to Change the Asia-Pacific*, Carlton: Melbourne University Press, 2015.

2   Geoffrey Blainey, *The Tyranny of Distance: How Distance Shaped Australia's History*, Melbourne: Macmillan, 1968.

NOTES

3   Allan Gyngell, *Fear of Abandonment*, Carlton: La Trobe University Press, 2021; Robert Menzies quoted in A.W. Martin, 'Menzies, Sir Robert Gordon (Bob) (1894–1978)', *Australian Dictionary of Biography, Volume 15: 1940–1980, Kem-Pie*, Carlton South: Melbourne University Press, 2000.

4   Allan Gyngell and Michael Wesley, *Making Australian Foreign Policy*, Port Melbourne: Cambridge University Press, 2007.

5   Department of Prime Minister and Cabinet, *Strong and Secure: A Strategy for Australia's National Security*, Commonwealth of Australia, Canberra, 2012.

6   N.K. Meaney, *Australia and the World: A Documentary History from the 1870s to the 1970s*, Melbourne: Longman Cheshire, 1985, p. 2.

7   Department of Defence, *Strategic Basis of Australian Defence Policy*, Canberra: Commonwealth of Australia, 1964, in Stephan Frühling (ed.), *A History of Australian Strategic Policy Since 1945*, Canberra: Defence Publishing Service, 2009, para. 1.

8   Coral Bell, *Dependent Ally: A Study in Australian Foreign Policy*, Melbourne: Oxford University Press, 1988.

9   Department of Defence, *Strategic Basis of Australian Defence Policy* [1964], in Frühling (ed.), *A History of Australian Strategic Policy Since 1945,* para. 6.

10 Department of Defence, *Australian Defence*, Canberra: Australian Government Publishing Services, 1976, p. 5.

11 Department of Defence, *The Defence of Australia*, Canberra: Australian Government Publishing Services, 1987; Paul Dibb, *Review of Australia's Defence Capabilities: Report for the Minister of Defence*, Canberra: Commonwealth of Australia, 1986.

12 Department of Defence, *Defending Australia*, Canberra: Commonwealth of Australia, 1994.

13 Department of Defence, *Australia's Strategic Policy*, Canberra: Commonwealth of Australia, 1997, p. 9.

14 Department of Defence, *Defence 2000: Our Future Defence Force*, Canberra: Commonwealth of Australia, 2000, p. x.

15 William Tow and Henry Albinski, 'ANZUS – Alive and Well After Fifty Years', *Australian Journal of Politics and History* 48:2 (2002), pp. 153–73, 162.

16 Quoted in Iain Henry, 'Playing Second Fiddle on the Road to INTERFET: Australia's East Timor Policy Throughout 1999', *Security Challenges* 9:1 (2013), pp. 87–112, 106.

17 Michael Cohen and Andrew O'Neil, 'Doubts Down Under: American Extended Deterrence, Australia, and the 1999 East Timor Crisis', *International Relations of the Asia-Pacific* 15:1 (2015), pp. 27–52.

18 Richard A. Higgott and Kim Richard Nossal, 'The International Politics of Liminality: Relocating Australia in the Asia-Pacific', *Australian Journal of Political Science* 32:2 (2010), pp. 169–86.

19 On Asia and 'otherness' in Australian history, see for example David Walker, *Anxious Nation: Australia and the Rise of Asia, 1850–1939*, St Lucia: University of Queensland Press, 1999.

NOTES

20 David Walker, 'Sinophobia 101: Why Is Australia's History of Anxiety About the Rise of China Still Relevant?', *Asialink*, 17 May 2022.

21 Lowy Institute Poll, Lowy Institute, 29 June 2022, https://poll.lowyinstitute.org/report/2022.

22 'Polling – Australian and Taiwanese Attitudes on China', The Australia Institute, Webpage, 22 August 2022, https://australiainstitute.org.au/wp-content/uploads/2022/08/Polling-August-2022-Australian-and-Taiwanese-attitudes-on-China-Detailed-Results-Web.pdf.

23 Helen Davidson, 'China's Decade Under Xi Jinping Explained in Seven Charts', *The Guardian*, 20 October 2022.

24 Nan Tian and Fei Su, *A New Estimate of China's Military Expenditure*, Stockholm: Stockholm International Peace Research Institute, 2021.

25 Feng Zhang, 'The Xi Jinping Doctrine of China's International Relations', *Asia Policy* 14:3 (2019), pp. 7–24.

26 'Australia Faces Real Threat of High-Intensity Conflict with China, Expert Warns', News.com.au, 8 August 2022; Michael Pezzullo, 'The Longing for Peace, the Curse of War', ANZAC Day Speech, Department of Home Affairs, 25 April 2021.

27 Peter Jennings, 'Eight Reasons That China Defeatism Is Misplaced', Australian Strategic Policy Institute, 21 November 2021, www.aspi.org.au/opinion/eight-reasons-china-defeatism-misplaced.

28 Diego Lopes da Silva, Nan Tian, Lucie Beraud-Sudreau, Alexandra Marksteiner and Xiao Liang, *Trends in World Military Expenditure*, Stockholm: Stockholm International Peace Research Institute, 2021.

29 Department of Defence, *Defending Australia in the Asia-Pacific Century: Force 2030*, Canberra: Commonwealth of Australia, 2009, p. 12; Department of Defence, *Defence White Paper 2013*.

30 Department of Prime Minister and Cabinet, *Strong and Secure*, pp. 7, 30, 38.

31 Department of Defence, *Australian Defence*, p. 5.

32 Department of Defence, *Defence White Paper 2013*, p. 7.

33 Department of Defence, *2016 Defence White Paper*, p. 45; ibid.

34 Department of Defence, *2016 Defence White Paper*, p. 45; Department of Foreign Affairs and Trade, *2017 Foreign Policy White Paper*, Canberra: Commonwealth of Australia, 2017, p. 83.

35 Ibid.

36 Department of Defence, *2016 Defence White Paper*, p. 33; Department of Defence, *2020 Defence Strategic Update*.

37 Commonwealth of Australia, *National Defence: Defence Strategic Review*, p. 45.

38 Department of Defence, *2016 Defence White Paper*, p. 122.

39 Ibid.

40 'Global Arms Trade: USA Increases Dominance; Arms Flows to the Middle East Surge, says SIPRI', Stockholm International Peace Research Institute, 11 March 2019.

41   Commonwealth of Australia, *National Defence: Defence Strategic Review*, p. 23.
42   Ibid.
43   Ibid.
44   Ibid.
45   Ibid., p. 25.
46   Ibid., p. 32.
47   Penny Wong, 'Special Lecture to the International Institute for Strategic Studies: A Shared Future: Australia, ASEAN and Southeast Asia', Speech, Singapore, 6 July 2022.
48   Gabriele Abbondanza, 'Australia the "Good International Citizen"? The Limits of a Traditional Middle Power', *Australian Journal of International Affairs* 75:2 (2021), pp. 178–96.
49   Commonwealth of Australia, *National Defence: Defence Strategic Review*.
50   Andrew Brown, 'The History of the Radford-Collins Agreement', Royal Australian Navy, n.d., www.navy.gov.au/history/feature-histories/history-radford-collins-agreement.
51   Ibid.
52   Ibid.
53   Commonwealth of Australia, Communications and the Arts, *Australian Sea Freight 2020–21*, Canberra: Department of Infrastructure, Transport, Regional Development, 2023.
54   Michael Beard, 'Protecting Australia's Maritime Trade: The Need to Plan Now to Bring the Future Into the Present', *Tac Talks* 1 (2021), n.p.
55   Hillary Briffa, Ian Hall, Alessio Patalano and Rebecca Strating, *Enhancing Maritime Security in the Indo-Pacific*, Nathan: Griffith Asia Institute, 2022.
56   Peter J. Martin, 'The Strategic Implications of "Sea Blindness" in the Australian LNG Trade Dynamic', *Australian Journal of Maritime and Ocean Affairs* 11:4 (2019), pp. 218–29; Michael Evans, *The Third War: Towards an Australian Maritime Strategy for the Twenty-First Century*, Russel: Directorate of Future Land Warfare, 2014.
57   Commonwealth of Australia, *National Defence: Defence Strategic Review*, p. 56.
58   Ibid., p. 57.
59   Department of Home Affairs, *Australian Government Civil Maritime Security Strategy*.
60   Ibid., p. 3.
61   Commonwealth of Australia, *Guide to Australian Maritime Security Arrangements: GAMSA*, Canberra: Maritime Border Command Canberra, September 2020.
62   Jade Lindley, Sarah Percy and Erika Techera, 'Illegal Fishing and Australian Security', Australian Naval Institute, Webpage, 4 January 2019, https://navalinstitute.com.au/illegal-fishing-and-australian-security.
63   Malcolm Turnbull, Keynote address at the 16th IISS Asia Security Summit, 3 June 2017.

64 Geoffrey Till, *Seapower: A Guide for the Twenty-First Century*, Oxon: Routledge, 2013.

65 Joanne Vince, 'The Twenty-Year Anniversary of Australia's Oceans Policy: Achievements, Challenges and Lesson for the Future', *Australian Journal of Maritime and Ocean Affairs* 10:3 (2018), pp. 182–94.

66 Joint Standing Committee on Foreign Affairs, Defence and Trade, *Australia's Maritime Strategy*, Canberra: Parliament of the Commonwealth of Australia, 2004, pp. iii, 2.

67 Commonwealth of Australia, *2020 Force Structure Plan*, Canberra: Department of Defence, 2020.

68 US Department of Defense, *2022 National Defense Strategy of The United States of America*, Washington, D.C.: Department of Defense, 2022.

69 Ibid., p. 12.

70 Christian Bueger and Tim Edmunds, 'Beyond Seablindness: A New Agenda for Maritime Security Studies', *International Affairs* 93:6 (2017), pp. 1293–311.

CHAPTER 2

1 UN Human Rights Office of the High Commissioner, 'Australia Violated Torres Strait Islanders' Rights to Enjoy Culture and Family Life, UN Committee Finds', press release, 23 September 2022, www.ohchr.org/en/press-releases/2022/09/australia-violated-torres-strait-islanders-rights-enjoy-culture-and-family; Climate Council, 'New Report: Rising Sea Levels Threaten Torres Strait Islanders, 30 June 2021.

2 Teisha Cloos, 'Government Denies Responsibility for Climate Change in Response to Torres Strait Eight', *National Indigenous Times*, 30 September 2001.

3 Jemima Garrett, 'Torres Strait Receives $26.2 million Funding for Coastal Protection', ABC News, 26 February 2014.

4 UN Human Rights Office of the High Commissioner, 'Australia Violated Torres Strait Islanders' Rights to Enjoy Culture and Family Life'.

5 For example, one study of South-East Australia's 2019–20 bushfires found that climate change contributed to the risk of intense fire weather by 30 per cent since 1900. Geert Jan van Oldenborgh et al., 'Attribution of the Australian Bushfire Risk to Anthropogenic Climate Change', *National Hazards Earth System Science* 21 (2021), pp. 941–60.

6 Australian Academy of Science, 'How Are Sea Levels Changing?', in *The Science of Climate Change: Questions and Answers*, Canberra: Australian Academy of Science, 2015.

7 Madeline Roache, 'The Mayor Fighting to Save Her Island Home from Climate Change', *Time,* 22 April 2019.

8 Torres Strait Island Regional Council, 'Boigu', Webpage, 2016, www.tsirc.qld.gov.au/communities/boigu; Torres Strait Island Regional Council, 'Saibai', Webpage, 2016, www.tsirc.qld.gov.au/communities/saibai.

9 T.B. Millar, 'The Defence of Australia', *Daedalus* 114:1 (1985), p. 278.

10 Andrew Carr, 'Australia's Archipelagic Deterrence', *Survival* 65:4 (2023), p. 79–100.

NOTES

11   3D Environmental, *Profile for Management of the Habitats and Related Ecological and Cultural Resource Values of Boigu Island*, Canberra: Torres Strait Regional Authority, January 2013.

12   Sean Dorney, *The Embarrassed Colonialist*, Sydney: Penguin Books/Lowy Institute, 2016.

13   Chris Urwin, Lynette Russell and Lily Yulianti Farid, 'Cross-Cultural Interaction Across the Arafura and Timor Seas: Aboriginal People and Macassans in Northern Australia', in Ian J. McNiven and Bruno David (eds), *The Oxford Handbook of the Archaeology of Indigenous Australia and New Guinea*, Oxford: Oxford Academic, 2021; Ian McNiven, 'Coral Sea Cultural Interaction Sphere', in ibid.

14   Bamblett, 'Before Australia', p. 21.

15   National Museum of Australia, 'Trade With the Makasar', Webpage, 29 September 2022, www.nma.gov.au/defining-moments/resources/trade-with-the-makasar.

16   Victor Briggs, *Seafaring: Canoeing Ancient Songlines,* Broome: Magabala Books, 2023.

17   James Oaten, 'Darwin Commemorates Sinking of a Japanese WWII Submarine I-124 by Australian Warship', ABC News, 13 September 2014.

18   See for example, Henry Frei, *Japan's Southward Advance and Australia: From the Sixteenth Century to World War II*, Honolulu: University of Hawaii Press, 1991.

19   Peter Dean, *MacArthur's Coalition: US and Australian Military Operations in the Southwest Pacific Area, 1942–1945*, Kansas: University Press of Kansas, 2018.

20   Joint Standing Committee on Foreign Affairs, Defence and Trade, *Australia's Maritime Strategy*, p. 8.

21   Dibb, *Review of Australia's Defence Capabilities*, p. 9.

22   Ibid., p. 15.

23   J.O. Langtry, 'Australia's Defence Policy in Transition', *Pakistan Horizon* 39:3 (1986), p. 66.

24   Department of Defence, *The Defence of Australia*, pp. vii, 1.

25   Ibid., p. viii.

26   Ibid., p. 19.

27   Ibid., p. 31.

28   Paul Dibb, David Hale and Peter Prince, 'Asia's Insecurity', *Survival* 41:3 (1999), p. 5–20.

29   James Cotton, 'East Timor and Australia – Twenty-Five Years of the Policy Debate', NAPSnet Special Reports, 21 September 1999, p. 1.

30   Commonwealth of Australia, *Torres Strait Fisheries Act 1984*.

31   Ibid.

32   Ibid.

33   Natasha Stacey, *Boats to Burn: Bajo Fishing Activity in the Australian Fishing Zone*, Canberra: ANU Press, 2007, p. 91.

34   Ibid., p. 1.

NOTES

35   Bruce Campbell, 'The Last Colonial Act: The Expulsion of Indonesian Fishermen from the North West Coast', in Jan Gothard (ed.), *Asian Orientations: Studies in Western Australia History*, Perth: University of Western Australia, 1995, p. 78.

36   Dibb, *Review of Australia's Defence Capabilities*, p. 38.

37   Millar, 'The Defence of Australia', p. 278.

38   Dibb, *Review of Australia's Defence Capabilities*, p. 15.

39   Department of Defence, *2020 Defence Strategic Update*.

40   OECD, *Fisheries and Aquaculture in Australia*, n.p.: OECD, January 2021.

41   Erin Parke, 'Piracy and Illegal Fishing Concerns Grow as Foreign Boats Return to Marine Park', ABC News, 18 December 2021; Erin Parke and Matt Brann, 'Pandemic-Fuelled Wave of Illegal Fishing Boats Prompts Call to Divert Border Force Resources', ABC News, 28 October 2021.

42   Ya Yen-Sun et al., *Road to Recovery: Assessing Job Risk and the Impact on the Most Vulnerable in Indonesia's Pandemic-Hit Tourism Industry*, Canberra; Australia Indonesia Centre, 2021.

43   Nadia Daly, 'South China Sea Dispute Sees Sea Cucumber Fishermen "Forced into Australian Waters"', ABC News, 10 March 2017.

44   Isabella Montecalvo, Philippe Le Billon, Chris Arsenault, and Milko Schvartzman, 'Ocean Predators: Squids, Chinese Fleets and the Geopolitics of High Seas Fishing', *Marine Policy* 152 (2023), pp. 4–6.

45   Aaron Smith, 'Chinese Fishing Plant in Torres Strait Raises Alarm for Australian Industry and Islanders', *The Guardian*, 26 November 2020.

46   Jeffrey Wall, 'China to Build $200-Million Fishery Project on Australia's Doorstep', *The Strategist*, 8 December 2020.

47   Daniel Flitton. 'Economy of Scales: Depleted Stocks Force Asian Fishermen Into Australian Waters', *The Sydney Morning Herald,* 25 February 2017.

48   Sebastian Strangio, 'Why China's "Island City" in Papua New Guinea Is a Mirage', *The Diplomat*, 9 September 2021.

49   Ashley Townshend and Toby Warden, 'Strengthening Coordination on Countering Maritime Coercion', in S. Jackman et al., *State of the United States: An Evolving Alliance Agenda*, Crawley: Perth USAsia Centre, 2021.

50   Department of Defence, 'Marine Rotational Force – Darwin', Webpage, accessed 17 January 2024, www.defence.gov.au/efence-activities/programs-initiatives/united-states-force-posture-initiatives/marine-rotational-force-darwin-initiative.

51   'United States Force Posture Initiatives', Department of Defence, Webpage, accessed 17 January 2024, www.defence.gov.au/programs-initiatives/united-states-force-posture-initiatives.

52   Commonwealth of Australia, *National Defence: Defence Strategic Review*, p. 32.

53   Peter Dean and Troy Lee-Brown, 'Littoral Warfare in the Indo-Pacific', Australian Army Research Centre, Webpage, 21 April 2021, https://researchcentre.army.gov.au/library/land-power-forum/

littoral-warfare-indo-pacific. The USMC use a common definition whereby the littoral is comprised of 'two segments: the seaward portion is that area from the open ocean to the shore that must be controlled to support operations ashore. The landward portion is the area inland from the shore that can be supported and defended directly from the sea.'

54 Department of Agriculture, *Australia's Second National Plan of Action to Prevent, Deter and Eliminate Illegal, Unreported and Unregulated Fishing*, Canberra: Commonwealth of Australia, 2014.

55 Hillary Mansour, 'Spike in Incursions Highlights Joint Australian and Indonesian Interests in Combating Illegal Fishing', *The Strategist,* 29 November 2021.

56 'Overview: Illegal, Unreported and Unregulated (IUU) Fishing', Department of Agriculture, Fisheries and Forestry, Webpage, accessed 17 January 2024, www.agriculture.gov.au/agriculture-land/fisheries/iuu/overview_illegal_unreported_and_unregulated_iuu_fishing#:~:text=%E2%80%8BIllegal%2C%20unreported%20and%20unregulated,or%20on%20the%20high%20seas.

57 Australian Border Force, 'Indonesia and Australia Conduct Joint Maritime Cooperation, Operation Gannet 5', Media Release, 21 April 2021, https://www.abf.gov.au/newsroom-subsite/Pages/indonesia-australia-joint-maritime-operation-21-05-2021.aspx.

58 Mansour, 'Spike in Incursions Highlights Joint Australian and Indonesian Interests in Combating Illegal Fishing'.

59 Department of Agriculture, *Australia's Second National Plan of Action to Prevent, Deter and Eliminate Illegal, Unreported and Unregulated Fishing*, Canberra: Commonwealth of Australia, 2014.

60 Dedi Supriadi Adhuri, James Fox and Natasha Stacey, 'Sailing South: Why Indonesian Fishers Risk Apprehension in Australian Waters', *The Conversation,* 7 December 2021.

61 Commonwealth of Australia and the Republic of Indonesia, *Agreement Between Australia and the Republic of Indonesia on the Framework for Security Cooperation,* Lombok, 13 November 2006, www.austlii.edu.au/au/other/dfat/treaties/2008/3.html.

62 Ewan MacAskill and Lenore Taylor, 'Australia's Spy Agencies Targeted Indonesian President's Mobile Phone', *The Guardian*, 18 November 2013; Michael Brissenden, 'Australia Spied on Indonesian President Susilo Bambang Yudhoyono, Leaked Edward Snowden Documents Reveal', ABC News, 13 November 2013; Katie Silver, 'Who Are the 10 Indonesians on Australian Spies' list?', ABC News, 18 November 2013.

63 Daniel Hurst, 'Australia and Indonesia Sign Spying Code of Conduct', *The Guardian*, 28 August 2014, www.theguardian.com/world/2014/aug/28/australia-and-indonesia-sign-spying-code-of-conduct.

64 Reuters Staff, 'Australia Recalls Ambassador to Indonesia after Executions', Reuters, 29 April 2105, www.reuters.com/article/uk-indonesia-executions-australia-idUKKBN0NJ2N820150428.

NOTES

65   Rebecca Strating, 'Ambassador's Return to Indonesia Shows his Recall was Futile', *The Conversation*, 12 June 2021.

66   Commonwealth of Australia and the Republic of Indonesia, *Joint Declaration on a Comprehensive Strategic Partnership between Australia and the Republic of Indonesia*, 31 August 2021, www.dfat.gov.au/geo/indonesia/Pages/joint-declaration-comprehensive-strategic-partnership-between-the-commonwealth-of-australia-and-republic-of-indonesia.

67   BBC News, 'Australia Considers Following the US on Jerusalem Embassy', BBC News, 16 October 2018.

68   Evan Laksmana, 'Why Does It Matter to Indonesia if Australia Moves Its Embassy to Jerusalem?', *The Strategist*, 23 November 2018.

69   Eryk Bagshaw and James Massola, 'Indonesia-Australia Free Trade Deal to be Activated by July', *The Sydney Morning Herald*, 7 May 2020.

70   Stuart Kaye, 'Indonesia's Archipelagic Sea Lanes: International Law and Practice,' *Naval Review* (2020), p. 1.

71   Notice Instituting Conciliation Under Section 2 of Annex V of UNCLOS by Timor-Leste, 11 April 2016, para. 4.

72   Mark Beeson and Andrew Chubb, 'Australia, China and the Maritime "Rules-based International Order": Comparing the South China Sea and Timor Sea Disputes,' *International Relations of the Asia-Pacific* 21:2 (2021), pp. 233–64.

73   Department of Foreign Affairs and Trade, *Australia and Timor-Leste Maritime Boundaries: Rules-Based Order in Action*, Canberra: Commonwealth of Australia, 2018.

74   Stephen Dziedzic, 'Timor-Leste Buys $484 Million Stake in Greater Sunrise Fields and Pushes for lng Pipeline', ABC News, 2 October 2018.

75   United Nations Compulsory Conciliation, 'In the Matter of the Maritime Boundary Between Timor-Leste and Australia (the "Timor Sea Conciliation")', 9 May 2018, annex 27, https://pcacases.com/web/sendAttach/2327.

76   Commonwealth of Australia, *Foreign Policy White Paper*, Canberra: Department of Foreign Affairs and Trade, 2017.

77   Simon Hewes and David Hundt, 'The Battle of the Coral Sea: Australia's Response to the Belt & Road Initiative in the Pacific', *Australian Journal of International Affairs* 76:2 (2022), pp. 178–93.

78   Australian Government, *Strengthening Australia's Northern Bases*, 27 April 2023.

79   Commonwealth of Australia, *National Defence: Defence Strategic Review*.

80   James Blackwell and Julie Ballangarry, 'Indigenous Foreign Policy: A New Way Forward?', *Australian Feminist Foreign Policy Coalition* 1 (April 2022).

81   Brendan Mounter and Charlie McKillop, 'Illegal Foreign Fishing Boats a "Threat" to Torres Strait Islander Commercial Fishers', ABC News, 31 January 2023.

82   Blackwell and Ballangarry, 'Indigenous Foreign Policy'.

83   'Indonesia, Australia Agree to Eradicate Illegal Fishing', *Antara News*, 1 April 2022.

84   Dio Suhenda, 'Indonesia to Lobby UN Over Lacking Supervision of Nuclear Technology', *Jakarta Post*, 3 August 2022.

85   Sam Bateman quoted in Marcus Hellyer (ed.), *Agenda for Change 2019: Strategic Choices for the Next Government*, Canberra: Australian Strategic Policy Institute, February 2019.

86   Ove Hoegh-Guldberg and Jamaluddin Jompa, 'Indonesia and Australia Are Sleeping Ocean Superpowers', *The Conversation*, 15 December 2016.

CHAPTER 3

1   Nancy Pelosi, 'Why I'm Leading a Delegation to Taiwan', *The Washington Post*, 3 August 2022.

2   Thomas L. Friedman, 'Why Pelosi's Visit to Taiwan Is Utterly Reckless', *The New York Times*, 1 August 2022.

3   Yue Honglin and Bai Yu, '中华人民共和国外交部声明（全文）' [Statement by the Ministry of Foreign Affairs of the People's Republic of China (in full)], People.cn, 2 August 2022.

4   David Speers, 'Anthony Albanese's Reaction to Nancy Pelosi's Taiwan Trip Was Dead Pan — But What He Didn't Say Spoke Volumes', ABC News, 4 August 2022.

5   Ibid.

6   Nancy Pelosi, 'Transcript of Pelosi Remarks Receiving Order of Propitious Clouds With Special Grand Cordon', Transcript of speech delivered at Taipei, Taiwan, 2 August 2022, https://pelosi.house.gov/news/press-releases/transcript-of-pelosi-remarks-receiving-order-of-propitious-clouds-with-special.

7   Quoted in Vincent Ni, 'Joe Biden Again says US Forces Would Defend Taiwan from Chinese Attack', *The Guardian*, 19 September 2022.

8   Tom Lowrey, 'Government and Opposition MPs to Visit Taiwan as Part of Australian Parliamentary Delegation', ABC News, 3 December 2022.

9   *An Appreciation of the Strategical Position of Australia*, Canberra: Commonwealth of Australia, 1946, part V.

10   'British Commonwealth Occupation Force 1945–52', Australian War Memorial, Webpage, 2 July 2021, www.awm.gov.au/articles/atwar/bcof.

11   Department of Defence, *Appreciation of the Strategic Position of Australia*, Canberra: Commonwealth of Australia, 1947, pt. 20.

12   'Treaties and Alliances', Ministry for Culture and Heritage of New Zealand, Webpage, 18 February 2020, https://nzhistory.govt.nz/war/new-zealand-forces-in-asia/nz-military-involvement.

13   Department of Defence, *Strategic Basis of Australian Defence Policy*, Canberra: Commonwealth of Australia, 1953, part II.

14   Mark E. Manyin, *The Senkakus (Diaoyu/Diaoyutai) Dispute: U.S. Treaty Obligations*, Washington, D.C.: Congressional Research Service, 2021.

15   Ibid.

NOTES

16   Hanyi Shaw, *The Diaoyutai Senkaku Islands Dispute: Its History and Analysis of the Ownership Claims of the P.R.C., R.O.C., and Japan*, Baltimore: School of Law of the University of Maryland, 1999; 'The Diaoyu Islands: The Owner and the Thief', Ministry of Foreign Affairs of the People's Republic of China, Webpage, 22 October 2012, www.fmprc.gov.cn/mfa_eng/topics_665678/diaodao_665718/201210/t20121022_701846.html.

17   Monika Chansoria, '1969 Report by UN Economic Commission for Asia and the Far East: A Turning Point in the Historical Debate Over Senkaku Islands', *Japan Review* 2:3 (2018), pp. 36–47.

18   'Treaty of Shimonoseki', USC US–China Institute, Webpage, accessed 17 January 2024, https://china.usc.edu/treaty-shimonoseki-1895.

19   Ibid.

20   Masaaki Kameda, 'Foreign Ministry's 1969 China Map Identifies Senkaku Islands by Japanese Name', *Japan Times*, 17 March 2015.

21   Daniel Tretiak, 'The Sino-Japanese Treaty of 1978: The Senkaku Incident Prelude', *Asian Survey* 18:12 (1978), pp. 1235–49.

22   Ozaki Shigeyoshi, 'The Senkaku Islands and Japan's Territorial Rights', Research paper, Review of Island Studies, 10 June 2013, www.spf.org/islandstudies/transfer/research/docs/a00001r.pdf.

23   'Senkaku Islands', Ministry of Foreign Affairs of Japan, Webpage, 2023, www.mofa.go.jp/region/asia-paci/senkaku/qa_1010.html.

24   Joel Atkinson, *Australia and Taiwan: Bilateral Relations, China, the United States, and the South Pacific*, Leiden: BRILL, 2012, pp. 17–40.

25   Department of Defence, *Strategic Basis of Australian Defence Policy*, Canberra: Commonwealth of Australia, 1959, pt. 7.

26   Ibid.

27   Atkinson, *Australia and Taiwan*, p. 22.

28   Gary Woodard, 'Australian Foreign Policy on the Offshore Crisis of 1954–55 and Recognition of China', *Australian Journal of International Affairs* 45:2 (1991), pp. 242–63.

29   David McLean, 'Australia in the Cold War: A Historiographical Review', *The International History Review* 23:2 (2001), pp. 299–321.

30   Atkinson, *Australia and Taiwan*, pp. 17–40.

31   Bec Strating, 'Maritime and Sovereignty Disputes in the East China Sea', The National Bureau of Asian Research, Webpage, 9 February 2021, www.nbr.org/publication/maritime-and-sovereignty-disputes-in-the-east-china-sea.

32   Minn Chung, 'Seoul Will Become a Sea of Fire . . .', *Bulletin of Concerned Asian Scholars* 26: 1–2 (1994), pp. 132–35.

33   Lee Teng-hui, 'Pres. Lee Teng-hui, Cornell University Commencement Address', USC US–China Institute, Webpage, 9 June 1995, https://china.usc.edu/pres-lee-teng-hui-cornell-university-commencement-address-june-9-1995.

34   Gary Klintworth, *Crisis Management: China, Taiwan and the United States – the 1995–96 Crisis and Its Aftermath*, Canberra: Commonwealth of Australia

NOTES

Information and Research Services, 24 March 1997.

35 Don Greenlees and Richard McGregor, 'Downer Warns China Over War Games', *The Australian*, 13 March 1996, p. 8.

36 'Japan-Australia Joint Declaration on Security Cooperation'.

37 Department of Defence, *Defending Australia in the Asia Pacific Century*, p. 95.

38 'Prime Minister Abbott and Prime Minister Abe Joint Statement: Special Strategic Partnership for the 21st Century', Ministry of Foreign Affairs of Japan, Webpage, 8 July 2014, www.mofa.go.jp/files/000044640.pdf.

39 Department of Defence, *Defence White Paper 2013*, p. 11.

40 Richard C. Bush, 'What the Historic Xi-Ma Meeting Could Mean for Cross-Strait Relations', *Brookings*, 9 November 2015.

41 Department of Defence, *Defence White Paper 2013*, p. 11.

42 Ibid.

43 George W. Bush, 'President Delivers State of the Union Address', Transcript of speech delivered at the United States Capitol, Washington, D.C., 29 January 2022, https://georgewbush-whitehouse.archives.gov/news/releases/2002/01/20020129-11.html.

44 Department of Defence, *Defence White Paper 2013*, p. 12.

45 'Senkaku Islands', Ministry of Foreign Affairs of Japan, Webpage, 2023, www.mofa.go.jp/region/asia-paci/senkaku/qa_1010.html.

46 Alan Taylor, 'Anti-Japan Protests in China', *The Atlantic*, 17 September 2012.

47 Taylor, 'Anti-Japan Protests in China'; G. E. Anderson, 'China's Anti-Japan Protests: Keeping the Automaker Damages at Home', *East Asia Forum*, 21 September 2012.

48 Nick Bisley and Brendan Taylor, *Conflict in the East China Sea: Would ANZUS Apply?*, Sydney: Australia-China Relations Institute at the University of Technology Sydney, November 2014.

49 Department of Defence, *2016 Defence White Paper*, p. 61.

50 'Statement by the Ministry of Foreign Affairs of the People's Republic of China', Ministry of Foreign Affairs of the People's Republic of China, 2 August 2022, www.fmprc.gov.cn/eng/zxxx_662805/202208/t20220802_10732293.html.

51 Gough Whitlam, 'Establishment of Diplomatic Relations With China', Department of Foreign Affairs, 22 December 1972, https://pmtranscripts.pmc.gov.au/sites/default/files/original/00003121.pdf.

52 'Questions and Answers Concerning the Taiwan (2): What Is the One-China Principle? What Is the Basis of the One-China Principle?', Mission of the People's Republic of China to the European Union, Webpage, 15 August 2022, http://eu.china-mission.gov.cn/eng/more/20220812Taiwan/202208/t20220815_10743591.htm.

53 Michael J. Green and Bonnie S. Glaser, 'What Is the U.S. "One China" Policy, and Why Does it Matter?', Center for Strategic and International Studies (CSIS), 13 January 2017, www.csis.org/analysis/what-us-one-china-policy-and-why-does-it-matter.

54   'Taiwan Relations Act', Pub. L No. 96–8, 93 STAT. 14, www.congress.gov/96/
      statute/STATUTE-93/STATUTE-93-Pg14.pdf.

55   'H.R.2479 – Taiwan Relations Act', 96th United States Congress (1979–80),
      www.congress.gov/bill/96th-congress/house-bill/2479.

56   Keoni Everington, 'Tsai Says Taiwan Already Independent, China Invasion
      "Very Costly"', *Taiwan News*, 16 January 2020, www.taiwannews.com.tw/en/
      news/3858329.

57   Ben Blanchard and Yimou Lee, 'Taiwan Opposition Chief in No Rush for
      China Meeting', Reuters, 2 March 2021.

58   'China: Law No. 34 of 2005, Anti-Secession Law', People's Republic of China,
      14 March 2015, www.refworld.org/docid/474403752.html.

59   Xi Jinping, '共圆中华民族伟大复兴中国梦 (全文)', [The Chinese Dream:
      Concentric Rejuvenation of the Chinese Nation (Full Text)], The Central
      People's Government of the People's Republic of China, 18 February 2014,
      www.gov.cn/ldhd/2014-02/19/content_2612763.htm.

60   Xi Jinping, 'Secure a Decisive Victory in Building a Moderately Prosperous
      Society in All Respects and Strive for the Great Success of Socialism with
      Chinese Characteristics for a New Era', Transcript of Speech at the 19th
      National Congress of the Communist Party of China, Beijing, China,
      18 October 2017, www.xinhuanet.com/english/download/Xi_Jinping's_report_
      at_19th_CPC_National_Congress.pdf.

61   'Full Text: The Taiwan Question and China's Reunification in the New Era', The
      Taiwan Affairs Office of the State Council and The State Council Information
      Office, August 2022, www.china.org.cn/china/2022-08/10/content_78365601.
      htm.

62   Up from 380 in 2020 to 1115 in 2022. 'Taiwan Incursion Updates', Missile
      Defense Advocacy Alliance, December 2022, https://missiledefenseadvocacy.
      org/missile-threat-and-proliferation/todays-missile-threat/
      taiwan-missile-updates.

63   Cheng-yi Lin, 'Taiwan: Surmounting New Security Threats', in Bryce Wakefield
      (ed.), *Taiwan, Cross-Strait Tension, and Security in the Indo-Pacific*, Canberra:
      Australian Institute of International Affairs, p. 7.

64   Michael Clarke and Matthew Sussex, 'Why "Strategic Ambiguity"
      Trumps "Strategic Clarity" on Taiwan', *Royal United Services Institute*,
      24 November 2021, https://rusi.org/explore-our-research/publications/
      commentary/why-strategic-ambiguity-trumps-strategic-clarity-taiwan.

65   'Taiwan Travel Act', Pub. L No. 115-135, 132 STAT. 341, www.congress.gov/
      bill/115th-congress/house-bill/535.

66   'Taiwan Allies International Protection and Enhancement Initiative
      (TAIPEI) Act of 2019', Pub. L. No. 116–35, 134 STAT, 278, www.congress.gov/
      bill/116th-congress/senate-bill/1678/text.

67   Michael M. Pompeo, 'Lifting Self-Imposed Restrictions on
      the U.S.–Taiwan Relationship', US Embassy and Consulates in

NOTES

China, 9 January 2021, https://china.usembassy-china.org.cn/
lifting-self-imposed-restrictions-on-the-u-s-taiwan-relationship.

68 Meredith Oyen, 'Biden Again Indicates That US Will Defend Taiwan
'Militarily' – Does This Constitute a Change in Policy?', *The Conversation*,
20 September 2022.

69 Qi Weiqun, 'Biden's Taiwan Policy Is the Most Dangerous Issue in China–US
Relations', *The Diplomat*, 10 June 2022.

70 Brendan Taylor, *Dangerous Decade: Taiwan's Security and Crisis Management*,
London: Routledge, 2019.

71 John Bolton quoted Lisa Murray and Mark Mulligan, 'Bolton Tells
Canberra to Build More Alliances and Let Japan Into AUKUS', *Australian
Financial Review*, 23 August 2022.

72 Cara Lyttle, 'Why Is the East China Sea a Potential Flashpoint for Japan and
China?', Investment Monitor, 26 September 2022, www.investmentmonitor.ai/
features/east-china-sea-japan-china-senkaku-islands.

73 Ibid.

74 'Typhoon Ends 157-Day Streak of Chinese Vessels Near Senkakus', *Japan Times*,
21 July 2021.

75 Junko Ogura and Simone McCarthy, 'Japan Says Chinese Coast Guard
Ships in Longest Violation of Its Territorial Waters in a Decade', *CNN World*,
26 June 2022.

76 Manyin, *The Senkakus (Diaoyu/Diaoyutai) Dispute*.

77 *Defense of Japan 2022*, Ministry of Defense Japan, 2022, www.mod.go.jp/en/
publ/w_paper/wp2022/DOJ2022_Digest_EN.pdf.

78 Justin McCurry and Tania Branigan, 'Obama Says US Will Defend Japan in
Island Dispute with China', *The Guardian*, 24 April 2014.

79 'East China Sea: What Australians Think', Australia-China Relations Institute
at the University of Technology Sydney (UTS), 19 January 2015, www.
australiachinarelations.org/content/east-china-sea-what-australians-think.

80 Ibid.

81 Nick Bisley and Brendan Taylor, *Conflict in the East China Sea:
Would ANZUS Apply?*

82 Franze-Stefan Grady, 'Australia Deploys P-8A Posiedon to Japan to Enforce
North Korea Sanctions', *The Diplomat*, 7 December 2018.

83 Tasha Wibawa, 'North Korea: Diplomatic Life Inside Pyongyang Can Be
"Superficial, Difficult, and Controlled"', ABC, 14 October 2018.

84 Jack Butcher, 'All Containment and No Engagement: Australia's Contemporary
Policy Towards the Democratic People's Republic of Korea', *Australian Journal
of Politics and History*.

85 See Aldo Borgu's comments in 'Downer Denies Taiwan Blunder', *The Age*,
20 August 2004.

86 Kevin Rudd, 'China/Taiwan', Radio interview with Geraldine Doogue, Australian
Labor Party, 19 July 2004, https://library.fes.de/aussies/2004/0704/20007990.html.

NOTES

87   Annabelle Quince, 'Taiwan: A Contested History', *Rear Vision*, ABC Radio National, 16 March 2008.

88   *2020 Strategic Defence Update*, Australian Department of Defence, p. 24.

89   Daniel Hurst, 'Dutton Dials Back Language on Australia Defending Taiwan in a Potential War with China', *The Guardian*, 6 March 2022.

90   Brendan Taylor, 'Taiwan: What Could, Should and Will Australia do?', *The Washington Quarterly* 45:3 (2022), pp. 131–46.

91   Peter Dutton, Minister for Defence, 'National Press Club Address', Canberra, 26 November 2021, www.minister.defence.gov.au/speeches/2021-11-26/national-press-club-address-canberra-act.

92   US Department of Defense, *2022 National Defense Strategy*.

93   Nick Bisley, et al., 'For a Progressive Realism: Australian Foreign Policy in the 21st Century', *Australian Journal of International Affairs* 76:2 (2002), pp. 138–60.

94   Hugh White, 'Reality Check: Taiwan Cannot Be Defended', *Australian Foreign Affairs,* 14 (2022), pp. 6–24.

95   Taylor, 'Taiwan'.

96   Ibid.

97   Stephen Dziedzic, 'Paul Keating Plays Down Prospect of Chinese Military Invasion of Taiwan, Urges Australia Not to Be Drawn Into Conflict', ABC, 10 November 2021.

98   Cameron Hill, 'Australia and the South China Sea: Debates and Dilemmas', Parliament of Australia, www.aph.gov.au/About_Parliament/Parliamentary_Departments/Parliamentary_Library/pubs/BriefingBook45p/SouthChinaSea#:~:text=In%20response%20to%20recent%20Chinese,%2C%20US%2Dled%20regional%20order.

99   Stephen McDonnell, 'East China Sea Row Escalates, as Wang Yi tells Julia Bishop that Australia has "Jeopardised Trust"', ABC, 7 December 2013.

100   Stephen McDonnell, 'East China Sea Row Escalates'.

101   Commonwealth of Australia, *Foreign Policy White Paper*. Australia: Department of Foreign Affairs and Trade, 2017, p. 47.

102   Nick Bisley and Brendan Taylor, *Conflict in the East China Sea: Would ANZUS Apply?*; 'Pragmatism Rules in Australia-China Relations, *Australian Financial Review*, 22 March 2015.

103   Nick Bisley and Brendan Taylor, *Conflict in the East China Sea: Would ANZUS Apply?*

104   'East China Sea: What Australians Think', Australia-China Relations Institute, University of Technology Sydney, 27 May 2015, www.uts.edu.au/acri/research-and-opinion/research-reports/east-china-sea-what-australians-think.

105   Hiroyuki Umetsu, 'Communist China's Entry into the Korean Hostilities and a U.S. Proposal for a Collective Security Arrangement in the Pacific Offshore Island Chain', *Journal of Northeast Asian Studies* 15 (1996), pp. 98–118.

106   Wilson VornDick, 'China's Reach Has Grown; So Should the Island Chains', Center for Strategic and International Studies, Asia Maritime

Transparency Initiative, 22 October 2018, https://amti.csis.org/chinas-reach-grown-island-chains.

107 Ibid.

108 Ibid.

109 Butcher, 'All Containment and No Engagement'.

110 'Vision Statement for a Secure, Peaceful and Prosperous Future Between the Republic of Korea and Australia 2014', Department of Foreign Affairs and Trade, accessed 17 January 2023, www.dfat.gov.au/geo/republic-of-korea/vision-statement-for-a-secure-peaceful-and-prosperous-future-between-the-republic-of-korea-and-australia.

111 'Australia-Republic of Korea Comprehensive Strategic Partnership', Department of Foreign Affairs and Trade, 13 December 2021, www.dfat.gov.au/geo/republic-of-korea/republic-korea-south-korea/australia-republic-korea-comprehensive-strategic-partnership.

112 'Treaty of Shimonoseki'; 'Australia-Republic of Korea Comprehensive Strategic Partnership', The Department of Foreign Affairs and Trade (DFAT), 13 December 2021, www.dfat.gov.au/geo/republic-of-korea/republic-korea-south-korea/australia-republic-korea-comprehensive-strategic-partnership.

113 'Japan-Australia Joint Declaration on Security Cooperation', Ministry of Foreign Affairs of Japan.

114 Japan-Australia Economic Partnership Agreement, The Department of Foreign Affairs and Trade, 2023, www.dfat.gov.au/trade/agreements/in-force/jaepa/japan-australia-economic-partnership-agreement; 'Agreement Between the Government of Japan and the Government of Australia Concerning the Transfer of Defence Equipment and Technology', signed by the Government of Japan and the Government of Australia, 8 July 1994, www.mofa.go.jp/files/000044447.pdf.

115 'Agreement Between the Government of Australia and the Government of Japan on the Security of Information', 17 May 2012 (entered into force 22 March 2013), www.austlii.edu.au/au/other/dfat/treaties/ATS/2013/15.html; 'Prime Minister Abbott and Prime Minister Abe Joint Statement "Special Strategic Partnership for the 21st Century"', Ministry of Foreign Affairs of Japan.

116 Michael Smith, 'Australia's ANZUS-style Defence Pact is New Territory for Japan', *The Australian Financial Review*, 23 October 2022.

117 'The United States Seventh Fleet', Commander, U.S. 7th Fleet, U.S. Department of Defense, 2023, www.c7f.navy.mil/About-Us/Facts-Sheet.

118 Thomas S. Wilkins, 'After a Decade of Strategic Partnership: Japan and Australia 'Decentering' from the US Alliance,' *The Pacific Review* 31:4 (2018), pp. 498–514; Shane Flanagan, 'Building Resilience in Japan-China Ties: A Role for Australia', Indo-Pacific Strategic Papers, *Centre for Defence and Strategic Studies*, (2017), pp. 1–27.

NOTES

119 Department of Foreign Affairs and Trade, 'Japan Country Brief', www.dfat.gov.au/geo/japan/japan-country-brief.

120 For example, a 2020 Pew Poll found that 61 per cent of respondents had 'unfavourable' views of mainland China, www.pewresearch.org/global/2020/05/12/in-taiwan-views-of-mainland-china-mostly-negative.

121 For example, a 2021 Australia Institute poll found that 68 per cent of respondents agreed that Taiwan should become independent if it could be done peacefully, 44 per cent even agreed even if China were to attack. 'Polling – Australian and Taiwanese attitudes to China', Australian Institute, 22 August 2022, https://australiainstitute.org.au/report/polling-australian-and-taiwanese-attitudes-to-china.

122 53 per cent of respondents agreed that 'China will Launch an Armed Attack' on Taiwan 'sometime', 5 per cent that it will 'soon'. Ibid.

123 59 per cent of respondents answered 'no' when asked 'Are your people prepared to go to war for independence/if China threatened?' Ibid.

124 62 per cent of respondents answered 'no' when asked 'Could your country successfully defend itself without international assistance?' Ibid.

125 22 per cent of respondents answered 'yes' when asked 'If China attacks your country, will US commit military to fight war?', while 34 per cent responded 'it depends', and 33 per cent 'no'. Ibid.

126 A Taiwanese election study in 2022 found that 28.7 per cent of respondents favour 'maintain status quo, decide at a later date', 28.5 per cent favoured 'maintain status quo indefinitely', and 25.4 per cent favoured 'maintain status quo, move towards independence'. Only 5.6 per cent favoured 'independence as soon as possible'. Election Study Center, National Chengchi University, 'Taiwan Independence vs. Unification with the Mainland (1994/12-2002/12)', https://esc.nccu.edu.tw/PageDoc/Detail?fid=7801&id=6963.

127 Anthony Albanese, 'Television interview – Piers Morgan Uncensored', Transcript, 3 May 2023, www.pm.gov.au/media/television-interview-piers-morgan-uncensored.

128 Secretary of the Department of Home Affairs Mike Pezzullo quoted in Andrew Greene, 'Home Affairs Secretary Mike Pezzullo Warns "drums of war" Are Beating in a Message to Staff', ABC, 26 April 2021.

129 Allan Behm et al., *Should Australia Go to War With China in Defence of Taiwan?*, The Australia Institute, July 2021.

130 Brendan Taylor, *Taiwan Flashpoint: What Australia Can Do to Stop the Coming Taiwan Crisis*, Sydney: Lowy Institute, 2020.

131 Taylor, 'Taiwan'.

132 Mark Harrison, *Rethinking Taiwan policy: History, Politics, Ideology*, Canberra: Australian Strategic Policy Institute, 2019.

133 Melissa Conley-Tyler, 'How Australia Can Help Taiwan Tackle Global Issues', *The Strategist*, 1 June 2021.

134 Allan Behm et al., *Should Australia Go to War With China in Defence of Taiwan?*

135 Duncan DeAeth, 'Republications Introduce Resolution for Calling for US to Recognize Taiwan', *Taiwan News*, 26 January 2023.

136 Glenn H. Snyder, *Alliance Politics*, Ithaca: Cornell University Press, 1997.

137 Iain Henry, 'What Allies Want: Reconsidering Loyalty, Reliability, and Alliance Interdependence', *International Security* 44:4 (2020), pp. 45–83.

138 'Joint Statement Australia-U.S. Ministerial Consultations (AUSMIN)' 2021, www.dfat.gov.au/geo/united-states-of-america/ausmin/ joint-statement-australia-us-ministerial-consultations-ausmin-2021.

139 Paul Dibb, 'Australia and the Taiwan Contingency', *The Strategist*, 6 February 2019; Mark Harrison, 'The Taiwanese Have Much to Teach Australians', *The Sydney Morning Herald*, 20 August 2022.

140 'Do you agree or disagree: Australia should act in accordance with our security alliance with the United States even if it means following them to war with China over the independence of Taiwan', Lowy Institute Poll [2022], poll. lowyinstitute.org/charts/war-over-taiwan.

141 'Military Action Under ANZUS', Lowy Institute Poll [2022], poll.lowyinstitute. org/charts/military-action-under-anzus.

142 John Lyons, 'What Would War With China Look Like for Australia? Part 1', *ABC News*, 20 February 2023; Allan Behm et al., *Should Australia Go to War with China in Defence of Taiwan?*

143 Donald Kirk, 'A Sad Reality of Pelosi's Visit: South Korea Won't Help Defend Taiwan', *The Hill*, 9 August 2022.

144 David Santoro and Ralph Cossa, *The World After Taiwan's Fall*, Pacific Forum, 2023.

145 'Memorandum on Formosa, by General of the Army Douglas MacArthur, Commander in Chief, Far East, and Supreme Commander, Allied Powers, Japan', Tokyo, 14 June 1950, https://history.state.gov/historicaldocuments/ frus1950v07/d86.

146 Quoted in Kathrin Hille, 'US Shows China Its Hand on Strategic Value of 'Unsinkable' Taiwan – Washington's Clear Statement of Island's Regional Security Role Part of Tougher Stance Towards Beijing', *Financial Times*, 29 December 2021.

147 Daniel Hurst, '"We Are in the Same Boat": Japan Urges Australia to Join Forces to Address Challenge of China', *The Guardian*, 21 July 2021.

148 Andrew Greene, 'Defence Department Silent on Latest Chinese Military Encounter with Australian Warship', *ABC News*, 13 July 2022.

149 George S. Capen, 'The Military Maritime Consultative Agreement', *Proceedings* 125:8:1 (1999), p. 158.

150 Nick Bisley and Brendan Taylor, *Conflict in the East China Sea: Would ANZUS Apply?*, Sydney: Australia-China Relations Institute, UTS, 2014.

151 Nick Derewlany, 'What Should Australia Be Doing in the East China Sea?', *The Diplomat*, 30 September 2016.

NOTES

CHAPTER 4

1   Commonwealth of Australia, *Parliamentary Debates: Senate,* 30 November 2017, p. 9297.

2   Daniel Hurst and Paul Karp, 'Australia to Pursue 'National Interest' When US Asks for South China Sea Action', *The Guardian,* 28 July 2020.

3   Anthony Galloway, 'Australia Will "Lose Next Decade" Unless It Stands Up to China: Dutton', *The Sydney Morning Herald,* 7 February 2022.

4   See for example Clive Hamilton, *Silent Invasion: China's Influence in Australia,* Melbourne: Hardie Grant, 2018.

5   Richard Oloruntoba et al., 'Conflict in the South China Sea Threatens 90% of Australia's Fuel Imports: Study', *The Conversation,* 22 August 2022.

6   US Department of Defense, *U.S. Department of Defense Freedom of Navigation Program Fact Sheet,* March 2015.

7   Paul Karp, 'Chinese Fighter Jet's Actions Near Australian Aircraft "Very Dangerous", Deputy PM Says', *The Guardian,* 4 June 2022.

8   Brendan Sargeant, 'Challenges to the Australian Strategic Imagination', *Centre of Gravity Series,* Canberra: ANU, 2018, p. 6.

9   Katherine Morton, 'China's Ambition in the South China Sea: Is a Legitimate Maritime Order Possible?', *International Affairs,* 92:4 (2016), pp. 909–40.

10   Elliot Brennan, 'Out of the "Slipstream" of Power? Australian Grand Strategy and the South China Sea Disputes,' Stockholm: Institute for Security and Development Policy, 2017.

11   Department of Defence, *The Defence of Australia,* p. 7.

12   Commonwealth of Australia, *Defence White Paper,* Canberra: Department of Defence, 2013.

13   Michael Wesley, 'Australia's Interests in the South China Sea,' in L. Buszynski and C. Roberts (eds), *The South China Sea and Australia's Regional Security Environment,* Canberra: National Security College, 2013.

14   Bill Hayton, *The South China Sea and the Struggle for Asia,* New Haven: Yale University Press, 2014.

15   This means that Indonesia does not view itself as having territorial disputes with China in the South China Sea.

16   Commonwealth of Australia, *Foreign Policy White Paper,* Canberra: Department of Foreign Affairs and Trade, 2017, pp. 46–47.

17   United Nations Convention on the Law of the Sea, Article 76.

18   Commission on the Limits of the Continental Shelf (CLCS), *Outer Limits of the Continental Shelf Beyond 200 Nautical Miles from the Baselines: Submissions to the Commission: Partial Submission by Malaysia in the South China Sea,* 2019, www.un.org/depts/los/clcs_new/submissions_files/submission_mys_12_12_2019.html.

19   People's Republic of China, *Note verbale: CML 17/2009,* 7 May 2009, www.un.org/Depts/los/clcs_new/submissions_files/mysvnm33_09/chn_2009re_mys_vnm_e.pdf.

NOTES

20 Zhiguo Gao and Bing Bing Jia, 'The Nine-Dash Line in the South China Sea: History, Status and Implications', *American Journal of International Law* 107:1 (2013), pp. 98–123.

21 Mira Rapp-Hooper, 'In Defense of Facts in the South China Sea', *Asia Maritime Transparency Initiative*, 2 June 2015, https://amti.csis.org/ in-defense-of-facts-in-the-south-china-sea.

22 Greg Poling et al., *Pulling Back the Curtain on China's Maritime Militia*, Centre for Strategic and International Studies, 18 November 2021, p. vii.

23 Ibid.

24 Permanent Court of Arbitration, *The South China Sea Arbitration Award*, PCA Case No. 2013–19, 12 July 2016.

25 Katherine Morton, 'China's Ambition in the South China Sea: Is a Legitimate Maritime Order Possible?', *International Affairs*, 92:4 (2016), pp. 909–40.

26 Congressional Research Service, *China Naval Modernization: Implications for U.S. Navy Capabilities – Background and Issues for Congress*, updated 20 January 2022, pp. 2, 5. https://sgp.fas.org/crs/row/RL33153.pdf.

27 Briffa et al., *Enhancing Maritime Security in the Indo-Pacific*, p. 3.

28 Thomas Shugart, *Australia and the Growing Reach of China's Military*, 2 August 2021, www.lowyinstitute.org/publications/ australia-and-growing-reach-china-s-military#_edn3.

29 Ibid.

30 Andrew Chubb, 'Is There a Problem with Australia's South China Sea Policy?' *China Matters Explores*, 2018, p. 3.

31 M. Taylor Fravel and Charles L. Glaser, 'How Much Risk Should the United States Run in the South China Sea?', *International Security* 47:2 (2022), pp. 88–134.

32 Ned Price, 'U.S. Support for the Philippines in the South China Sea', *Department of State Press Release*, 13 February 2023, www.state. gov/u-s-support-for-the-philippines-in-the-south-china-sea-3.

33 Bisley and Taylor, *Conflict in East China Sea*.

34 Department of Defence, *2016 Defence White Paper*, p. 57.

35 Sam Bateman, 'What Are Australia's Interests in the South China Sea?', *The Strategist*, Australian Strategic Policy Institute, 28 May 2015.

36 Christian Wirth, 'Whose 'Freedom of Navigation'? Australia, China, the United States and the Making of Order in the 'Indo-Pacific', *The Pacific Review*, 32:4 (2019), pp. 475–504.

37 United Nations Conference on Trade and Development, Evolution of the World's 25 Top Trading Nations, Table, 2021, https://unctad.org/topic/ trade-analysis/chart-10-may-2021.

38 CSIS, 'How Much Trade Transits the South China Sea?', ChinaPower, 2 August 2017, https://chinapower.csis.org/much-trade-transits-south-china-sea.

39 Johnathan Kearsley, '"There It Was, China's List of Grievances": How 9News Got the Dossier at the Heart of the Latest Diplomatic Scuffle Between Canberra and Beijing', *9news*, 23 November 2020.

NOTES

40   Reuters, 'Chinese Port Bans Imports of Australian Coal, Sending Dollar Tumbling', *The Guardian,* 21 February 2019.

41   Yan Zhuang, 'Sailors Stranded for Months as China Refuses to Let Ships Unload Australian Coal', *The New York Times*, 26 December 2020, www. nytimes.com/2020/12/26/business/coal-ships-china-australia.html; Natalie Klein, 'Australia's Maritime Security Challenges: Juggling International Law and Informal Agreements in a Rules-based International Order', *United States Naval War College International Law Studies,* forthcoming.

42   Ben Butler, 'Australia's Supply Chain Issues Likely to Continue Despite Drop in Covid Cases', *The Guardian,* 13 February 2022.

43   Hugh White, *How to Defend Australia,* Melbourne: La Trobe University Press, 2019.

44   James Borton, *Dispatches from the South China Sea: Navigating to Common Ground,* Universal Publishers, 2022.

45   Elizabeth Mendenhall et al., 'Climate Change Increases the Risk of Fisheries Conflict', *Marine Policy* 117 (July 2020), pp. 103954.

46   U. Rashid Sumaila et al., *Sink or Swim: The Future of Fisheries in the East and South China Seas*, Hong Kong: ADM Capital Foundation, 2021.

47   Ibid.

48   Ibid.

49   Robert Glasser, 'The Rapidly Emerging Crisis on Our Doorstep', *Australian Strategic Policy Institute Strategic Insights,* April 2021.

50   Schreer and Huxley, cited in Brendan Taylor and William Tow, 'Australia Debates the South China Sea: Is There a Third Way?' in Andrew Carr (ed.), *The South China Sea: Middle Power Perspectives*, Centre of Gravity series paper 27, Canberra: Australian National University, 2016, pp. 2–5.

51   James Goldrick, 'Why Australia Must Send Its Navy to Assert Freedom to Operate in the South China Sea', *The Interpreter,* 29 October 2015.

52   Sam Roggeveen, 'Fierravanti-Wells' Outburst Tells More Than Just a China Story', *The Interpreter,* 7 June 2019; Anna Henderson, 'South China Sea: Stephen Conroy Denies Remarks on China 'Bullying' Designed to Stir Up Tensions', ABC News, 14 July 2016.

53   Malcolm Turnbull, *A Bigger Picture,* Richmond: Hardie Grant, 2020, pp. 423–24.

54   Julian Ku, 'The US Navy's "Innocent Passage" in the South China Sea May Have Actually Strengthened China's Sketchy Territorial Claim', *Lawfare,* 4 November 2015.

55   See for example, Department of Foreign Affairs and Trade, *Joint Statement on the Establishment of a Strategic Partnership Between Australia and Viet Nam,* 15 March 2018, www.dfat.gov.au/geo/vietnam/Pages/joint-statement-on-the-establishment-of-a-strategic-partnership-between-australia-and-viet-nam; Department of Foreign Affairs and Trade, *Joint Statement on the Eighth Australia-Indonesia Foreign and Defence Ministers' 2+2 Meeting,* 10 February 2023, www.foreignminister.gov.au/minister/penny-wong/media-release/

joint-statement-eighth-australia-indonesia-foreign-and-defence-ministers-22-meeting; Department of Foreign Affairs and Trade, *Joint Statement: 5th Australia-Malaysia Annual Foreign Ministers' Meeting,* 5 May 2023, www.foreignminister.gov.au/minister/penny-wong/media-release/joint-statement-5th-australia-malaysia-annual-foreign-ministers-meeting; 'The Philippines-Australia Ministerial Meeting – Joint Ministerial Statement', Department of Foreign Affairs and Trade, accessed 17 January 2024, www.dfat.gov.au/geo/philippines/philippines-australia-ministerial-meeting-joint-ministerial-statement.

56 Commonwealth of Australia, *Defence White Paper,* Canberra: Department of Defence, 2013, pp. 8, 11.

57 Commonwealth of Australia, *Foreign Policy White Paper,* pp. 46–47.

58 Asia Maritime Transparency Initiative, *Arbitration Support Tracker,* 2021, https://amti.csis.org/arbitration-support-tracker.

59 See Douglas Guilfoyle, 'The Rule of Law and Maritime Security: Understanding Lawfare in the South China Sea', *International Affairs* 95:5 (2019), pp. 999–1017.

60 Australian Government, No. 20/026, New York, 23 July 2020, www.un.org/depts/los/clcs_new/submissions_files/mys_12_12_2019/2020_07_23_AUS_NV_UN_001_OLA-2020-00373.pdf.

61 Christian Wirth, 'Whose 'Freedom of Navigation'? Australia, China, the United States and the making of order in the 'Indo-Pacific', *The Pacific Review*, 32:4 (2019), pp. 475–504.

62 United States White House, *Indo-Pacific Strategy of the United States,* 2022, www.whitehouse.gov/wp-content/uploads/2022/02/U.S.-Indo-Pacific-Strategy.pdf. See also Oriana Skylar Mastro, 'Chinese Intentions in the South China Sea', Essay, 2020–2021 Wilson China Fellowship, 2021, https://fsi-live.s3.us-west-1.amazonaws.com/s3fs-public/documents/mastro_paper.pdf.

63 Paul Karp, 'Australia "Pretending" to Stand Up to China over Disputed Islands, Labor Says', *The Guardian*, 13 July 2016.

64 Department of Defence, *2020 Defence Strategic Update.*

CHAPTER 5

1 Michael Shoebridge, 'Djibouti Shows What Sogavare's Deal with China Really Means', *The Strategist,* 11 April 2022.

2 See: Joanne Wallis, *Pacific Power? Australia's Strategy in the Pacific Islands,* Melbourne: Melbourne University Press, 2017.

3 John Howard, quoted in Mark Forbes, 'Pacific Leaders Back Australian Role', *The Age*, 9 August 2004; Department of Defence, *Defence White Paper 2013*, p. 25; Alex Hawke, 'Australia's Focus on the Pacific – Keynote Speech to the AIIA National Conference', Canberra, 17 October 2019, www.internationalaffairs.org.au/australianoutlook/australias-focus-on-the-pacific-minister-of-international-development-and-the-pacific-hon-alex-hawke-mps-keynote-speech-to-the-aiia-national-conference; Scott Morrison, 'Australia and the Pacific: A New Chapter', Lavarack Barracks, Townsville, 8 November 2018, www.pm.gov.au/media/address-australia-and-pacific-new-chapter.

NOTES

4   Meg Taylor, 'Griffith Asia Lecture 2019', Brisbane, Griffith University, 11 November 2019, www.forumsec.org/2019/11/12/griffith-asia-lecture-2019-delivered-by-the-secretary-general-of-the-pacific-islands-forum-dame-meg-taylor.

5   Frank Chung, '"Australia Must Ready Solomon Islands Invasion" to Stop China Security Deal', *The Courier Mail*, 25 March 2022.

6   Manasseh Sogavare, 'Prime Minister Statement to Parliament', 29 March 2022.

7   Cait Storr, '"Imperium in Imperio": Sub-Imperialism and the Formation of Australia as a Subject of International Law', *Melbourne Journal of International Law* 19:1 (2018), p. 335.

8   Quoted in Adam Morton, 'Fiji PM Frank Bainimarama Slaps Down Liberal MP John Alexander's Climate Advice', *The Guardian*, 8 May 2019.

9   Neville Meaney, 'Australia's Foreign Policy: History and Myth', *Australian Outlook,* 23:2 (1969), p. 173.

10   British Government, Arthur Phillip's first commission, 12 October 1786, in *Historical Records of New South Wales, Vol. 2, Part 2: Grose and Paterson, 1793–1795*, Sydney: Government Printer, 1893.

11   House of Representatives, *Australian Parliamentary Debates*, 6 (1901–02), pp. 7079–91.

12   Ibid.

13   *Security Treaty Between Australia, New Zealand and the United States of America [ANZUS]*, San Francisco, 1 September 1951, part. 4.

14   Department of Defence, *Force Structure Review*, Commonwealth of Australia, Canberra, 1991, 28.

15   'Protecting and Advancing Australia's Interests in the Pacific Islands', Paper attached to Cabinet submission, 'Review of Australia's Policy Towards the Pacific Islands', NAA: A 11502, 2003/38457, 23 September 2000, pt. 1.

16   Department of Defence, *Defence 2000*, p. 44.

17   Gareth Evans, 'Australia in the South Pacific', Address to the Foreign Correspondents' Association, Sydney, 23 September 1988, *Australian Foreign Affairs Record*, 59:9 (1988), pp. 347–50, 350, 349.

18   Department of Foreign Affairs and Trade, *Advancing the National Interest: Australia's Foreign and Trade Policy White Paper*, Canberra: Commonwealth of Australia, 2003, p. 93.

19   John Howard, 'Address to the Australian Strategic Policy Institute, Westin Hotel, Sydney', 18 June 2004, https://pmtranscripts.pmc.gov.au/release/transcript-21325.

20   Department of Defence, *Defence Capability Plan 2004–2014*, Canberra: Commonwealth of Australia, 2003.

21   Kevin Rudd, 'Port Moresby Declaration', 6 March 2008, https://pmtranscripts.pmc.gov.au/release/transcript-15802.

22   Department of Prime Minister and Cabinet, *Strong and Secure*, pp. 7, 38, 30.

23   Department of Defence, *Defence White Paper 2013*.

NOTES

24   Department of Defence, *2016 Defence White Paper*.

25   Quoted in Pacific Beat, 'Chinese Military Base in Pacific Would Be of 'Great Concern', Turnbull Tells Vanuatu,' ABC News, 10 April 2018.

26   Pacific Islands Forum, 'Boe Declaration on Regional Security', Niue, 5 September 2018, www.forumsec.org/2018/09/05/boe-declaration-on-regional-security.

27   Christopher Pala, 'How Eight Pacific Island States Are Saving the World's Tuna', *Foreign Policy*, 5 March 2021.

28   Joanne Wallis et al., 'Mapping Security Cooperation in the Pacific Islands', *Department of Pacific Affairs Research Report 1*, 2021, pp. 7–8.

29   Chang Sen Yu, 'The Pacific Islands in China's Dtrategy for the 21st Ventury', in *2014–2015 Dayangzhou lanpi shu [2014–2015 Blue Book of Oceania]*, 2nd ed., Beijing: Social Sciences Academic Press, 2015.

30   Rohan Fox and Matthew Dornan, 'China in the Pacific: Is China Engaged in 'Dept-Ttrap Diplomacy'?', *DevPolicy*, 8 November 2018.

31   'Pasifika' meaning peoples of the Pacific Islands. Māori, the Indigenous people of New Zealand, have historical ancestral ties to the Pacific Islands and significant cultural and linguistic similarities, but are considered separate from Pasifika.

32   Nick Sas, Tim Swanston, and Chrisnrita Aumanu-Leong, 'Solomon Islands PM Blasts the United States After Missing Pacific Leaders' Summit at White House', ABC News, 27 September 2023.

33   Nic Maclellan, '"Macron-ising" the Pacific', *Islands Business*, 14 June 2018.

34   Meg Taylor, 'Keynote Address: The China Alternative: Changing Regional Order in the Pacific Islands', University of the South Pacific, Port Vila, 8 February 2019, www.forumsec.org/keynote-address-by-dame-meg-taylor-secretary-general-the-china-alternative-changing-regional-order-in-the-pacific-islands.

35   Ibid.

36   Steven Ratuva, 'Pacific Island Agency in the Global Game of Competitive Geo-political Bidding', *Australian Outlook*, 6 June 2019, www.internationalaffairs.org.au/australianoutlook/pacific-island-agency-in-the-global-game-of-competitive-geo-political-bidding/; Derek Futaiasi, et al., *Lalaga, tithiki, talia vata: Pacific Islands Weaving Statecraft, Adelaide Papers on Pacific Security 02/2023*, Adelaide: University of Adelaide, 2023.

37   Quoted in Daniel Hurst, 'Samoa's PM Says China Expectation of Pacific-Wide Deal "Something We Could Not Agree To"', *The Guardian*, 2 June 2022.

38   'Joint Statement from the Hon Fiamē Naomi Mataʻafa, Prime Minister of Samoa and Senator Penny Wong, Australia's Minister for Foreign Affairs', 2 June 2022, https://samoa.embassy.gov.au/files/apia/Joint%20Statement%20-%20Visit%20by%20Minister%20Wong%20to%20Samoa%202-3%20June%202022.pdf.

NOTES

39   Meg Taylor, 'Address – 2018 State of the Pacific Conference', Canberra: Australian National University, 8 October 2018, www.forumsec.org/keynote-address-by-dame-meg-taylor-secretary-general-the-china-alternative-changing-regional-order-in-the-pacific-islands.

40   Epeli Hau'ofa, 'Our Sea of Islands', *The Contemporary Pacific* 6:1 (1994), pp. 148–61.

41   Pacific Islands Forum, *2050 Strategy for the Blue Pacific Continent*, Suva: Pacific Islands Forum Secretariat, 2022, www.forumsec.org/wp-content/uploads/2022/08/PIFS-2050-Strategy-Blue-Pacific-Continent-WEB-5Aug2022.pdf.

42   Greg Fry and Sandra Tarte (eds.), *The New Pacific Diplomacy*, Canberra: ANU Press, 2015.

43   Drawn from Joanne Wallis, 'Strategic Competition in the Pacific Islands', in Lynn Kuok and Tim Huxley (eds.), *Asia-Pacific Regional Security Assessment 2021*, London: International Institute for Strategic Studies, 2021, pp. 115–34.

44   Malcolm Turnbull, 'Media Release – Pacific Islands Forum in Samoa', 6 September 2017, https://pmtranscripts.pmc.gov.au/release/transcript-41165.

45   Benjamin Felton, 'Australia's Pacific Support Vessel: What to Make of ADV Reliant', *Australian Defence Magazine*, 4 August 2022.

46   Anthony Galloway, 'Defence Looks at Chinese Plane Blocking Australian Aid Plane in Vanuatu', *The Sydney Morning Herald*, 15 April 2020.

47   Scott Morrison, 'Australia and the Pacific: A New Chapter', Lavarack Barracks, Townsville, 8 November 2018, www.pm.gov.au/media/address-australia-and-pacific-new-chapter.

48   Scott Morrison, 'Address, University of the South Pacific', Suva, 18 January 2019, www.pm.gov.au/media/address-university-south-pacific-fiji.

49   Former Marshall Islands Foreign Minister Tony de Brum quoted in Nick O'Malley, 'Australia Is a Pacific Island – It Has a Responsibility', *The Sydney Morning Herald*, 21 September 2014.

50   Former Australian High Commissioner to Samoa Sara Moriarty, *Australia in the World: Episode 30*, Podcast, 3 October 2019, www.internationalaffairs.org.au/australianoutlook/australia-in-the-world-episode-30.

51   Winston Peters, 'Shifting the Dial, Eyes Wide Open', Speech to the Lowy Institute, Sydney, 2 March 2018.

52   Joanne Wallis, 'The Enclosure and Exclusion of Australia's "Pacific Family"', *Political Geography* 106 (2023), p. 102935.

53   Tracey Banivanua Mar, *Violence and Colonial Dialogue: The Australian-Pacific Indentured Labor Trade*, Manoa: University of Hawaii Press, 2006.

54   Henrietta McNeill, 'Deportation as a Neo-Colonial Act: How Deporting State Influence Extends Beyond the Border', *Political Geography*, 102 (2023), p. 102845.

55   Joanne Wallis and Anna Powles, *Smooth Sailing? Australia, New Zealand and the United States Partnering in – and With – the Pacific Islands*, Canberra: Australian Strategic Policy Institute, 2023.

NOTES

CHAPTER 6

1   Christian Bouchard and William Crumplin, 'Neglected No Longer: the Indian Ocean at the Forefront of World Geopolitics and Global Geostrategy', *Journal of the Indian Ocean Region* 6:1 (2010), p. 26.

2   'Australia and the Indian Ocean Region', Australian Government Department of Foreign Affairs and Trade, accessed 30 March 2022, www.dfat.gov. au/international-relations/regional-architecture/indian-ocean/Pages/indian-ocean-region.

3   Sergei DeSilva-Ranasinghe, 'Why the Indian Ocean Matters', *The Diplomat*, 2 March 2011.

4   Andrew C. Winner and Peter Dombrowski, 'Introduction: American Strategy in the Indian Ocean', in Peter Dombrowski and Andrew C. Winner (eds), *The Indian Ocean and US Grand Strategy: Ensuring Access and Promoting Security*, Washington, D.C.: Georgetown University Press, 2014, p. 6.

5   R.S. Aswani, 'Non-Traditional Maritime Security Threats in the Indian Ocean Region: Policy Alternatives', *Journal of Public Affairs*, 22:2 (2022), p. 1.

6   Sam Bateman and Anthony Bergin, *Our Western Front: Australia and the Indian Ocean*, Canberra: Australian Strategic Policy Institute, 2010, p. 12.

7   Peter Hannam, 'WA's Offshore Gasfields Pay Almost No Royalties and Stoke Carbon Emmisions, Report Finds', *The Guardian*, 17 January 2022.

8   Mark Noonan and Elizabeth Williams, 'Combating Maritime Transnational Crime: An Australian Perspective', *Journal of the Indian Ocean Region*, 12:1 (2016), p. 46.

9   Sam Bateman and Anthony Bergin, *Our Western Front*, p. 33.

10   Marles, 'Securing Australia's Sovereignty'.

11   Department of Defence, *An Appreciation of the Strategical Position of Australia*, Canberra: Commonwealth of Australia, 1946.

12   Department of Defence, *Strategic Basis of Australian Defence Policy* [1964], pt. 34.

13   Department of Defence, *Strategic Basis of Australian Defence Policy*, Canberra: Commonwealth of Australia, 1968, pt. 37.

14   Sam Bateman and Anthony Bergin, *Our Western Front: Australia and the Indian Ocean*, Australia: Australian Strategic Policy Institute, 2010, p. 13.

15   Parliament of the Commonwealth of Australia, *Report from the Joint Committee on Foreign Affairs on the Indian Ocean Region*, December 1971, p. 34.

16   Department of Defence, *Strategic Basis of Australian Defence Policy*, Canberra: Commonwealth of Australia, 1971.

17   Ibid., pt. 105.

18   Department of Defence, *Strategic Basis of Australian Defence Policy*, Canberra: Commonwealth of Australia, 1971, pt. 105.

19   Ibid., pt. 140.

20   Parliament of the Commonwealth of Australia, *Australia and the Indian Ocean Region*, November 1976, p. 171.

NOTES

21   Parliament of the Commonwealth of Australia, *Australia and the Indian Ocean Region*, November 1976, p. 182.

22   Department of Defence, *Australian Defence*.

23   Ibid., p. 6.

24   Kim Beazley and Ian Clark, *Politics of Intrusion: The Super Powers and the Indian Ocean*, Sydney: Alternative Publishing Cooperative Limited, 1979.

25   Department of Defence, *The Defence of Australia*, p. viii; Kim Beazley, 'The Two Ocean Navy', in R. Bruce (ed.), *Australia and the Indian Ocean: Strategic Dimensions of Increasing Naval Involvement, Studies in Indian Ocean Maritime Affairs, No 1*, Perth: Centre for Indian Ocean Regional Studies, Curtin University of Technology, 1988, pp. 920.

26   Department of Defence, *The Defence of Australia*, p. 10.

27   Auriol Weigold, 'Engagement Versus Neglect: Australia in the Indian Ocean, 1960–2000', *Journal of the Indian Ocean Region* 7:1 (2011), 32–51.

28   Ian Hall, 'Australia's Fitful Engagements of India', in Ian Hall (ed.), *The Engagement of India: Strategies and Responses,* Washington DC: Georgetown University Press, 2014, p. 130.

29   Senate Standing Committee on Foreign Affairs, Defence, and Trade, *Australia-India Relations: Trade and Security*, Canberra: Commonwealth of Australia, 1990, p. ix.

30   Ibid., p. ix–x.

31   Department of Defence, *Defending Australia*, p. 86.

32   Ibid., p. 91.

33   Australian Department of Foreign Affairs and Trade, *India's Economy at the Midnight Hour: Australia's India Strategy*, Canberra: Australian Government Publishing Service, 1994.

34   Christian Wagner, 'The Indian Ocean Rim – Association for Regional Co-operation (IOR-ARC): the Futile Quest for Regionalism?', *Journal of the Indian Ocean Region* 9:1 (2017), p. 10.

35   Department of Defence, *Defence 2000*, p. 20.

36   Department of Defence, *Defending Australia in the Asia Pacific Century*, p. 12.

37   Ibid., p. 37.

38   Ibid., p. 52.

39   Ibid., p. 96.

40   Australian Senate Foreign Affairs, Defence and Trade Committee, *The Importance of the Indian Ocean Rim for Australia's Foreign, Trade and Defence Policy*, June 2013, p. 200.

41   Kevin Rudd, 'Australia's Foreign Policy Looking West', *Journal of the Indian Ocean Region* 7:1 (2011), p. 132.

42   Department of Defence, *Defence White Paper 2013*, p. 7.

43   Ibid., p. 8.

44   David Brewster, *Australia's Second Sea: Facing Our Multipolar Future in the Indian Ocean*, Australia: Australian Strategic Policy Institute, 2019, p. 15.

45   Department of Defence, *Defence White Paper 2013*, p. 2.

46   Ibid., p. 7.

47   Ibid., p. 65.

48   Ibid., p. 16.

49   Julie Bishop, 'Australia's Economic Diplomacy: Our Prosperity, Global Prosperity', Media release, 18 August 2014, www.foreignminister.gov.au/minister/julie-bishop/media-release/australias-economic-diplomacy-our-prosperity-global-prosperity.

50   Department of Defence, *2016 Defence White Paper*, pp. 61–62.

51   Ibid., p. 120.

52   Ibid., p. 135.

53   Ibid., p. 62.

54   Daniel Hurst, 'It's Unprecedented for Dutton to Label a Chinese Spy Ship Sailing Outside Australia's Territory 'An Aggressive Act', *The Guardian*, 13 May 2022.

55   Lee Jones and Shahar Hamieri, *Debunking the Myth of 'Debt-trap Diplomacy': How Recipient Countries Shape China's Belt and Road Initiative*, London: Chatham House, 2020, p. 14.

56   Deborah Brautigam, 'A Critical Look at Chinese 'Debt-Trap Diplomacy': The Rise of a Meme', *Area Development and Policy* 5:1 (2020), pp. 1–14.

57   Lauren Frayer, 'Why a Chinese Ship's Arrival in Sri Lanka Has Caused Alarm in India and the West', *National Public Radio*, 19 August 2022.

58   H.I. Sutton, 'Chinese Ships Seen Mapping Strategic Seabed in Indian Ocean', *Naval News*, 22 January 2021.

59   Caitlin Campbell, *Highlights from China's New Defence White Paper, 'China's Military Strategy'*, US-China Economic and Security Review Commission Issue Brief, 1 June 2015, www.uscc.gov/sites/default/files/Research/Issue%20Brief_Highlights%20from%20Chinas%20New%20Defense%20White%20Paper_Campbell_6.1.15.pdf.

60   China Aerospace Studies Institute, *In Their Own Words: Foreign Military Thought*, Science of Military Strategy, U.S. Air University, 2013, p. 310.

61   Alicia Garcia Herrero, 'Will the Belt and Road Initiative Be Another Casualty of the Pandemic?', *Georgetown Journal of International Affairs*, 11 November 2022.

62   Dinakar Peri, 'Extra-Regional Fishing Fleets Present in Indian Ocean: Navy', *The Hindu*, 13 November 2022.

63   Chris Wilcox et al., *A Review of Illegal, Unreported and Unregulated Fishing Issues and Progress in the Asia-Pacific Fishery Commission Region*, Hobart: Commonwealth Scientific and Industrial Research Organisation, 2021, p. 53.

64   Rushali Saha, 'Prioritizing the Indian Ocean in US Indo-Pacific Strategy', Stimson Center Policy Memo, 3 February 2023, www.stimson.org/2023/prioritizing-the-indian-ocean-in-us-indo-pacific-strategy.

65 Donald Trump, *National Security Strategy of the United States of America*, December 2017, https://trumpwhitehouse.archives.gov/wp-content/uploads/2017/12/NSS-Final-12-18-2017-0905.pdf, p. 46.

66 The White House, *Indo-Pacific Strategy of the United States*, February 2022, www.whitehouse.gov/wp-content/uploads/2022/02/U.S.-Indo-Pacific-Strategy.pdf.

67 Van Jackson, 'America Needs an Economic Peace Strategy for Asia', Essay, National University of Singapore, https://ari.nus.edu.sg/app-essay-van-jackson.

68 David Brewster, 'Indian Ocean Base Race: India Responds', *The Interpreter*, 15 February 2018.

69 Abhijit Singh, 'The U.S. Navy in the Indian Ocean: India's 'Goldilocks' Dilemma', *War on the Rocks*, 11 May 2021.

70 ReCAAP Information Sharing Centre, *Executive Director's Report 2021*, www.recaap.org/resources/ck/files/reports/ED%20Report/ReCaap_ExecutiveDirectorsReport2021.pdf, p. 10.

71 Commonwealth of Australia, *Guide to Australian Maritime Security Arrangements*.

72 World Wide Fund for Nature, *Unregulated Fishing on the High Seas of the Indian Ocean*, November 2020, www.wwf.eu/?1014116/Unregulated-fishing-on-the-high-seas-of-the-Indian-Ocean, 5.

73 P. Anagha, 'Impact of Climate Change on the Blue Economy of the Indian Ocean Region: Case Study of the Fisheries Sector', *Vivekananda International Foundation*, 9 September 2022.

74 Darshana M. Baruah, 'What Island Nations hHave to Say on Indo-Pacific Geopolitics', *Carnegie Endowment for International Peace*, 23 March 2022, https://carnegieendowment.org/2022/03/23/what-island-nations-have-to-say-on-indo-pacific-geopolitics-pub-86700.

75 Dani Cooper, 'Forests of the Sea in Western Australia Slashed by Marine Heatwave', ABC News, 8 July 2016.

76 Emma Larkin, 'Controlling Irregular Migration in the Asia-Pacific: Is Australia Acting Against Its Own Interests?', *Asia & the Pacific Policy Studies* 4:1 (2017), p. 86.

77 Ibid.

78 Helen Ware, 'Who Are Australia's 'Boat People', and Why Don't They Get on Planes?', *The Conversation*, 25 July 2012.

79 Australian Department of Foreign Affairs and Trade, *Plan of Action for the Implementation of the Joint Declaration on Maritime Cooperation Between the Government of Australia and the Government of the Republic of Indonesia*, February 2017, www.dfat.gov.au/sites/default/files/indonesia-australia-maritime-cooperation-action-plan.pdf.

80 Michael R. Pompeo, 'Trump Administration Diplomacy: The Untold Story', Speech at the Heritage Foundation President's Club Meeting, Washington, United States, 22 October 2019, https://translations.state.gov/2019/10/22/

secretary-michael-r-pompeo-at-the-heritage-foundation-presidents-club-meeting-trump-administration-diplomacy-the-untold-story.

81   'Chapter Six – Australia's Response to Nuclear Tests in South Asia', Parliament of Australia, Australian Federal Government, www.aph. gov.au/Parliamentary_Business/Committees/Senate/Foreign_Affairs_ Defence_and_Trade/Completed_inquiries/1999-02/nuclear/report/c06.

82   David Brewster, 'Australia and India: The Indian Ocean and the Limits of Strategic Convergence', *Australian Journal of International Affairs* 64:5 (2010), pp. 549–65, 551.

83   Stephanie March, 'Uranium Deal: PM Tony Abbott in India to Sign Nuclear Cooperation Agreement', ABC News, 4 September 2014; Nigam Prusty, 'India and Australia Seal Civil Nuclear Deal for Uranium Trade', Reuters, 5 September 2014.

84   'Framework for Security Cooperation between Australia and India 2014', Department of Foreign Affairs and Trade, Australian Federal Government, 18 November 2014, www.dfat.gov.au/geo/india/Pages/ framework-for-security-cooperation-between-australia-and-india-2014.

85   'Joint Statement on a Comprehensive Strategic Partnership between Republic of India and Australia', Department of Foreign Affairs and Trade, Australian Federal Government, 4 June 2020, www.dfat.gov.au/geo/india/joint-statement-comprehensive-strategic-partnership-between-republic-india-and-australia.

86   'Joint Declaration on a Shared Vision for Maritime Cooperation in the Indo-Pacific Between The Republic of India and the Government of Australia', Department of Foreign Affairs and Trade, Australian Federal Government, 4 June 2020, www.dfat.gov.au/geo/india/ joint-declaration-shared-vision-maritime-cooperation-indo-pacific-between-republic-india-and-government-australia.

87   'Prime Minister's Speech at the East Asia Summit, 4 November 2019', Ministry of External Affairs, Government of India, 4 November 2019, www.mea.gov.in/Speeches-Statements.htm?dtl/32171/ Prime_Ministers_Speech_at_the_East_Asia_Summit_04_November_2019.

88   'Australia-India Indo-Pacific Oceans Initiative Partnership: Grant Round 1', Australian High Commission New Delhi, Australian Federal Government, https://india.highcommission.gov.au/ndli/AIIPOIP.html.

89   Sumit Ganguly, 'India's Endangered Democracy', *Journal of Democracy* 32:4 (2014), pp. 177–80.

90   Abhijit Singh, 'The U.S. Navy in the Indian Ocean: India's 'Goldilocks' Dilema', *War on the Rocks*, 11 May 2021, https://warontherocks.com/2021/05/ the-u-s-navy-in-the-indian-ocean-indias-goldilocks-dilemma.

91   David Brewster, 'Australia Begins to Step It Up in the Northeast Indian Ocean', *The Interpreter*, 2 March 2022, www.lowyinstitute.org/the-interpreter/ australia-begins-step-it-northeast-indian-ocean.

92   Department of Defence, *2020 Defence Strategic Update*, p. 6.

NOTES

93   Commonwealth of Australia, *National Defence: Defence Strategic Review*, p. 46.

94   The White House, 'Fact Sheet: Quad Leaders' Tokyo Summit
2022', 23 May 2022, www.whitehouse.gov/briefing-room/
statements-releases/2022/05/23/fact-sheet-quad-leaders-tokyo-summit-2022.

95   'Quad Leaders' Joint Statement', Hiroshima, Japan, 20 May 2023, www.
whitehouse.gov/briefing-room/statements-releases/2023/05/20/quad-
leaders-joint-statement/#:~:text=We%2C%20the%20countries%20of%20
the,United%20States'%20APEC%20host%20year.

96   M.R. Khan et al., 'High-Density Population and Displacement
in Bangladesh', *Science* 372:6548 (2021), pp. 1290–93.

CHAPTER 7

1   Australian Antarctic Program, *20th Anniversary of the Hawke Government's Action
to Protect Antarctica*, 14 December 2009, www.antarctica.gov.au/news/2009/20th-
anniversary-of-the-hawke-governments-action-to-protect-antarctica.

2   It should be noted that some definitions view the ocean as beginning
60 degrees latitude south, where it meets the Pacific, Atlantic and Indian
oceans: Klaus Dodds, *The Antarctic: A Very Short Introduction*, Oxford: Oxford
University Press, 2012, p. 5.

3   Foreign Affairs, Defence and Trade References Committee, *Australia's Future
Activities and Responsibilities in the Southern Ocean and Antarctic Waters*,
Australian Senate, October 2014, p. 2.

4   Marigold Black and Peter Dortmans, 'Not So Quiet on the Southern Front', *The
Interpreter*, 18 February 2022.

5   Karen N. Scott, 'Maritime Security and Shipping Safety in the Southern
Ocean,' in Natalie Klein, Joanna Mossop and Donald Rothwell (eds), *Maritime
Security: International Law and Policy Perspectives from Australia and New
Zealand*, Oxon: Routledge, 2010, p. 117.

6   Dodds, *The Antarctic*, pp. 23, 25.

7   Christopher Joyner, *Antarctica and the Law of the Sea*, Netherlands: Martinus
Nijhoff Publishers, 1992, p. 50.

8   Dodds, *The Antarctic*, p. 52.

9   W.M. Bush, *Antarctica and International Law: A Collection of Inter-state and
National Documents*, London: Oceana Publications, 1982, p. 143.

10   Elizabeth Buchanan, 'Australia's Southern Flank: Antarctica', in Brooklyn et al.
(eds), *Australia on the World Stage*, pp. 185–86.

11   Dodds, *The Antarctic*, p. 35.

12   Joyner, *Antarctica and the Law of the Sea*, p. 197. Although as Kaye and
Rothwell note, those sovereign claims are 'as good as any other claim that
may be made to the continent'. Stuart Kaye and Donald Rothwell, 'Australia's
Antarctic Maritime Claims and Boundaries', *Ocean Development of
International Law* 26 (1995), p. 195-226.

13   Donald Rothwell, Karen Scott and Alan Hemmings, 'The Search for 'Antarctic
Security', in Alan Hemmings, Donald Rothwell and Karen N. Scott (eds),

NOTES

Antarctic Security in the Twenty-First Century: Legal and Policy Perspectives, Oxon: Routledge, 2012, p. 2.

14   Dodds, *The Antarctic.*

15   Elizabeth Buchanan, 'Australia's Southern Flank: Antarctica', p. 188.

16   Patrizia Vigni and Francesco Francioni, 'Territorial Claims and Coastal States', in Klaus Dodds, Alan Hemmings and Peder Roberts (eds), *Handbook on the Politics of Antarctica,* Cheltenham: Edward Elgar Publishing, 2017, p. 245.

17   Karen N. Scott, 'Maritime Security and Shipping Safety in the Southern Ocean', in Natalie Klein, Joanna Mossop and Donald R. Rothwell (eds.), *Maritime Security: International Law and Policy Perspectives from Australia and New Zealand,* London and New York: Routledge, 2010, p. 118.

18   Bernard H. Oxman, 'Antarctica and the New Law of the Sea', *Cornell International Law Journal* 19:2 (1986), article 4; Joyner, *Antarctica and the Law of the Sea,* p. 75.

19   Commonwealth of Australia, Continental Shelf Submission of Australia: Executive Summary, 2004, www.un.org/Depts/los/clcs_new/submissions_files/aus04/Documents/aus_doc_es_web_delivery.pdf.

20   Commonwealth of Australia, *Seas and Submerged Lands (Limits of Continental Shelf) Proclamation 2012,* 24 May 2012.

21   'Key Challenges and Achievements', *Convention for the Conservation of Antarctic Marine Living Resources,* www.ccamlr.org/en/organisation/key-challenges-and-achievements.

22   'History', *Convention for the Conservation of Antarctic Marine Living Resources,* www.ccamlr.org/en/organisation/fishing-ccamlr.

23   'Key Challenges and Achievements', *Convention for the Conservation of Antarctic Marine Living Resources,* www.ccamlr.org/en/organisation/key-challenges-and-achievements.

24   Commonwealth of Australia, 'Introducing the Commission for the Conservation of Antarctic Marine Living Resources', *Australian Antarctic Program,* www.antarctica.gov.au/about-antarctica/law-and-treaty/ccamlr/australias-primary-goal-within-ccamlr.

25   Bernard P. Herber, 'The Common Heritage Principle: Antarctica and the Developing Nations', *The American Journal of Economics and Sociology* 50:4 (1991), p. 365.

26   Nengyu Liu, 'What Are China's Intentions in Antarctica?', *The Diplomat,* 14 June 2019.

27   Elizabeth Buchanan and Rebecca Strating, 'Why the Arctic Is Not the 'Next' South China Sea', *War on the Rocks,* 5 November 2020.

28   Buchanan, 'Australia's Southern Flank: Antarctica', p. 194.

29   Elizabeth Buchanan, 'Antarctica in the Gray Zone', *Australian Journal of International Affairs* 76:3 (2022), p. 324.

30   China's Bei Dou satellite system, Russia's GLONASS, the United States' GPS and the EU's Galileo are just some systems with receiving stations in Antarctica. Buchanan, 'Australia's Southern Flank: Antarctica', p. 192.

NOTES

31   Klaus Dodds, 'Five Inconvenient Truths About the Antarctic', *OUP blog*,
      18 March 2013.
32   Department of Defence, *2016 Defence White Paper*, p. 53.
33   Cassandra Brooks, 'Why Are Talks Over an East Antarctic Marine Park Still
      Deadlocked?', *The Conversation*, 3 November 2017.
34   Ibid.
35   Foreign Affairs, Defence and Trade References Committee, *Australia's Future
      Activities and Responsibilities in the Southern Ocean and Antarctic Waters*,
      October 2014, p. 12.
36   Maurice Huguenin, Ryan Holmes and Matthew England, 'Drivers and
      Distribution of Global Ocean Heat Uptake Over the Last Half Century', *Nature
      Communications* 13:4921 (2022).
37   Peter Davis et al., 'Suppressed Basal Melting in the Eastern Thwaites Glacier
      Grounding Zone,' *Nature* 614 (2023), pp. 479–85.
38   Jamie Seidel, 'Melting "Doomsday" Glacier Could Leave Most of Inhabited
      Australia Underwater", News.com.au, 21 February 2023.
39   Karen N. Scott, 'Maritime Security and Shipping Safety in the Southern Ocean,'
      in Natalie Klein, Joanna Mossop and Donald R. Rothwell (eds), *Maritime
      Security: International Law and Policy Perspectives from Australia and New
      Zealand,* London and New York: Routledge, 2010, p. 11.
40   Foreign Affairs, Defence and Trade References Committee, *Australia's Future
      Activities and Responsibilities in the Southern Ocean and Antarctic Waters*,
      Australian Senate, October 2014.
41   Australian Antarctic Programme, *Australian Antarctic Strategy and 20 Year
      Action Plan*, Canberra: Commonwealth of Australia, 2016.
42   Ibid.
43   Department of Defence, *2016 Defence White Paper*.
44   Ibid.
45   Department of Foreign Affairs and Trade, *2017 Foreign Policy White Paper*,
      p. 85.
46   Australian Antarctic Program, *RSV Nuyina – Australia's New Icebreaker*, www.
      antarctica.gov.au/about-antarctica/history/transportation/shipping/rsv-nuyina.
47   Henry Belot, 'Australia's New $528m Icebreaker Research Vessel
      Nuyina Suffers Another Setback', *The Guardian*, 31 January 2023;
      Australian Antarctic Programme, 'RSV Nuyina Prepares for a Busy
      Year Ahead', 24 April 2023, www.antarctica.gov.au/nuyina/stories/2023/
      rsv-nuyina-prepares-for-a-busy-year-ahead.
48   Matt Hickman, 'Scientists Push Back Against Australia's Multibillion-Dollar
      Antarctic Airport', *The Architect's Newspaper,* 4 January 2021.
49   Foreign Affairs, Defence and Trade References Committee, *Australia's Future
      Activities and Responsibilities in the Southern Ocean and Antarctic Waters*,
      Australian Senate, October 2014.
50   Ibid.

NOTES

Dan Smith, 'Antarctic Cargo Ship *Happy Diamond*, Chartered to Replace Beleaguered Icebreaker *RSV Nuyina*, Runs Aground off Mawson Station", ABC, 20 February 2023.

52 Ibid, p. 26.

53 Foreign Affairs, Defence and Trade References Committee, *Australia's Future Activities and Responsibilities in the Southern Ocean and Antarctic Waters,* October 2014, p. 19.

54 Ibid., p. ix.

55 Claire Young, 'Antarctica: Working a Rules-Based System', *The Interpreter,* 16 February 2021.

56 Australian Antarctic Program, *Momentum Builds for Southern Ocean Protection,* 29 April 2021, www.antarctica.gov.au/news/2021/momentum-builds-for-southern-ocean-protection.

57 Rebecca Strating, 'Assessing the Maritime "Rules-based Order" in Antarctica', *Australian Journal of International Affairs* 76:3 (2022), pp. 286–304.

58 Anthony Bergin, 'Australian Oceans and Antarctic Policy', *Agenda for Change 2016: Strategic Choices for the Next Government,* Canberra: ASPI, 2016.

59 Elizabeth Buchanan, 'Antarctica in the Gray Zone', *Australian Journal of International Affairs* 76:3 (2022), p. 336.

60 Sam Bateman, 'Regional Navies and Coastguards: Striking a Balance Between "Lawships" and Warships' in Geoffrey Till and Jane Chan (eds), *Naval Modernisation in Southeast Asia,* Oxon: Routledge, 2013.

61 Foreign Affairs, Defence and Trade References Committee, *Australia's Future Activities and Responsibilities in the Southern Ocean and Antarctic Waters,* October 2014, pp. 77–78.

62 Buchanan, 'Antarctica in the Gray Zone', p. 337.

63 Foreign Affairs, Defence and Trade References Committee, *Australia's Future Activities and Responsibilities in the Southern Ocean and Antarctic Waters,* October 2014,

64 Daniel Bray, 'The Geopolitics of Antarctic Governance: Sovereignty and the Strategic Denial of Australia's Antarctic Policy', *Australian Journal of International Affairs* 70:3 (2016), pp. 256–74.

65 Elizabeth Buchanan, 'Australia's Scrapping of Antarctic Aerodrome Could Pave the Runway for China', *The Strategist,* 30 November 2021.

66 Foreign Affairs, Defence and Trade References Committee, *Australia's Future Activities and Responsibilities in the Southern Ocean and Antarctic Waters,* October 2014, p. ix.

CHAPTER 8

1 Commonwealth of Australia, *National Defence: Defence Strategic Review,* p. 11.

2 Glenn H. Snyder, *Alliance Politics,* Ithaca: Cornell University Press, 1997.

3 Ibid, p. 8.

4 Ted Hopf, 'The Logic of Habit in International Relations', *European Journal of International Relations* 16:4 (2010), pp. 539–61.

NOTES

5   Mark Kenny, 'Defence Expansion Would Break the Budget if Australia Ditches US Alliance: Angus Houston', *The Sydney Morning Herald*, 21 February 2017.

6   Marles, 'Securing Australia's Sovereignty'.

7   David Vallance, 'The "Somewhat" Conundrum: Lack of Communication Bedevils AUKUS Support", *The Interpreter*, 21 June 2021.

8   Anthony Albanese, 'Address to the National Press Club', Canberra, 22 February 2023, www.pm.gov.au/media/address-national-press-club.

9   Aubrey Allegretti, 'Size of UK's Nuclear Submarine Fleet Could Double Under AUKUS Plans', *The Guardian*, 14 March 2023.

10 Marles, 'Securing Australia's Sovereignty'.

11 AP4D, 'A Joint Agenda for Maritime Security', *Blue Security*, 1 (2023).

12 Jennifer Parker, *An Australian Maritime Strategy: Resourcing the Royal Australian Navy*, Australian Strategic Policy Institute, 2023, p. 5.

13 Ibid, p. 5.

14 John Saunders, 'We Need a Navy to Protect Our Supply Routes', *The Strategist*, 16 February 2018.

15 Gareth Hutchens, 'Australia Loses Another Oil Refinery, Leaving Our Fuel Supply Vulnerable to Regional Crises', ABC, 11 February 2021.

16 James Blackwell, 'The Future Of Foreign Policy Is First Nations. Where Then Are Our Voices?', *Australian Outlook*, 5 August 2022, www.internationalaffairs.org.au/australianoutlook/the-future-of-foreign-policy-is-first-nations-where-then-are-our-voices.

17 Ibid.

INDEX

INDEX

INDEX

INDEX

INDEX

INDEX

INDEX

INDEX

INDEX

White, Hugh 85
white papers 3, 6, 13, 24
    see also entries under defence white
    paper
Whitlam, Gough 42, 74
Whitsun Reef 104
Widodo, Joko 54, 63, 64
Wilkins, Hubert 193–4
women, empowerment of 166–7
Wong, Penny 5, 22, 66, 83, 143
Woodside 42
World Health Assembly 91
World Trade Organization 112
World War I 12, 68, 128
World War II 12, 20, 23
    and China 69, 72
    consequences of 22–3, 68–72, 99,
      128, 160

and Japan 25, 34, 37–9, 69, 106, 128,
    138
and Korea 70, 71
and the north seas 37–40
in the Pacific 128, 137–8
and rules-based order 23
and shipping 224
and United Kingdom 70
and USA 23, 25, 38–9, 69
see also Coral Sea
WYW Holding Limited 49

Xi Jinping 15–16, 76, 79, 138, 227

Yemen 157
Yeonpyeong Island 77
Yoon Suk Yeol 220
Yudhoyono, Susilo Bambang 54

Milton Keynes UK
Ingram Content Group UK Ltd.
UKHW012324110424
440929UK00003B/135